Remaking College

Remaking College

Innovation and the Liberal Arts

Edited by
Rebecca Chopp, Susan Frost,
and Daniel H. Weiss

Johns Hopkins University Press
Baltimore

© 2014 Johns Hopkins University Press
All rights reserved. Published 2014
Printed in the United States of America on acid-free paper

Johns Hopkins Paperback edition, 2016

9 8 7 6 5 4 3 2 1

Johns Hopkins University Press
2715 North Charles Street
Baltimore, Maryland 21218-4363
www.press.jhu.edu

The Library of Congress has cataloged the hardcover edition of this book
as follows:

Remaking college : innovation and the liberal arts / edited by Rebecca
Chopp, Susan Frost, Daniel H. Weiss.
      pages   cm
  Includes bibliographical references and index.
   ISBN 978-1-4214-1134-7 (hardcover : acid-free paper) —
ISBN 978-1-4214-1135-4 (electronic) — ISBN 1-4214-1134-2 (hardcover :
acid-free paper) — ISBN 1-4214-1135-0 (electronic)
   1. Small colleges—United States.   2. Education, Humanistic—
United States.   I. Chopp, Rebecca S., 1952–   II. Frost, Susan.
III. Weiss, Daniel H.
   LB2328.32.U6R46   2013
   370.11'2—dc23   2013010160

A catalog record for this book is available from the British Library.

ISBN-13: 978-1-4214-1978-7
ISBN-10: 1-4214-1978-5

Special discounts are available for bulk purchases of this book.
For more information, please contact Special Sales at 410-516-6936
or specialsales@press.jhu.edu.

Johns Hopkins University Press uses environmentally friendly book
materials, including recycled text paper that is composed of at least
30 percent post-consumer waste, whenever possible.

Contents

Preface

The essays gathered within this volume represent a shared vision of liberal arts colleges in the United States at a time of profound change and in the face of great opportunity. The twenty contributors are all sitting presidents or other educational leaders who have reflected carefully on the future of liberal arts education and the responsibility of liberal arts colleges to the future of higher education in the United States and around the world.

This project began as a collaboration between Rebecca Chopp and Daniel H. Weiss, who, with the support of the Andrew W. Mellon Foundation, convened a number of our colleagues for a conference held in April 2012 at Lafayette College called "The Future of the Liberal Arts College in America and Its Leadership Role in Education around the World." The objective of the forum was to provide a context for thinking together about issues that were emerging as game-changers for us all. Although we recognized that all institutions—public and private, large and small—are facing comparable challenges, we held the view that liberal arts colleges, by virtue of their scale and their focused mission, are especially well positioned to lead in developing new approaches for an uncertain future. The conference was intended to support the development of shared learning, innovative thinking, and bold proposals as part of a comprehensive process of review and assessment.

Although we imagined a small audience for the meeting, we were greatly surprised that more than two hundred presidents, faculty members, professional staff, students, board members, and others attended. The meeting attracted so much interest because the issues that were being discussed were widely acknowledged to be urgent and consequential. These included the problems of a distressed economic model and the related issue of declining affordability, the purposes of a liberal education in a world increasingly focused on professional training and vocationalism, the challenges and opportunities presented by new technologies and changing demographics, and the place of the small residential liberal arts college within our vast educational system.

The essays that constitute this volume are an outgrowth of the presentations made at the Lafayette/Swarthmore conference. As we proceeded toward publication, we were grateful to enlist a third partner, Susan Frost, a seasoned writer, higher education leader, and conference presenter. She shared our belief that these chapters offer a valuable resource for communicating the many ways in which liberal arts colleges are engaging the world and, in so doing, have become centers of innovation.

Those of us who work as presidents and other leaders at liberal arts colleges recognize the importance of this moment in higher education, and we understand the power of a strong foundation in the liberal arts for transforming people and communities. At the same time, we who oversee budgets, personnel, academic programs, admissions, and all of the other components of our institutions know that this is a time of great challenge and of public criticism. In many ways, this book explores the nature of this dualism in a changing environment and the ways in which liberal arts colleges are evolving, even transforming, to meet the needs of individuals and society. To remain effective educational leaders in such a challenging environment, our institutions must adapt, and we must embrace change. Within the pages of this book, we make the case that this is exactly what we are doing.

Acknowledgments

It is a pleasure to thank friends and colleagues who have supported this project. Earlier versions of the essays gathered here were first presented at the Lafayette/Swarthmore conference "The Future of the Liberal Arts College in America and Its Leadership Role in Education around the World" held on the campus of Lafayette College in April 2012. Support for that conference and the subsequent work leading to this volume was generously provided by the Andrew W. Mellon Foundation. Phil Lewis and Gene Tobin at Mellon provided significant leadership to this project and contributed substantively to our deliberations. Marie Enea handled many details of the conference with grace and remarkable effectiveness, even with a significantly larger than anticipated attendance.

We are especially grateful to our contributors, all of whom have great demands on their time, for their steadfast and enthusiastic commitment to this project. Greg Britton at the Johns Hopkins University Press has taken a lively interest in this project from the outset. He was present at our conference and has provided thoughtful counsel and advice in bringing this volume to press. Numerous editors worked on the project; Hal Jacobs deserves special mention.

We would like to express our deep and abiding gratitude to Olivia Smith, who has kept all of us on track and on schedule—a most challenging task—and who has provided outstanding editorial guidance in improving each essay and in bringing the essays together into this volume.

Remaking College

Updating the Liberal Arts Mission for the Twenty-First Century

Residential liberal arts colleges may well be among the most resilient institutions in our culture. Indeed, the colleges represented in this book are among the oldest continuing institutions in the United States. With considerable fortitude and adaptability, they have continued through times of financial recession and depression, wars and conflicts of all sizes, the rise and decline first of the agrarian culture and then of industrialization, several technological revolutions, and massive shifts in cultural norms and practices that have occurred throughout U.S. history. Over the course of the past two hundred years, critics have boldly and frequently proclaimed the irrelevancy and predicted the extinction of the liberal arts college. The reader of this book will find little to support such critics and their forecasts. Today many liberal arts colleges are not only surviving and flourishing but are also places to discover innovative ideas and practices in knowledge creation and democratic community. The contemporary residential college is a surprising case study in flexibility, strength, and irrepressibility, all key components of the kind of resiliency that individuals and institutions need in the twenty-first century.

If these chapters address the question "How are liberal arts colleges faring in the current environment?" the answer must be that they seem to be invigorated by current challenges and opportunities. When times get tough, it appears, liberal arts colleges get creative, resourceful, and wise. To live, work, or visit a contemporary residential liberal arts college is to discover an environment teeming with intensity and innovation. Faculty and students are pushing academic boundaries out of the classroom and into cutting-edge research in the sciences, community-based courses that cross a range of disciplines, and problem-based courses that address the major issues of the day, for example; and leaders are debating the value of competing priorities and how resources should be allocated.

At the same time, the wisdom conveyed through traditional models of teaching, learning, and research continues to be practiced. Students learn and live in a culture that applies both rigor and agility to experiencing the fullness of knowledge. This effort is constantly reinforced and expanded by a residential community that is inclusive and diverse, well-rounded and cosmopolitan, and oriented toward helping students learn the skills, values, and commitments they need to build democratic communities.

Of course, the difficult challenges that liberal arts colleges face must be taken with the utmost seriousness. Some of these issues, perhaps most important the challenges of the financial model, have no easy or clear answers. But, as these chapters show, even as academic communities craft options, consider alternatives, and deal with increasingly complex situations, incredible innovation is occurring within these institutions. Whether it be updating the mission, developing new institutional structures, addressing issues of governance, or reimagining the residential experience, our authors join with Bill Bowen in concluding: "There is more to hope than to fear."

As these chapters powerfully suggest, the twofold mission of liberal arts colleges—to provide a holistic educational formation for young adults and to serve the democratic good of associative living—is adapting, evolving, and transforming in substance and style because of technology, governance, partnerships with universities and other entities, and even the sheer scope of what one considers the social good. The first part of this mission relates to developing the individual for a life of success, satisfaction, and service. The heart of this formation is teaching students how to think critically and creatively. "Critical thinking" is the heart and soul of liberal arts education, but these essays propose that its shape in the twenty-first century is evolving and may be, in some ways, transformed in quite dramatic ways. As David Oxtoby and Wendy Hill suggest, the twenty-first century seems to be exploding with interdisciplinary courses, programs, centers, and even memorandums of understanding for faculty members whose work bridges more than one discipline.

Innovation in knowledge and the desire to embrace critical thinking as problem solving offer an expansion of critical thinking to include both disciplinary and cross-disciplinary ways of understanding. As Brian Rosenberg demonstrates, some models of critical thinking are being transformed through problem-based learning in centers. An area of what we might call ambiguous transformation for how we understand critical thinking is technology. Kevin Guthrie details the radical changes that technology offers our education model, especially in terms of how we bundle teaching and learning practices. What can be bundled, technology can unbundle; the result is challenging to the assumptions of liberal arts colleges. Other authors, such as Adam Falk and Dan Porterfield, view the impact of technology as, at best, a pedagogical tool in the evolution of our work with students and caution us that technology can also threaten deep thinking, emotional wellness, and the ability to connect to others.

The second part of the mission—serving the social good—is likewise expanded. The mission is now not United States centric but focused on educating students from across the world who will, in turn, serve the world. Jane McAuliffe insists that the radical internationalization of Bryn Mawr is a transformation, but it is one that upholds the college's mission to advance the role of women—now the role of women around the world. But this is not to say that these colleges are not addressing domestic issues. A residential college provides what John McCardell calls a comprehensive, seamless, and relevant environment to shape the individual. Ron Crutcher demonstrates how such an environment can address the challenges of diversity and of globalism in new ways.

Is the mission the same, evolving, or transformed? In one sense, this is a living tradition rather than a dead traditionalism: changes are guided by mission, and in turn the mission is continually adapted to changing times. But in another sense, as Rebecca Chopp suggests, residential liberal arts education may serve as a bold experiment in the design of knowledge and in incubating intentional communities in the twenty-first century—an education that counters the current focus on vocational training as well as the weakening of community ties and models of democracy.

Developing New Structures for Sustainability and Growth

Given the economic climate of the past five years, it is perhaps understandable that one of the issues receiving the greatest attention lately is that of the ever-increasing cost of attending college and the related problem of the sustainability of the economic model. As Catharine Hill, Jill Tiefenthaler, and Suzanne Welsh outline in their chapter on economics and affordability, our system is undergoing an enormous transition that will affect its various sectors differently. Within this challenging environment, they identify specific ways in which liberal arts colleges can address these issues while maintaining their historical commitments to undergraduate education.

Although the economic issues are complex, they are well understood by most educational leaders. The economic model is changing—and changing quickly—

in ways that are likely to result in greater differentiation between sectors of the higher education system. According to Weiss and Catharine Hill, Tiefenthaler, and Welsh, this means that liberal arts colleges must assume greater control of operating expenses while maintaining our important and historical commitment to providing need-blind financial aid in order to ensure access to all who qualify for admission regardless of their ability to pay. This will almost certainly not be the case for other sectors within our system—including public institutions and the for-profit sector—as they face greater pressure to align tuition expenses with graduate outcomes and, in so doing, to improve graduation rates while reducing overreliance on student debt.

The problem of escalating costs and declining affordability is not the only challenge facing us, however. The transformational impact of technological innovation on both teaching and research is even more immediate and dramatic. All of the authors represented here believe strongly in the enduring resilience of the high-touch educational model, while agreeing with Guthrie that the Internet and networked technologies have unleashed a powerful new force on higher education even if we do not yet understand the impact this will have on liberal arts colleges in the United States. Falk believes these technological changes to be more incremental than transformational as they advance the work of liberal arts colleges. Comparing the current technological wave to other transformational moments—such as the development of the printing press or educational television—Falk sees incremental change being built around the enduring educational principles of liberal arts colleges, especially the primacy of human interaction in undergraduate education. He also warns of the prohibitive economic consequences of perpetual investment in leading-edge technologies. In his chapter on the cultural and intellectual impact of technology on students, especially those at liberal arts colleges, Porterfield helps us to understand how to harness the educational potential while doing what we can to limit its dehumanizing aspects.

The impact of communications technology can also be felt as the learning environment, like the outside world, shifts from a hierarchical, disciplinary-based learning model to one that is more integrative and open to collaboration across academic fields and disciplines. David Oxtoby observes that such integrative approaches have become the hallmark of scholarship in the twenty-first century, although he acknowledges that most liberal arts colleges have not kept pace with these changes. Still, largely as a result of the smaller size and traditional emphasis on teaching, liberal arts colleges offer new opportunities to foster interdisciplinary innovation. These include new forms of institutional collaboration such as those practiced within the Claremont group and a refreshed focus on topics, challenges, and issues rather than fields. Presidential leadership is needed to build the necessary bridges for sustainable interdisciplinary teaching.

Wendy Hill sees liberal arts colleges as well positioned to succeed in fostering interdisciplinary approaches because of their strong foundation in balancing teaching, learning, and research. The benefits include higher cognitive skills, increased sensitivity to ethical issues, and greater tolerance for ambiguity. In order to achieve these substantial educational benefits for their students, liberal arts colleges are finding new and innovative ways to evolve toward a more integrative model, and they are doing so within the economic constraints of the new normal.

Several authors directly address the related theme of building networks and partnerships to engage with other educational institutions, think tanks, nonprofit organizations, and neighborhoods to integrate knowledge and real-world experience for the sake of students and humanity. Three types of alliances are described: those designed to strengthen the academic core, those aimed at expanding scope and reach, and those created to cut costs or share administrative effort. Carol Christ, Jane McAuliffe, Oxtoby, Rosenberg, and McCardell describe, for example, partnerships that help students gain valuable professional experience, learn firsthand how to assist communities in developing nations, and contribute to research in disciplines not represented on their campus. They also describe partnerships that help institutions reduce their investment in library materials and accomplish a variety of administrative savings.

Christ explains that outreach has "deep roots" in the traditions of liberal arts colleges, and now these roots are expanding as colleges align themselves closer with their neighbors, peers, and larger research universities. Because no one college can offer everything, academic partnerships are becoming "even more central to the design of the education we offer." Chopp believes that this shift could encourage students to change their view of their own role in the educational process from being "consumers of knowledge" to being "co-creators of knowledge with faculty." McAuliffe sees the work of presidents as "not only providing new content in our classrooms but also moving ourselves and our students into external networks of action and discovery." Because faculty and students are at the center of a college's mission, they should also be at the center of collaborative arrangements and partnerships. Crutcher, Rosenberg, and McCardell encourage leaders to engage students and faculty intentionally and meaningfully in this work. Rosenberg cautions, however, that these collaborations should not be add-ons or afterthoughts. They will have lasting influence only if they affect the heart of a student's work.

As liberal arts colleges continue to define their unique role, leaders of colleges recognize that collaboration with scholars at larger research institutions will remain a valuable option for some students. Tobin recommends that alliances be considered carefully in light of contributing to each other's respective mission. He writes, "Research universities have the resources and infrastructure that would enable liberal arts colleges to expand their curricular offerings and provide their faculties with interesting scholarly opportunities, and liberal arts colleges have much to share with their university colleagues about getting undergraduates involved in research."

Partnerships and alliances that contribute directly to the educational mission by modeling the collaborative arrangements that mark the world our students will enter are encouraged. Wendy Hill, McCardell, and Oxtoby advise leaders to recognize the importance of faculty commitment to successful partnerships and to encourage tenure and promotion structures that recognize faculty's contributions to such arrangements. As McCardell writes, "Adroit administrators will find the best fit for each faculty member's particular skills and will especially encourage faculty interested in the lives students lead outside the classroom to play a significant role in those lives, thereby broadening the understanding of professional development and rewarding leadership."

While it is still critical for students to learn how to work independently, it is also becoming essential for them to learn to contribute to a team of peers. On campus, experience within a cooperative arrangement at the institutional level might hold valuable learning opportunities for students. As Oxtoby explains, "Faculty members can serve as models to their students when it comes to teaching students to become good citizens of the country and the world." Authors agree that, as alliances are formed, the collaborative leadership required to sustain them should be open and transparent—and realistic—about their mission and aims. For example, it is unrealistic to expect deans, department chairs, and vice presidents to add inventing and sustaining collaborative arrangements to an already full work assignment. Thus, it might be wise to start a potentially long-term relationship with an alliance that does not affect the academic core. When trust is established, such alliances are more likely to succeed.

Of course, partnerships and alliances range widely in terms of what it takes to sustain to them. Several authors describe how technology can add value as an alliance takes hold. Christ, for example, writes about the advantage of "blended courses, combining face-to-face with web-transmitted classwork." But technology alone is not enough. Falk and Porterfield remind leaders that successful collaborative arrangements and partnerships depend on human relationships and face-to-face interactions to develop a lasting sense of trust.

Changing Views on Governance, Leadership, and Communication

Governance is becoming both more focused and more flexible in the twenty-first century as a result of changing dynamics in organizations and changing requirements of decision making. As Susan Frost and Shelly Storbeck argue, governance operates in a new culture of participation in which our constituents—board members, faculty, students, alumni, and partners—want to be engaged and invested in processes that relate directly to their concerns. Leaders focus their efforts on specific, rather than comprehensive, strategies, involving constituents who express interest or have particular talents to offer.

In a series of interviews with presidents, board leaders, and leaders of faculty governance, Frost and Storbeck learned that governance practices in liberal arts colleges are evolving, and most believe this is happening not a moment too soon. Although our highly structured consultative processes have served well, we now need more flexible, timely ways to take advantage of opportunities, decide how the campus should evolve, shape the academic program to sustain excellence in the face of rising costs and growing need, and accomplish other strategic decision making. As Rosenberg observed, the extent to which liberal arts colleges are prepared to focus on quality, distinctiveness, and social purpose will determine their future health. In other words, decision makers—including the president, the board, and the faculty—should ask: How good are our programs and the educational experience we offer? How are we distinctive from our neighbors and peers? How powerfully do we—and our students and alumni—contribute to the common good? Rosenberg cautions that leaders need to demonstrate "that the education we provide has positive outcomes, that it differs in beneficial ways from the education offered in other kinds of institutions (including the virtual), and that it contributes to the collective good."

By detailing the kinds of decisions liberal arts colleges encounter as they meet new kinds of opportunities and demands, several authors illuminate new requirements of governance processes. For example, Christ discusses the power of collaborative arrangements, and Wendy Hill explains how interdisciplinary teaching and scholarship are changing faculty roles. Taking advantage of these types of change—change that could, if accomplished well, improve the foundation of liberal arts education and make a college more distinctive and competitive—requires productive, flexible alignment among the president, board, and faculty. Evolving from a slow, more traditional governance process to a quicker, more dynamic form takes time, as several presidents observed.

Transparency and openness are also key requirements. In fact, Joanne Creighton offers this advice to entering presidents: "Do not enter office with full-fledged vision. Vision is the ability to see what is there and imagine what more might be if an institution were to realize its unique genius and full potential." She recommends that new presidents begin by leading a strategic planning process.

As our authors described governance on their campuses, new collaborative forms repeatedly came to light. We are encouraged, for example, that presidents are extending innovative practices used to guide the college through the recession to increase strength now that management is on a more even keel. Frost and Storbeck describe how one president among those they surveyed routinely forms board members and faculty members into short-term strategic teams. Designed to accomplish one or two specific aims, these teams are particularly helping board members become more deeply attached to the institution as they make important contributions.

At the same time, leaders are exploring ways to use well-defined boundaries to structure and add discipline to sometimes rowdy collaborative governance practices. When boundaries are loose, it is easier for board members to set aside helpful protocols—a potential danger about which several leaders caution. Creighton, an experienced president of three institutions, advises leaders to "maintain boundaries with the board and blur the lines with faculty and draw them together to shape the priorities of the institution." She also stresses the importance of shared governance and the central role faculty should play in curriculum development and academic appointments. Rosenberg agrees that shared governance is important but draws on his experience to recommend that shared governance works best in small groups. He argues that leaders should do more to centralize decisions that can influence the direction of an institution and rely more heavily on representative forms of governance for other types of decisions.

Overall, the authors describe a president's role in governance that is evolving. Whereas in the past, leaders presided over well-orchestrated meetings organized around well-anticipated issues, now leaders are called on to manage, interpret, and encourage decision making on new kinds of questions and issues as they unfold. Weiss and Creighton call for leaders to focus planning efforts and manage expectations by making practices and outcomes transparent to all stakeholders. So, too, did Frost and Storbeck find in their interviews with presidents, board leaders, and faculty members that there are high expectations from all constituents for transparency and open communication.

Engaging the Power of the Residential Experience

The residential liberal arts college is an intense, complex learning and living community. One distinguishing characteristic of the colleges featured in these essays is that the majority of students not only reside on the campuses in which they take classes but also participate in and are responsible for a rich community life. A student may be on the debate team, play club rugby, and occasionally perform in one of the theater groups. Another student may serve as an academic tutor, be a varsity swimmer, and lead the jazz group. Habits of discipline, respect for others, and learning to build consensus are nurtured through community practices. McCardell observes in his chapter that such a residential experience gives students opportunities to experience challenge and to gain self-confidence.

It is therefore not surprising, as Chopp notes, that residential liberal arts colleges report significant alumni satisfaction with the overall experience; for many alumni the residential experience was nearly as important as the classroom experience. Being able to continue a classroom debate over lunch or spend a late-night session with roommates discussing perspectives brought together from various classes or just exploring the big topics or merely humorous ones is enjoyable, enriching, and formative. Many alumni note the rich friendships they developed in athletics, in cultural groups, or simply from living together. Weiss describes the powerful professional and social networks that alumni enjoy throughout their lives. Students note that alumni continue these intense feelings of community, offering current students many ways to engage with alumni through internships and mentoring programs, among other means.

The residential experience serves individual students and provides a deep connection with alumni. As Chopp explains, it also serves, in a way quite distinct in American education, the democratic community, or what John Dewey called "associative living." When residential liberal arts colleges claim that they excel at shaping the democratic citizens for tomorrow, they rely not only on what students learn in the classes but also, as Rosenberg articulates, on the habits for democratic participation and even leadership cultivated outside the classroom. Students learn to pursue their individuality in the context of nurturing community and to build community by respecting the needs and talents of others.

A number of authors pick up on the idea of "intentional community" introduced by Chopp. The notion that residential campuses should be thought of as intentional communities means that issues such as diversity and inclusivity, sustainability, and being a world citizen can be intentionally addressed not only in classes but also in daily living experience. The authors are concerned about social challenges that range from civic discourse to living as world citizens and believe that the residential campus provides a tremendous opportunity for experimenting with new models of community for the twenty-first century and for shaping students around the practices and virtues necessary for life in a global, technological world. Crutcher, for example, cites a variety of strategies his campus is using to help students to "develop a repertoire of strategies for living in an intercultural, global world." As Crutcher and others caution, the practice of ignoring how students interact or live together in residential housing must end. We must now claim the opportunity that a comprehensive residential community provides in order to prepare leaders who can address the problems of tomorrow.

Envisioning a Promising Future

While the essays gathered here are intended to inform and stimulate debate on a wide range of pressing issues, the authors also describe a promising future for liberal arts colleges as they lay out approaches that are innovative and indeed often visionary. Their views are informed in large part by their own experiences at institutions with diverse cultures and resources, sometimes leading to different approaches and outcomes. Rather than weakening the case for the future of liberal arts colleges, these contrasting views show how important it is to understand— and respect—an institution's culture and resources before pursuing new ideas or options. One common area of agreement is that while much work is underway, more needs to be done both within the liberal arts college sector and throughout the system.

These chapters also show how liberal arts institutions are remaking college— in guiding the development of thoughtful and engaged graduates who serve our communities, our nation, and the world in myriad ways. For our institutions to thrive and our system to prosper, we must continue—and even accelerate—our efforts to innovate and communicate effectively as we work together to ensure that we have an educational system worthy of the dynamic opportunities ahead.

PART I / Reimagining the
Liberal Arts College in America

CHAPTER 1

Remaking, Renewing, Reimagining

The Liberal Arts College Takes Advantage of Change

Rebecca Chopp

PRESIDENT, SWARTHMORE COLLEGE

The "distinctively American" tradition of residential liberal arts colleges rests on the foundation of an early social charter between American higher education and democratic society.[1] Simply put, the story goes like this: Sixteen years after the Pilgrims landed on the shore of Plymouth Harbor, Harvard was founded. As the frontier of the rapidly expanding United States moved west, new communities organized colleges as soon as they were able. In the 1860s, the great land-grant universities emerged with an even stronger focus on meeting the needs of individuals and communities. With each wave of development, higher education evolved to serve one great mission: educating leaders and citizens to realize their individual potential and build their capacity to serve in a democratic society. These dual goals—supporting the development of the individual and cultivating the common good—are inextricably linked through the belief in and practices of freedom. In the American narrative, freedom combines the pursuit of individual passion or fulfillment with service to the common good. Individuals are free to be themselves, but this freedom, as expressed in a wide variety of ways, is *for,* not *from,* service to the common good. Over time, the main components of this historical narrative became consolidated into three primary principles that form the foundation of what we know as residential liberal arts education: critical thinking, moral and civil character, and using knowledge to improve the world.[2]

First, *critical thinking,* rather than mastery of technical or codified knowledge, is the heart and soul of a liberal arts education. Our tradition requires that we encourage students to refine their capacity for analytic thinking; ask difficult questions and formulate responses; evaluate, interpret, and synthesize evidence; make clear, well-reasoned arguments; and develop intellectual agility. It is both "art" and "science" in that students are educated not only to master knowledge but to create new modes of performance, production, or design and find connections and discover new ideas and perspectives. Critical thinking helps students learn how to learn, preparing them for a lifetime of work, service, and well-being, no matter what professions, vocations, and lifestyles they choose. Society is served by the ongoing expansion of intellectual capital that is both self-critical and innovative within personal, cultural, economic, and political realms but that also advances the common good.

Second, residential liberal arts colleges *cultivate a moral and civic character* in students in terms of both their individual choices and their contribution to the common good. Moral character does not mean mastery of a defined code of ethics but rather the cultivation of habits and characteristics that reinforce moral behavior individually as well as communally. Athletics, arts, as well as political, activist, and cultural groups on campus have a powerful impact on students and serve as vehicles for individual and communal development. Many of these colleges offer special leadership development programs, and nearly all would cite a history and goal of educating individuals who contribute to their fields and their communities. The cultivation of character, combined with the development of critical thinking, creates capacities in the individual for what John Dewey liked to call "associative living."[3] An education that cultivates the responsible expression of individual freedoms in the context of nurturing the common good is essential to strengthening democratic communities.

Third, *using knowledge and virtue to improve the world* is the ultimate aim of an education that serves individual and communal freedom. Liberal arts education is renowned for educating people to serve the world in multiple expressions, styles, and practices, whether through theater or the arts, economic analysis, scientific discovery, creative writing, the development of social policy, or historical interpretation. While the area of focus may be very limited and precise, the whole point of critical thinking and of cultivating moral character is to live well and to serve the common good. This twofold "ultimate" mission is the raison d'être of liberal arts education that, as William Sullivan has noted, expresses the best of the Western tradition: "The whole classical notion of a common *paideia,* or moral-civic cultivation, rested on the assertion that growth and transformation of the self toward responsible mutual concern is the realistic concern of public life"[4] (emphasis mine). In this tradition, individual flourishing is defined both as the pursuit of one's passions and as service to others, and this capacity to fulfill the self by fulfilling one's obligations to the common good requires intellectual and moral formation in the context of a community. In this tradition public service includes those who serve directly in fields such as public policy, education, non-profit work, or health care as well as those who contribute to a robust culture through business or the arts, research in basic sciences that one day might benefit others, or volunteer leadership in their communities.

Although new chapters in the history of liberal arts education unfold and the plot thickens, through the centuries the same anchors—of academic quality, community, and using knowledge to improve the world—propel our colleges forward. The great narrators of education have envisioned this social charter time and time again, underscoring the point made so well by Thomas Jefferson: "I look to the diffusion of light and education as the resource to be relied on for ameliorating the condition, promoting the virtue, and advancing the happiness of man."

Each small liberal arts college is a distinct expression of this social compact, and the resulting tapestry of knowledge and social responsibility for the development of the individual and the cultivation of the common good supports, promotes, and expands freedom in its many expressions in this country. Through the willingness to encourage critical and creative thinkers—those who can combine self-reflection, disciplined action, and community building—we advance freedom of thought and expression as well as personal and social responsibility. As historian William Cronon notes, the act of making us free also binds us to the communities that gave us our freedom in the first place and, significantly, makes us responsible to those communities in ways that limit our freedom. In the end, it turns out that liberty is not about thinking or saying or doing whatever we want. It is about exercising our freedom in such a way as to make a difference in the world—and make a difference for more than just ourselves.[5]

Three Critiques of the Liberal Arts

For nearly as long as liberal arts colleges have existed, its critics have announced that this type of education fails to relate to the contemporary world. Today's critics cite a long list of issues and pressures facing education, including technological innovation, globalism, the traditional structure of academic disciplines, environmental and financial sustainability, and changing demographics. From these pressing issues, some critics have concluded that the very sustainability of the liberal arts is at stake and predict the demise of this type of education is around the next technological, financial, or demographic corner.

These dire warnings tend to fall into three categories. The first asserts that education should be focused on job training, job procurement, and long-term financial security for students. Indeed, since the mid-1980s, most parents and prospective students indicate that the main purpose of education is to find a high-paying job and enjoy financial stability.[6] Once the quest for a certain salary becomes the paramount and sometimes the only reason to go to college, education becomes job training in its mission and practices.

The second critique follows from the first and asserts that liberal arts education is a hopelessly romantic endeavor designed to give privileged students cultivated tastes for an outdated, elite life under the guise of leadership. Rather than seeing education in terms of human development that appreciates and sustains human culture as well as supports the common good, education is seen as a leisurely commodity for individuals who, by virtue of family or business connections, are already assured of a high station in life. In this view of what it means to be human, young adults are not cultivated so much as prepped and pampered, and the common good is seen not primarily as the arena of culture in which arts and politics flourish but one in which a social and economic order must be sustained.

The third category weaves through the former two, suggesting that liberal arts education is, plainly speaking, too expensive in terms of both cost and the experience it provides. In evaluating whether college is worth the cost, skeptics conclude that the sticker price is not justified because the relative "returns" do not directly translate into specific training or expertise. In other words, the value of developing the individual and contributing to the common good does not balance the sheer cost of the "product."

Critics offer this argument routinely despite overwhelming evidence that college graduates attain, on average, higher incomes over the course of their careers and have more rather than fewer career options.[7] That data, coming from U.S. Treasury Department's "The Economic Case for Higher Education" (2012), reports on the income level of graduates of all colleges and universities, not just liberal arts colleges. When surveyed, employers indicate that the top skills they want in new employees include critical thinking, the ability to innovate, and the ability to work on teams with members of diverse groups.[8]

Alumni of, admittedly, top liberal arts colleges offer other evidence that contradicts the critics' claim. A study by Hardwick Day notes that alumni of colleges belonging to the Annapolis Group (130 selective, independent liberal arts colleges in the United States) are more likely than any other group to have graduated in four years or less, giving them a head start on their careers. More than any other group, these alumni are more likely to rate their undergraduate experience as "excellent" and to give higher overall satisfaction ratings. They credit their undergraduate experience with helping them develop a broad range of important life skills (problem solving, making effective decisions, thinking analytically, writing effectively, speaking effectively, working as part of a team, and leadership abilities). They rate their college as highly effective in helping them obtain their first job or gain admission to graduate school and report that their education continues to help them with career changes or advancement. Crediting the overall quality and breadth of their academic preparation more frequently, they believe they are better prepared than graduates of other institutions they've encountered since college.[9]

Being Proactive about the Liberal Arts

In response to these critiques, defenders of the liberal arts have been increasingly vocal, offering eloquent apologias, or philosophical and historical defenses, against the critics. Andrew Delbanco's book *College: What It Was, Is, and Should Be* addresses issues and pressures on liberal education but also defends its importance for economic prosperity for the individual and the country and for an inclusive democratic citizenship, as well as to create capacity for what Jefferson called "the pursuit of happiness." In *Cultivating Humanity* and *Not for Profit,* Martha Nussbaum argues for the importance of the tradition of the liberal arts to prepare "world citizens" who think critically, at least in part, through their ability to cultivate the capacity for empathy developed through humanities and the arts.[10]

I applaud the eloquent apologias based on our proud tradition, a tradition that is not only alive but also evolving. But to make the case for liberal arts, we need to assert a more proactive claim about our special relevance for linking knowledge, community, and freedom in the future. Although the critics' conclusions may be reductionist, we are not recused from the task of making a case for the liberal arts as a leader of change for education.

Our response to our critics and to the public in general should be not only about the history and philosophy of the liberal arts but also about its relevance in the twenty-first century for the United States and the world. The case we must make for liberal arts education is that the residential educational setting serves as an incubator for intellectual agility and supports the creation of new models of engagement to help both individuals and communities survive and flourish in this century. These principles stand as fresh reinterpretations of our tradition and enable us to impress upon our students that they have an obligation to use their talents to improve the world. The importance of this type of education rests on its long and unique tradition and on what it can offer in a world in which learning to navigate the new may be far more important than the ability to master the old.

While our current liberal arts residential colleges do live up to the apologias so eloquently offered about them, it is nonetheless the case that colleges also express an incredible degree of evolutionary, and even revolutionary, change in how knowledge is produced, interpreted, transmitted, taught, learned, and lived. Contemporary residential liberal arts colleges not only offer "community" as the environment for learning, but they do so by creating bold cultural experiments, some utopian in nature, of how to live out democracy and educate leaders. Our liberal arts residential communities serve as incubators or pilots of new ways to link knowledge, freedom, and democracy on a global stage. These colleges express the tradition of residential education through the ongoing reinterpretation of critical thinking, community living, and working to improve the world. And it is this current expression of the tradition, as much as the history and the philosophy, that we must use to make our case for the liberal arts.

This story of transformation and paradigm change deserves a powerful voice. If representatives of liberal arts colleges could write a joint case statement, it would emphasize the value of what we have always done well and would continue to guide this evolution through naturally occurring changes in structures, cultures, and practices. I suggest that we begin by reinterpreting the social charter that makes up the twin components of the liberal arts:

- First, we must expand our definition of what critical thinking is and how it is nurtured and learned and redefine how students and faculty engage one another in *knowledge design* through the dynamic interactions of teaching, learning, and scholarship.
- Second, we must extend the distinct role our campuses play as *intentional communities* within the broader public, especially as we focus on educating students in the practical virtues of building inclusive, sustainable, and civil democratic communities and on cultivating the next generation of ethical leaders.

Imagining the Future of Knowledge

As roads once paved the way to great centers of learning that were concentrated in distant corners of the world, so now do new forms of social organization and technology. In Thomas Friedman's image, technology has flattened the globe, making it possible for anyone with a laptop and a Wi-Fi connection to have access to the world's most brilliant minds.[11] We might summarize the current period as a shift from a bounded bureaucracy in which knowledge was divided into fixed disciplines to a porous network in which knowledge is fluid and collaborative. A byproduct of this shift is that individuals are finding new ways to organize and form community as well as to teach and learn. We are beginning to call this social learning.

Social learning does not rely on linear knowledge transfer. Rather, it is based on the premise that, as Brown and Adler put it, we "understand content through conversation and grounded interaction around problems or actions." Twenty-first century social learning goes well beyond traditional modes of participation to include the ways professors show students how to "be" a physicist, for example, as they are learning the content of that field. In the past, students might have spent years accumulating substantive knowledge before they were qualified to join a "community of practice," but now they are invited in at the outset.[12]

The current generation of students is ready for this form of engagement. They live in a world with few boundaries and compartments, where they multitask and tweet throughout the day and night. Partly because of this open access and wide range of interactions, they want more and better forms of problem-centered, real-world-based, digitally informed learning. Our faculty members want to work with students on projects and programs that welcome new, often interdisciplinary ways to organize knowledge and develop deeper connections between theory and practice. It is exciting to watch the myriad ways that this transformation is taking place in and out of the classroom.

Our students and faculty are not waiting for institutions to act. They are already participating in *knowledge design,* a concept aimed at placing creativity and agility at the heart of learning and scholarship by embracing new learning platforms and recognizing the power of visualization and the remixing of knowledge. Many of our most energized and passionate faculty members and students are involved in knowledge design now, either in small projects or programs or in large-scale institutes or centers. For example, at Swarthmore College a faculty member has used a specific problem faced by a nonprofit group to teach statistics to math-resistant students, and a philosopher and biologist have partnered to teach an introductory environmental course on "nature" in the field rather than in the classroom or lab.

To encourage these exciting possibilities, we will have to develop creative ways to structure old and new forms of faculty work while also making it easier for students to integrate many forms of learning and navigate the curriculum. We will have to reinvent the structures and cultures of education to match the forms of social and participatory learning, teaching, and knowledge creation that will dominate the twenty-first century. We are beginning to support new models of teaching and learning to help our students innovate, work in teams across many fields, and "design" as well as master ideas, solutions, products, and performances. In short, we are combining the discipline of critical thinking with the more organic processes of creative activity.

One step in this evolving process would be to frame critical thinking as knowledge design. In this reality, students would experience college as an engagement that takes them from the world in which they live, embeds them in communities of practice, and moves them from being consumers of knowledge to being co-creators of knowledge with faculty.

How do we frame and claim the expansion of knowledge design that is already in our midst? An experience at my institution made me keenly aware of these possibilities. Recently, Swarthmore finished a fifteen-month strategic-planning process, an experience that included an audit of globalization activities across the campus. We found, to our surprise, that we have lots of global connections that had never been gathered together, seen, or appreciated as a whole. As we explored what we should be doing globally, we discovered that we were already doing it! In other areas, Swarthmore has enjoyed an incredible expansion of practices in teaching, research, and learning among our faculty, students, staff, and alumni. We found many dots to connect and many emerging trends to support among both old and new ways of creating knowledge and using knowledge to improve the world.

During this process, I shifted my own framework from simply thinking that we are honing the skill of critical thinking to realizing that we are, at least in part, expanding how we understand critical thinking as it relates to the process of designing knowledge. Can we imagine our institutions as design studios—places where knowledge is invented, remixed, and performed? Places where critical and innovative thinking are constantly colliding and blending? Would recognizing our institutions as incubators of knowledge shift the way we think about departments and programs, about requirements and majors? Can we excite the public with the news that although liberal arts schools are few in number, we serve a critical function in a democracy as places that sustain and strengthen knowledge? There is no logical or practical need to assert that we provide the only type of education that does this. Indeed, all types of education, including the type provided by community colleges and research universities, must contribute to this goal. Our claim is not that we are the only ones capable of designing knowledge, but that we do so in a distinct fashion and with great effectiveness.

Even as the design of knowledge changes, we need to maintain key traditions in scholarship, teaching, and learning. Faculty members help students pick focused areas of study that shape their progress through structured semesters and well-defined academic years. Students attend classes face to face with their fellow students and teachers. They drop by their professors' offices to discuss complex problems. We need to support transformative changes even as we encourage traditional practices. We need to talk about knowledge in ways that are anchored in tradition even as we fuel emerging change.

Cultivating the Moral Individual and the Common Good

The second component of any compelling narrative needs to include a strong claim about residential community. The liberal arts derive uniqueness and strength from the intense coexistence, collision, and even comingling of curricula and extracurricular aspects to create an experience that is about the formation of individuals within community. We who live in these institutions understand that this form of education transforms students through their engagement in the academic enterprise and also in an intense and stimulating life outside the classroom 24/7.

This reality offers an immense opportunity for our students, faculty, and staff—one that very few other institutions can meet. Our country is in desperate need of what the liberal arts can offer. A serious crisis deeply linked to the failure of individuals in democratic communities to find common ground is leading many citizens to lose faith in their leaders, in their democratic institutions, in their communities that are increasingly polarized, and in a long-held sense of the common good. Current practices of democratic community such as tolerance, respect for others, and open debate are becoming anemic and are unable to provide the robust support that a thriving society needs. Just as knowledge must be free to shift to a participatory model, freedom in the social and moral sphere must shift from the unintentional consumer to the intentional community.

As liberal arts colleges become more agile, we must also imagine new models of community life, build their prototypes, and train students to convey them into the future. By offering what I call *intentional community,* we can frame our liberal arts narrative to create new models of engagement for the twenty-first century. Institutions that support intentional community would teach and promote civil discourse, civic virtues, inclusiveness, and a sustainable life together as well as the development of a fuller life for each individual. One outcome for colleges and universities would be to supplant the overarching focus on a consumer model that is so prevalent on campuses today.

At Swarthmore College we have identified three arenas in which to model our own intentional community: expanding our concept of diversity to become a more inclusive community; shaping our culture as a space of civility and civil discourse across and beyond our own various interest groups and ideologies; and living, as much as possible, as a community that promotes sustainable living both environmentally and fiscally. If the new narrative of education is to find a home in the evolving structures of knowledge design, we have to recognize that our unique opportunity to design a residential experience is critical to our *entire* educational program. In fact, our residential communities are nothing less than a way to offer new models of community for the twenty-first century. Why does this particular kind of residential incubator work so well? How might we claim its full value and go on to imagine it working even more effectively in order to model it in communities around the country and world?

Despite the challenges we all experience, especially in the economic realm, there are emerging trends and creative practices on which to build. Many liberal arts colleges are renewing efforts to engage students in practices of civility. Efforts at diversity are expanding from an exclusive focus only on minority students and are calling upon all students, staff, and faculty to build upon a more diverse population and experiment with inclusive community models. And sustainability is becoming more widely interpreted to include not only environmental protection but also economic efficiency and the cultural practices of new generations of students and staff who support a variety of sustainable practices.

Using Knowledge to Improve the World

It is the unique combination of developing the individual and cultivating the common good that allows residential liberal arts colleges to incubate the future, to show us what is possible, to create trajectories of new ways of being and doing in the world. Yet, as already stated, while these colleges have a special role within higher education, they are certainly not the ultimate or only type of higher education needed. Certain students, given their talents and passion, will flourish in this environment, and others will not.

My argument is that residential liberal arts colleges—as bold experiments in knowledge design and intentional community—have much to contribute to making the world a better place. By developing models of intentional community around some of our most difficult issues, for example, they will advance the common good. Other types of institutions will contribute to individual flourishing and further the common good in other ways.

My argument includes, inevitably, a type of meritocratic stance, since these schools are small and, despite the generous amounts of financial aid provided by many of them, not always affordable. Over the years, liberal arts colleges have worked hard, and largely succeeded, at becoming more diverse and inclusive not only to extend opportunities to those once excluded but also to provide the most robust residential community for all students. But given the relatively small populations that attend—3 to 6 percent of all students, depending on how one counts—we are limited to graduating a small, diverse group of students despite the great resources invested. These students, of course, have an obligation to use their talents to flourish as individuals and in serving the common good, just as educators have a responsibility to infuse them with a moral understanding of freedom and democracy.

Some might wonder why one would choose this type of education. Does one really wish to rely on a type of incubator for common good as the starting point of a lifelong educational process? Students who will benefit most from this type of education are those who embrace the boundless nature of acquiring and creating knowledge and welcome the challenge of living intentionally. So if this type of education is a fit for a particular student's talents, desires, and character, then it is more than worthwhile. Indeed, for some students it is the *most* fruitful environment for education.

Renewing the Mission of the Residential Liberal Arts College

The task of renewing our devotion to the common good and teaching the art and science of community building is, in my judgment, one of the most critical goals for higher education and one of the hardest to achieve in the years ahead. To achieve this goal, we need to understand that our mission is to support both the development of the self and the development of community. We must invent or reinvent educational practices that embrace virtue and practical wisdom as well as intellect and aesthetics; we must affirm the right of education to set standards for behavior, expectations of values, and commitment to the common good.

We also need to encourage individuals to exercise their freedom to enhance current models of values and community, a charge that will simultaneously foster community and innovation. To become an intentional community, one that portrays a new vision of the beloved community for the United States as well as for the world, we need to demand more of our students, faculty, and staff to make a commitment to life together, and we must set high standards for behavior inside and outside of the classroom.

Ultimately, the future of the residential liberal arts college rests on both its traditions and its relevance to the twenty-first century. Simply put, the relevance rests on the bold experiment that continually underpins the design of knowledge and life together in intentional community. Liberal arts colleges, in this way, provide a hopeful future, developing the leaders who will aspire to bring all that they have learned about how to think, create, and live into practice throughout their personal, professional, and civic lives.

NOTES

1. The term "distinctively American" is borrowed from the title of the volume *Distinctively American: The Residential Liberal Arts College,* ed. Steven Koblik and Stephen R. Graubard (New Brunswick, NJ: Transaction Publishers, 2000). Interestingly, the residential liberal arts college is now being emulated in countries such as Ghana, France, England, and China.

2. Women, slaves, and certain groups of immigrants were not counted as individual citizens at the founding of the country. The principles identified as the foundation of the social charter—critical thinking, the formation of moral and civic character, and using knowledge to improve the world—allowed the ongoing redefinition of freedom, democracy, and the common good. This work continues today.

3. John Dewey, "Creative Democracy: The Task before Us," in *John Dewey: The Political Writings,* ed. Debra Morris and Ina Shapiro (Indianapolis, IN: Hackett, 1993).

4. William M. Sullivan, *Reconstructing Public Philosophy* (Berkeley: University of California Press, 1982), 168.

5. William Cronon, "Only Connect: The Goals of a Liberal Education," *American Scholar* 67, no. 4 (Autumn 1998): 73–80.

6. See, for instance, Kate Zernike, "Making College 'Relevant,'" *New York Times,* Jan. 3, 2010, www.nytimes.com/2010/01/03/education/edlife/03careerism-t.html?pagewanted=1&em.

7. Victor E. Ferrall Jr., *Liberal Arts at the Brink* (Cambridge, MA: Harvard University Press, 2011); Debra Humphrey and Anthony Carvavale, "The Economic Value of Liberal Education," www.aacu.org/leap/documents/LEAP_MakingtheCase_Final.pdf.

8. See, e.g., the study by Peter D. Hart & Associates commissioned by AAC&U, www.aacu.org/leap/businessleaders.cfm.

9. See the Hardwick Day study prepared for the Annapolis Group: http://collegenews.org/news/2011/liberal-arts-college-graduates-feel-better-prepared-for-lifes-challenges-study-finds.html.

10. Andrew Delbanco, *College: What It Was, Is, and Should Be* (Princeton, NJ: Princeton University Press, 2012); Martha C. Nussbaum, *Cultivating Humanity: A Classical Defense of Reform in Liberal Education* (Cambridge, MA: Harvard University Press, 1997), and *Not for Profit: Why Democracy Needs the Humanities* (Princeton, NJ: Princeton University Press, 2010).

11. Thomas L. Friedman, *The World Is Flat* (New York: Farrar, Straus and Giroux, 2007).

12. John Seely Brown and Richard Adler, "Open Education, the Long Trail and Learning," *Educause,* January/February 2009, 16–32.

CHAPTER 2

Challenges and Opportunities in the Changing Landscape

Daniel H. Weiss

PRESIDENT, HAVERFORD COLLEGE

The greatest challenge facing higher education today—both for individual in-stitutions and for the system as a whole—lies in the ability of its leaders and key stakeholders to realize an academically compelling, publically comprehensible, and economically sustainable vision in an environment of profound uncertainty. The major factors driving this uncertainty are well known to all who maintain an interest in American colleges and universities: a distressed and (presumably) unsustainable economic model; the proliferation of dazzling and potentially transformative technologies; a seismic demographic shift in college-eligible students; and increased public skepticism about the purpose and value of a college education, or more cynically, a college degree. Collectively, these factors are likely to have an impact on the mission and purposes of higher education comparable to, if not greater than, that of the GI Bill on college enrollments following the Second World War or, shortly thereafter, the impact of government-sponsored research on the rise of the American research university. In some ways we might compare the current situation to the so-called revolution of the 1960s, which achieved, among other changes, coeducation as normative at most selective institutions, the "democratization" of the curriculum, and the emergence of community colleges as an essential part of the national system of higher education.[1]

In order to conceive of what such a leadership vision might encompass for liberal arts colleges, it would be useful to assess more closely the precipitating factors that are driving much of this change as well as the disparate and complex competitive environment within which liberal arts colleges currently operate.

Precipitating Factors
Economics

Clearly, the most obvious and long-standing problem facing higher education has been the dramatic, and presumably unsustainable, rate of increase in college tuitions and fees. Even after adjusting for inflation, during the last twenty years tuition and fees at private four-year colleges and universities have increased by 280 percent, while that for public institutions has increased 370 percent.[2] It is for good reason that many families no longer believe that they can afford to send their children to college. Whereas in 1992 educational costs represented 30 percent of median family income, by 2012 the number had risen to 55 percent and is continuing to rise.[3] The problem of escalating costs is highly complex and, perhaps not surprising, poorly understood by the public and even by many key stakeholders. The impact, however, is becoming increasingly clear to all.

Following the economic downturn of 2008, the connected problems of rising costs and declining affordability have attracted much attention from leaders in higher education, economists, and the national media. Once thought to be largely the consequence of shortsighted management practices and an excessive focus on consumerism, the root causes of these financial problems are now generally recognized to be systemic and cumulative. I will review briefly five major factors: (1) the skilled labor productivity problem, also known as "cost disease"; (2) the cost premium for investing in quality and innovation; (3) the consequences of an overheated competitive environment; (4) historical management practices; and (5) the impact of increasing market demand.

First identified by William Baumol and William Bowen in their study on the economics of the performing arts, the cost disease problem in higher education has received much recent attention, including a comprehensive study on rising college costs by Robert Archibald and David Feldman.[4] Put briefly, the problem concerns the costs associated with supporting a highly skilled workforce in labor-intensive industries such as higher education or the performing arts. Since at least the 1970s, industrial productivity gains have lifted the overall economy, and therefore the standard of living, for a highly educated workforce. Whereas productivity improvements have generally led to substantial salary gains for skilled workers—clearly benefitting some more than others—this has not been the case in labor-intensive industries such as higher education. For skilled labor in higher education, including especially professors and administrators, salaries have grown to keep pace with the general economy, but productivity growth significantly lags behind that of other sectors. As a result, educational costs per student have inevitably risen faster than the overall economy.[5] Increasing faculty productivity would be very difficult under the current system without either increasing class size or redirecting faculty away from research and service and toward increased teaching loads. Of course, modest gains can and have been achieved, primarily through the use of technology, but options are limited unless performance goals for faculty are to be modified.

Another structural problem that cannot easily be resolved concerns the need for continued investment in educational resources that simply do not track with increases in the cost of living. Colleges and universities, even those that do not pursue research as their highest institutional priority, must invest substantially in laboratory and scientific equipment; books, periodicals, and other scholarly materials; and digital media and technology, as well as the staff required to oversee and maintain these resources. Whereas it is now generally recognized that technology-related expenses inevitably grow at rates well in excess of inflation on college campuses just as they do in most other business sectors, it is also true that other expenses are equally difficult to control. One notable example concerns the troubling rate of growth in acquisition costs for periodicals. The average increase for periodical subscriptions at leading small colleges has been close to 8 percent per year for the past decade.[6] In light of this challenge, and in order to control library acquisition costs overall, many schools have had to reduce book acquisition expenditures to balance budgets, a practice that has further eroded a difficult market for academic books.

Another area of concern that has generated much attention is the financial impact of an overheated competitive environment. In order to keep pace with real and perceived competitors, for example, institutions have invested in campus improvements intended to heighten eye appeal for those with a consumer's mentality. These kinds of expenses have attracted much attention from critics, including Andrew Hacker and Claudia Dreifus, who proclaim, "The colleges are caught in an extravagant amenities race, tripping over each other to provide luxuries, large and small, especially aimed at seventeen-year-old applicants."[7] There is little doubt that many colleges and universities are guilty of some pandering to young applicants, but it is also true that competitive pressure has been a good thing for many college students and their families. Such pressures have driven the creation of innovative academic programs, the acquisition of state-of-the-art facilities and resources, and most of all, the implementation of new financial aid programs that have substantially reduced or even eliminated affordability as a problem for many low-income families and even some with middle incomes. At Lafayette and a great many peer institutions, this commitment to economic access has resulted in rates of growth in financial aid budgets well in excess of growth in overall operating expenses. Although sponsoring institutions and many students have benefitted greatly from these programs, the associated expense growth trajectories are clearly unsustainable over the long term.

The fourth factor concerns historic management practices that have placed too great an emphasis on inputs rather than outcomes—or to put it differently, on more rather than better.[8] Institutions across the spectrum—public and private, large and small, highly selective and those with open admissions—have long-standing management practices and institutional planning processes that were predicated on the generation of incremental resources rather than the reallocation of existing ones. Largely as the result of emerging reaccreditation pressures, most colleges and universities have now begun to develop better methods for measuring the quality of outcomes, which, in turn, has led to better decision making about cost management and resource reallocation.

A final, crucial factor that has contributed to the problem of rising costs is the fact that market demand and other forms of external support have continued to grow in the face of rising tuition rates and other market pressures. During the past several decades, most of the selective public and private institutions have experienced significant growth in college applications and, equally, in other forms of external support, including rising levels of philanthropic giving from alumni, parents, and others; private foundation support; and government-sponsored research. All of these groups have, in one form or another, sent a signal that they believe their investments to be worthwhile or they would not have chosen to sustain them. Even as prices have risen at rates well in excess of the cost of living, and there is more and more talk of the affordability crisis, applications at the most selective institutions have continued to rise. During the past several decades, the most expensive private—and increasingly, public—institutions have experienced ever-increasing levels of interest in them. Seen in this way, it would be correct to observe that the market has rewarded more and better programs, increased numbers of faculty, and even more campus amenities. Only recently has there been evidence that demand is shifting in important ways for many sectors of the higher education system.

Because colleges and universities serve their missions best by operating in a highly competitive environment, performance in the market will continue to be crucial in helping leaders determine how best to allocate resources and plan for the future. For a very long time we have lived in an environment that rewarded ever more institutional growth and program enhancement. Perhaps those days are now behind us. The market has many ways of making clear what it values.

Technology

It is increasingly evident that near and intermediate-term advances in technology are likely to exert a more substantial impact on the direction and practices of higher education than any of the other leading factors outlined in this essay.[9] Yet we must also acknowledge that the specific consequences for liberal arts colleges and other sectors of the higher education system remain unclear at best. Drivers of change in education are closely related to the general impact of technological progress in our society as a whole. Because the value of technology to the educational work of faculty and students continues to improve, there is increased demand for new resources, which in turn has provided powerful incentives for investment in new businesses to serve these markets.[10] Within our complicated and disparate educational system there is clear evidence that new technologies are ably and efficiently replacing distressed labor-intensive approaches. For example, the development of cost-effective and educationally compelling interactive technologies, including cognitive tutors and other systems, has now provided exciting new platforms for individualized teaching on a very large scale. Student demand for innovative, flexible, and cost-effective new technologies will continue to drive the market just as consumer demand has driven the general technology market.

Because of the demonstrable value of these technologies for research and teaching, they will continue to find their way onto college and university campuses across the spectrum of institutions, even if the specific details of a financially sustainable business model has not yet emerged. The proliferation of new businesses and learning platforms will surely continue, and some will have a transformative impact on us all (if only we knew which ones). As we follow these developments, our institutions will need to make new investments, some with considerable uncertainty, even as we continue to realign our organizations to keep pace.

These changes, dramatic as they are, will require liberal arts colleges to think carefully about how technological changes in higher education can enhance the quality and effectiveness of their particular offerings within their distinctive model. Administrators and faculty will need to consider the following questions as they develop their own institutional plans:

1. What is the appropriate role of technology for institutions that focus on individual mentorship of students and close interaction with faculty?

2. What is the best method for thoughtful and cost-effective planning?
3. How do we make sure to acknowledge—and even optimize—generationally distinct learning approaches?
4. What are the right kinds of investments in a constrained financial environment?

Changing Demographics

A major demographic shift is now underway in the United States that will have a profound impact on the character, constitution, and competitiveness of liberal arts colleges. According to the U.S. Census Bureau, within ten years minorities will comprise more than half of all children, a number that is expected to rise to 62 percent by the middle of this century. By 2050 the Hispanic and Asian populations are projected to double, while the black population will see modest rates of growth. As a result, the longstanding educational goal of increasing diversity within the small college sector is likely also to become a strategic necessity. Because many of these students will be the first generation in their families to go to college, finding ways to attract them to small private institutions that focus on a liberal arts education will not be easy. The problem is complicated further because many of these students will come from geographic areas that are traditionally underserved by liberal arts colleges, including the South and the West, while areas of traditional enrollment strength, including New England and the Middle Atlantic regions, will see significant decreases in college eligible populations.[11]

Public Skepticism

As a consequence of the factors described above and surely of others, public concern has been rising about the value of an investment in higher education and, more generally, about the direction and integrity of our postsecondary educational system. These concerns find expression in the national media on a daily basis, and they extend beyond finances to include the costs—financial and otherwise—of intercollegiate athletics; the failure of graduates to find satisfactory employment even as they face unmanageable student debt; and, for many, the questionable long-term benefits of a liberal education rather than a more focused pre-professional one. As David Scobey has recently written, "This crisis of legitimacy . . . has fueled the atmosphere of distrust that pervades public debates over higher education, the current rash of calls for external assessment and accountability, and rising skepticism about the 'value proposition' that social and familial investment in higher education offers."[12]

Some critics have gone farther, describing the current environment as an emerging crisis comparable to those of the health care system or financial services. Mark Taylor has pointed out that "there are disturbing similarities between the dilemma colleges and universities have created for themselves and conditions that led to the collapse of major financial institutions supposedly too secure to fail."[13] In *Academically Adrift: Limited Learning on College Campuses,* a recent study that received a great deal of media coverage, Richard Arum and Josipa Roksa raise troubling questions about the amount of real learning that is occurring on the campuses of American colleges and universities.[14] They see a growing disconnect between institutional objectives and undergraduate academic learning. In one form or another, the volume of these criticisms is rising for the general public as well as for various stakeholders, including state and federal governments, foundations, and the media.

Moreover, the problem has been exacerbated by a growing disconnect between college leaders and the public on these very issues, especially concerning the value and affordability of a college degree.[15] Those on the inside who are closest to the debate have much greater knowledge of complicated financial aid resources that significantly reduce the real cost of attending college, and they have benefitted from the opportunity to see the long-term benefits of a college education on a great many individuals and society as a whole. Prospective students and their parents, as well as recent graduates and the public, inevitably have a more circumscribed perspective on these difficult issues.

Whatever the merit of these criticisms may be, the issue of public skepticism and loss of trust is real and highly consequential. If college and university leaders do not engage these criticisms more directly, develop meaningful and appropriate actions to respond, and communicate more effectively about them, the problems are likely to increase, leading to further erosion of trust. The consequences will be serious indeed, including possible loss of market share to lower-cost alternatives, the prospect of increased government regulation, and potential further reductions than we have already seen in government funding as well as other forms of external support. Finally, the most invidious consequence of diminished public trust will be damage to the crucial but fragile partnership between colleges and their many stakeholders. As this problem escalates, we will see more and more evidence of public criticism and distrust, which inevitably will detract from the ability of colleges to provide a challenging and comprehensive learning experience for their students.

Institutional Category	No. Institutions (approx.)	Admissions	Curricular Emphasis	Outlook
1 Most selective liberal arts colleges	100	Highly selective	Liberal arts	Strong/stable
2 Research innovators / global leaders	50	Highly selective	Diverse	Strong/stable
3 National universities—public and private	50	Selective	Diverse	Challenging
4 Providers of social mobility		Open	Vocational	Enrollment strong / funding precarious
Community colleges	1,100			
Regional publics	500			
5 Regional private colleges	500+	Moderately / less selective	Liberal arts / preprofessional	Precarious
6 For-profit providers	700+	Open	Vocational/ preprofessional	Strong / high growth / increased government scrutiny

The Competitive Environment

Within the large and disparate universe of colleges and universities in the United States, the impact of these four precipitating factors will vary significantly by the type of institution and the particular markets they serve. Without doing injustice to the richness and heterogeneity of institutions within our system, we might distinguish between six general categories of schools from the vantage point of the undergraduate student (see table, facing page). In segmenting the higher education market in this way, I recognize that in some cases I have blurred important distinctions between individual institutions and in others distinguished between schools that otherwise have much in common. In focusing on the competitive environment for undergraduates, I have considered four distinguishing characteristics: (1) the kinds of students who attend; (2) curriculum and academic programs offered; (3) sources of institutional distinctiveness for undergraduates; and (4) institutional success factors.

Most Selective Liberal Arts Colleges

Offering a student-centered environment with substantial opportunities for leadership, close work with faculty, and outstanding resources dedicated to undergraduates, these colleges have consistently achieved outstanding results as measured by student and alumni satisfaction, graduation rates, and professional outcomes. Faculty members are expected to be actively engaged in research that advances their disciplines but that also complements the institution's focus on undergraduate education. Many of these colleges are able to compete for the best students in the United States and around the world, and they support them by offering financial aid comparable to that offered by the leading research universities. Success factors include significant endowment levels per student, strong annual giving and major gift programs, outstanding faculty who are dedicated to mission, and highly developed campus infrastructures. In addition to the significant resources dedicated to undergraduates, these schools are distinguished by an excellent record of graduate outcomes and strong alumni networks dedicated to supporting the college.

Research Innovators

Representing the gold standard of American universities, these institutions are among wealthiest and most widely respected in the world. The universities in this group, including the Ivies, MIT, and Johns Hopkins, as well as a few of the leading flagship public universities, have vast resources, diverse academic offerings, and a research focus that generally privileges graduate students and professional schools. Because of their prestige, the quality of their students and faculty, and the wealth of opportunities they offer, undergraduate admission is intensely competitive, even if for the most part the programs that serve them represent a niche within a larger institution. Success within this group depends on the effective management of a complex funding system including, in addition to tuition, large endowments, research grants and indirect cost recoveries, philanthropic support, and other revenue-producing operations. Notwithstanding their emphasis on graduate and professional education and the research demands that often circumscribe the kind of faculty engagement seen in selective liberal arts colleges, these schools have been national leaders in the area of undergraduate education. Because they are global institutions with substantial resources, what they do has reverberated throughout the system. Demand for undergraduate admission to these universities is only likely to increase.

Public and Private National Universities

Offering a traditional university experience for undergraduates, these schools offer a wide range of academic programs; a more balanced faculty commitment to research and teaching; opportunities for professional training in engineering, business, and education; and, very often, highly visible and expensive intercollegiate athletics programs. Admission to these universities is moderately selective. As opposed to small liberal arts colleges, the student experience is characterized more by opportunities for participation than for leadership, and class sizes tend to be large. The private schools in this group are very expensive, relying primarily on tuition revenues, with supplemental income coming from endowments and research funding. Success factors include a strategic vision that enhances institutional distinctiveness, signature programs that offer competitive advantage or at least greater visibility, and strong fiscal management. The outlook for these schools is more uncertain, given ongoing financial challenges from state funding sources for public institutions and from continued pressure on pricing increases for both public and private schools. Although these institutions are large and collectively serve a significant portion of undergraduates in the United States, they will be challenged to maintain quality and enrollments in the face of increasing competitive and financial pressures.

Providers of Social Mobility

Offering open admissions and a low cost of attendance, community colleges and regional public universities represent the largest number of schools in the American system.[16] These schools emphasize pre-professional and vocational academic programming designed to help graduates secure employment and begin careers. Many of these students are among the first generation in their families to attend college. This sector has benefitted significantly from the demographic changes outlined above and therefore has experienced rapid growth. Institutional success depends on a clear and comprehensible value proposition, careful management of costs, stable sources of public funding, and geographic proximity to their students, since most of those enrolled are commuters. This sector is likely to see continued enrollment growth even as it struggles with serious funding shortages tied to state budget cuts.

Regional Private Colleges

With generally more limited resources, regional and local markets for student enrollments, and significant pressures on tuition pricing, regional private colleges will continue to face significant challenges in the face of a difficult economy and the proliferation of competitive options available to prospective students. These schools focus on providing a traditional small college experience that includes relatively small classes, a student-centered environment, and a faculty dedicated primarily to teaching. Thus far, many of these schools have been able to survive by meeting enrollment targets while limiting growth in discount rates, by careful control of operating costs, and, increasingly, by offering degrees in preprofessional fields. Faculty at these schools are generally required to carry heavier teaching loads than that required at other four-year schools, and their salaries fall well below benchmarks for universities and leading liberal arts colleges.[17] Notwithstanding these challenges, these colleges succeed in providing many students with a strong and highly valued small college experience, a supportive educational community, and significant opportunities for student engagement. In light of the precipitating factors outlined above, it is likely that some of these schools will be struggling for their survival in the coming decade.

For-Profit Providers

Offering flexible on-line programs primarily for nontraditional students, the for-profit sector has experienced rapid growth in the past decade but has recently experienced weakened demand and increased government scrutiny for its financial practices, particularly with regard to management of student loans.[18] This sector has achieved success by offering relatively lower cost and flexible programs leading to vocational and pre-professional degrees. Unlike other sectors, these businesses have a highly flexible cost structure due primarily to reliance on part-time faculty who do not hold tenure. The for-profit business model requires aggressive advertising, a market-driven curriculum that serves well-defined consumer needs, and ease of access toward a degree. It is likely that this area will continue to experience market share growth in the foreseeable future.

An Opportunity to Lead

Over the next decade, the four precipitating factors discussed above are likely to result in dramatic change across the system, although the particular impact will vary for each of the groups described above. With more limited resources and greater pressure on pricing, we should expect to see greater differentiation than we have seen thus far, both across sectors and between individual institutions. As they are called upon to achieve specific institutional objectives with greater resource constraints, colleges will inevitably have to make more clearly defined choices, and this will drive greater levels of institutional risk taking and differentiation in the market. Over the long term, greater heterogeneity should serve the public more effectively by encouraging innovation and offering a wider range of college choices for prospective students.[19] However, these market and financial pressures are also going to result in consolidation; clearly some of the more than four thousand institutions serving undergraduates today will not survive. Greatest risk will be to regional private colleges and perhaps some regional public universities as well. One factor that is not yet clear to anyone is the long-term impact of computer-based instruction, both on institutional practices and on the system as a whole.

Within this complex and dynamic competitive environment, the most well-funded and selective liberal arts colleges are especially well positioned to lead in advancing undergraduate education because of their strong and diversified resource base, the capacity to adapt more quickly to change, their proven educational model, and their continued focus on the needs of undergraduates. However, such an opportunity to lead will not be easy. Success will depend on the degree to which these colleges are able to build on six areas of distinction that have traditionally contributed to an outstanding educational experience and an enduringly valuable investment. In addition, they will need to maintain a strong focus on several key success practices.

Six Areas of Distinction

1. *Formative Educational Experience:* For many small colleges, the pressure to enhance the curriculum with pre-professional training continues to increase, usually in response to perceived market needs in a down economy. Yet we know that our graduates will change jobs, and even careers, several times throughout their lifetimes and that they will be served best with an education that helps them to develop the critical skills needed to function effectively in a rapidly changing environment, including the ability to read carefully, think critically, communicate effectively, and reflect carefully on an ethical dimension. Most important, they will need to become highly skilled lifetime learners. A liberal education is for many students the most effective means of achieving these skills and helping them realize strong graduate outcomes. Since so many other schools in the system offer ample pre-professional training for those who seek it, there is little incremental value for liberal arts colleges to redirect their resources away from a proven educational model to produce a duplicative one.

2. *Comprehensive Learning Environment:* As Rebecca Chopp, John McCardell, and others in this volume have argued, the distinguishing characteristic of most liberal arts colleges is their capacity to create learning environments that integrate the curricular, extracurricular, and cocurricular experiences for all students. In so doing, they aspire to what Chopp calls the "cultivation of character," using the development of critical thinking, a civic perspective, and service to the world as critical components in building intentional communities that can serve as incubators for linking knowledge, freedom, and democracy.

3. *Engaged Faculty:* Perhaps the most important component of the small college experience for students is the opportunity to work closely with faculty within the classroom and in other contexts and in so doing to build mentoring relationships that endure well beyond their college years. In my experience, the best faculty members at these institutions select small colleges because they believe in the complementarity of teaching and research, and they value these relationships as much as do the students. Finding the right balance between research and teaching varies not only by the institution and academic discipline but also by the intellectual interests of the faculty member. However, it is important to recognize the value of research to the teaching mission and to support it accordingly. Moreover, the commitment of the best faculty to the small college environment extends beyond their teaching and academic contributions to the institution itself through serious engagement in shared governance. More than any other institu-

tions within our system, small colleges depend on faculty involvement in governance and community leadership.

4. *High Impact Learning Practices:* These include first-year seminars, learning communities, writing intensive courses, undergraduate research, service learning experiences, and capstone projects among others. In his 2008 study of high impact learning practices, George Kuh noted that these practices are powerful because they increase the frequency of meaningful interactions with faculty and peers, induce students to spend more time and effort on research, writing, and analytic thinking, and involve students in more hands-on and collaborative forms of learning.[20] While these kinds of educational opportunities can and should be offered to all undergraduates regardless of the kind of institution they attend, small colleges are particularly well positioned to ensure that all students have such highly meaningful experiences.

5. *Outstanding Postgraduate Outcomes:* The leading liberal arts colleges have historically done an outstanding job of helping their graduates to develop meaningful careers by engaging with them throughout their college years in careful advising and close mentoring. Graduates are therefore well prepared to make informed decisions about graduate school or careers, and they have the support they need to help them along.

6. *Powerful Alumni Network:* Although they are not unique in offering their students access to an extensive and extraordinarily productive alumni network, the elite liberal arts colleges do this from a position of special advantage. These colleges can often provide access to a vast network of support for professional and social opportunities that are otherwise unavailable to students and alumni. In addition to the long-term benefit of membership in such a group, these networks also supplement the college learning environment by providing valuable internship opportunities and through meaningful engagement on campus.

Key Success Practices

Although there is considerable uncertainty and even anxiety about the changes ahead for higher education, there is less doubt about the effectiveness of the liberal arts college model in producing outstanding and well-documented educational results. In order to build on this record of achievement, to anticipate as much as possible the changes that lie ahead, and to lead the nation and the world in providing innovative, enduring, and relevant education for life in the twenty-first century, several key success practices will be essential:

- Developing a compelling institutional vision that enhances all six areas of distinction.
- Implementing careful and prudent financial management practices to limit reliance on fee increases. Budgeting growth rates beyond 1–2 percent above CPI is not likely to be sustainable.
- Incorporating technology into the overall vision, including operational practices and academic planning. Involve students and faculty in the process.
- Focusing planning efforts and management practices on outcomes and make them transparent to all stakeholders.
- Maintaining a strong and visible commitment to the values of shared governance, even as decision-making cycles become shorter. Make clear what is needed from all constituencies.
- Engaging more actively in communication and advocacy with the public on all of the educational issues of concern to them. Make a compelling case for the purposes and enduring value of liberal arts colleges.

If, in the face of much uncertainty, liberal arts colleges can contribute to society, as they always have in the past, by graduating highly intelligent and ethically grounded individuals who are capable learners, productive team members, and effective communicators, and if they can do so without imposing undue financial hardship on most of their students or their families, they will persevere through the challenges before us and help us to navigate whatever lies ahead.

NOTES

Work on this essay was completed during my tenure as president of Lafayette College. I would like to express my thanks to my colleagues there who helped in significant ways with this project, including especially Ed Ahart, exemplary board chair and trusted friend.

1. Christopher Jencks and David Riesman, *The Academic Revolution* (Garden City, NY: Doubleday, 1968).

2. "Trends in College Pricing," 2011 Report of the College Board, http://trends.collegeboard .org.

3. "Higher Education Is Key to Economic Growth and Competitiveness—But Can the U.S. Retain Its Edge?" www.standardandpoors.com/ratingsdirect.

4. William Baumol and William Bowen, *Performing Arts: The Economic Dilemma* (New York: Twentieth Century Fund, 1966), and Robert B. Archibald and David H. Feldman, *Why Does College Cost So Much?* (New York: Oxford University Press, 2011).

5. This point is also made in William Bowen's excellent essay, "Thinking about Tuition," reprinted in *Ever the Teacher: William G. Bowen's Writings as President of Princeton* (Princeton, NJ: Princeton University Press, 1987), 530.

6. www.educationadvisoryboard.com (22852D).

7. Andrew Hacker and Claudia Dreifus, *Higher Education? How Colleges Are Wasting Our Money and Failing Our Kids—and What We Can Do about It* (New York: Times Books, 2010), 119.

8. See, e.g., www.economist.com/node/21541398/print.

9. See Taylor Walsh, *Unlocking the Gates: How and Why Leading Universities Are Opening Up Access to Their Courses* (Princeton, NJ: Princeton University Press, 2011). See also Lawrence S. Bacow, William G. Bowen, et al. "Barriers to Adoption of Online Learning Systems in U.S. Higher Education," sr.ithaka.org/research-publications/barriers-adoption-online-learning-systems-us-higher-education.

10. Nick DeSantis, "A Boom Time for Education Start-Ups," *Chronicle of Higher Education*, March 18, 2012.

11. All data from U.S. Census Bureau, Population Division and U.S. Department of Education, National Center for Education Statistics.

12. David Scobey, "Civic Engagement and the Copernican Moment," Foreseeable Futures #11, Position Papers from Imagining America, 8.

13. Mark Taylor, *Crisis on Campus: A Bold Plan for Reforming Our Colleges and Universities* (New York: Knopf, 2010).

14. Richard Arum and Josipa Roksa, *Academically Adrift: Limited Learning on College Campuses* (Chicago: University of Chicago Press, 2011).

15. See the Pew Research Center Report, "Is College Worth It?" http://pewresearch.org/pubs/1993.

16. In 2009, public two-year colleges represented 26 percent of full-time undergraduate enrollments in the United States, while public four-year colleges represented 44 percent. See www.collegeboard.org/trends.

17. See the recent study on financing of liberal arts colleges by Lucie Lapovsky, http://lapovsky.com/wp-content/uploads/2012/06/Case-lib-arts-colleges-21412.pdf.

18. According to the College Board, market share for private for-profits increased from 6 percent to 11 percent between 2000 and 2009, www.collegeboard.org/trends.

19. This point was made by Bowen in "Thinking about Tuition," 534.

20. Quoted in *The LEAP Vision for Learning: Outcomes, Practices, Impact, and Employer's Views* (AAC&U, 2011), 15.

PART II / An Opportunity to Lead

CHAPTER 3

Economics and Affordability

Catharine Bond Hill
PRESIDENT, VASSAR COLLEGE

Jill Tiefenthaler
PRESIDENT, COLORADO COLLEGE

Suzanne P. Welsh
VICE PRESIDENT FOR FINANCE AND TREASURER, SWARTHMORE COLLEGE

At a time when the cost of a college education is rising and household incomes are declining, university and college leaders are faced with some difficult questions about the price and affordability of higher education. Indeed, President Barack Obama emphasized this very point in his 2012 State of the Union address, saying, "Let me put colleges and universities on notice: If you can't stop tuition from going up, the funding you get from taxpayers will go down. Higher education can't be a luxury—it is an economic imperative that every family in America should be able to afford."[1]

How do we propose an effective response to this challenge? One way is for leaders at liberal arts colleges to define and explain the issues. In particular, it is important to recognize that there are more than four thousand institutions of higher education in the United States, including community colleges, public two- and four-year colleges and universities, private non-profit colleges and universities, and a rapidly growing for-profit sector—all with economic models that differ in important ways. While some issues facing these sectors are similar, each faces a variety of unique challenges.

It is also important to remember that many people—including some of the press—do not understand the difference between cost, price, and net price, and yet these distinctions help define the issues facing different sectors and could inform solutions.[2] For some institutions, cost is the main issue and, given other revenue streams, drives price and net price. For other institutions, price is the main issue as schools push up tuition charges to offset declining revenues from other sources.

We want to clarify some of the challenges facing American higher education generally, and liberal arts colleges in particular, and to propose possible paths forward, keeping in mind the specific issues faced by different types of institutions. We start by presenting data on the higher education sector in the United States and discussing the challenges it is facing broadly. We then present data on a representative selective liberal arts college (based on the data of twelve liberal arts colleges[3]), highlighting the particular challenges of this one segment of American higher education. Finally, we discuss some possible policy responses—some that our sector can adopt, some that would have to be implemented by others (but where we might play a role), and some that could be imposed on us.

The Economics of Higher Education

To understand the new economic reality facing higher education generally, we need to recognize some of the forces shaping higher education in the United States today. An article in the science magazine *Seed* described the current situation succinctly: "Our world is not the stable workhorse we once presumed it to be. Financial markets are inherently volatile; seemingly healthy ecosystems can collapse suddenly; the favorable window of life-supporting conditions that humans currently enjoy is an anomaly in the cosmic history of the planet. Change, sometimes in the form of radical, transformative shifts, is the defining characteristic of our existence."[4]

Applying these ideas to higher education, one could say that the decades before the Great Recession, when we could count on a steady stream of endowment earnings, philanthropy, and tuition increases, were the anomaly, and we are unlikely to see that kind of stability again. Now we are in a period of enormous transition, with institutions trying to do more with less while continuing to make sure that students and faculty receive the resources, support, and encouragement they need. Given that most colleges and universities have streamlined their operations and are doing all they can to ensure access, the next step may be educating the public—especially students, parents, alumni, and boards—of our efforts to support the traditions and values that have made the U.S. system of higher education the gold standard across the world.

Demand and Supply

Higher education is one of the largest industries in the United States and one of this country's top service exports. More than four thousand degree-granting institutions are spread across the country, educating 21 million students and employing 3.4 million people. Public colleges and universities represent 40 percent of all U.S. institutions of higher education and enroll 76 percent of all college students. Nonprofit private institutions comprise 38 percent of all institutions and educate 15 percent of undergraduates, while liberal arts colleges educate 6 percent of all undergraduates. The growing sector of for-profit institutions (22 percent of all institutions in the United States) now educate 9 percent of undergraduates.[5] Global rankings of postsecondary institutions show that the United States still leads globally with fifteen of the top twenty universities. Liberal arts colleges in particular are emulated throughout the world as interest in "American-style" higher education grows.[6]

Over the last several decades, both supply and demand have shaped the market price of a college education. On the demand side, three trends have led to an increase over the last thirty years. First, the demographic bulge resulting from the Baby Echo-Boom, or Baby Boomlet, led to more high school graduates from 1992 to 2009. Second, despite the fact that the Baby Boomlet has ended, an increase in the rate of those going to college has translated into continued growth. From 2009 to 2020, total enrollment in higher education is expected to increase 13 percent. This enrollment growth will include a 45-percent increase for Hispanics, a 25-percent increase for both black students and Asian / Pacific Islanders, and only a 1-percent increase for students who are white. The enrollment of first-time freshmen is expected to increase 11 percent.[7]

What is motiving this increase in college goers? Likely, it is the increasing value of a college degree. As the U.S. Treasury Department reported in "The Economic Case for Higher Education" (2012), a college graduate earned 64 percent more in 2011 than a high school graduate in median weekly earnings ($1,053 compared to $638). According to the report, today's earnings gap is the highest since 1915, the earliest year these estimates were tracked. Today a college degree is key to economic mobility. In fact, according to one source, "attaining a college degree quadruples the likelihood that a child born to parents on the bottom rung of the income ladder will make it to the top."[8]

Additionally, the unemployment gap between those with a college degree and those without a degree has increased. According to a September 2012 article by Thomas Friedman in the *New York Times,* the unemployment rate was 4.1 percent for people with four years of college, 6.6 percent for those with two years, 8.8 percent for high school graduates, and 12.0 percent for dropouts. Friedman echoes the sentiments of many pursuing the promise of higher education: "If you want a decent job that will lead to a decent life today *you* have to work harder, regularly reinvent yourself, obtain at least some form of postsecondary education, make sure that you're engaged in lifelong learning and play by the rules."[9] Even in 2008/ 09, during the worst part of the economic downturn, unemployment for all college graduates remained at 5 percent, a level that economists often consider to be full employment.

And finally, on top of the growing national market for higher education is students' demand to attend the most selective institutions, increasing the relative demand for the top colleges and universities. According to Caroline Hoxby, a Stanford economist, students are looking for schools that offer advantages in terms of both resources and peers. In the past, students were likely "to attend a local college regardless of their abilities and its characteristics. Now, their choices are driven far less by distance and far more by a college's resources and student body. It is the consequent re-sorting of students among colleges that has, at once, caused selectivity to rise in a small number of colleges while simultaneously causing it to fall in other colleges."[10]

Hoxby goes on to show that this integration of the higher education market has not only changed the peer experience for students but has also altered the investment choices of institutions as well as both the tuition students pay and the subsidies they receive. Although tuition is increasing at the most selective schools, students are gaining even more from attending them. Because these institutions are able to direct substantial revenues from large endowments and alumni giving toward the academic program and student services, spending on each student is significantly more than the price of full tuition.

Several factors are also affecting the supply or cost structure of higher education, leading to rising expenses that show no sign of abating. The increasing demand for highly skilled labor that causes people to want a college degree also makes it more expensive to employ such labor. Higher education is one of the most intense industries in terms of the percentage of employees with advanced degrees. And unlike many industries—financial services, for example, where gains in technology have streamlined the labor force—technological improvements in higher education have added to, rather than decreased, costs. For example, in the 1990s institutions wired every residence hall for Internet access; then, less than a decade later, they needed to make additional investments to make the campus wireless. While computers have eliminated the need for typists, they have created the need for IT specialists at a greater expense.

The increasing need for financial aid adds to the economic pressure on institutions. Financial aid has grown as schools seek out greater diversity in their student populations, an effort that benefits society as a whole and enriches learning in and out of the classroom. As more entering students come from a wider range of racial, ethnic, and socioeconomic backgrounds, institutions are called on to help them with generous financial aid packages and other resources needed to make a smooth transition to college. Financial aid reduces net revenues, while other resources increase expenditures and therefore costs. Many institutions, worrying about the impact of debt burden on students, have substituted additional grant aid for loans for low-income and first-generation students, putting further pressure on financial aid resources.

Rising Tuition

As a result of growing demand, decreasing public appropriations, and rising costs, college tuition has consistently increased above inflation over the past thirty years. As figure 1 shows, since 1981 the average inflation-adjusted tuition and fees at a public four-year institution has gone up 368 percent as compared to 281 percent at a private four-year college. While private institutions remain significantly more expensive than their public counterparts, in the last decade the annual inflation-adjusted tuition increase at private nonprofit four-year institutions was 2.6 percent, compared to 6.1 percent per year at four-year publics.[11]

Why has tuition increased more rapidly at public institutions in the past decade? Because state governments must decrease appropriations when the economy is weak and tax revenues decline, public institutions require tuition increases to maintain quality. For private institutions, on the other hand, tuition tends to increase when family incomes rise.

Declining family income is another trend driving concerns about the rising costs of tuition. While family incomes increased, in real terms, in the 1980s and 90s (with the most significant income gains skewed toward the top of the income distribution), families in all income groups saw their real incomes fall between 2000 and 2010, the "lost" decade (see fig. 2).

Making matters more difficult for students and families is the somewhat confusing issue of gross tuition and fees, or the "sticker price," versus net tuition costs. For example, in 2011 the average sticker price for tuition and fees at a private four-year college was $28,500, but the average price students paid was $12,970. According to one source, that's close to what students paid, on average, in the 2001/02 school year in inflation-adjusted dollars.[12]

It is also important to note that all college students receive a subsidy, not just

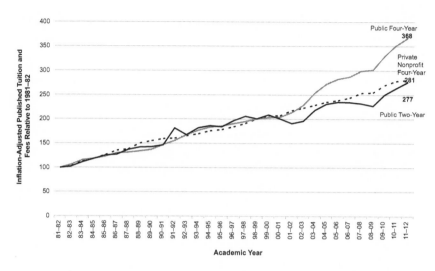

Figure 1. Inflation-Adjusted Tuition and Fees Relative to 1981–82. *The College Board, Annual Survey of Colleges. NCES, Integrated Postsecondary Education Data System (IPEDS), 2012.*

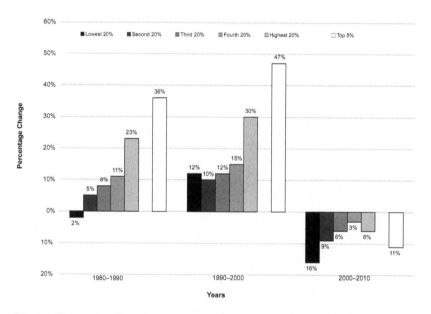

Figure 2. Percentage Growth in Mean Family Income by Quintile in Constant 2010 Dollars. *US Census Bureau, Current Population Survey, 2011, Table F-1, Table F-3, and FINC-01; calculations by authors. http://www.census.gov/cps/.*

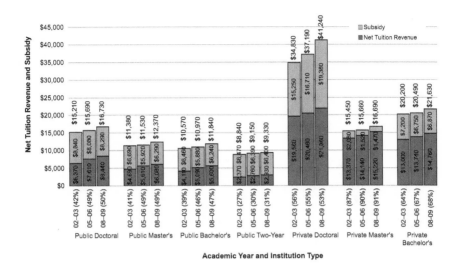

Figure 3. Net Tuition Revenues, Subsidies, and Educational Expenditures per FTE Student in Constant 2009 Dollars. *College Board, Annual Survey of Colleges, 2012.*

those who get financial aid (see fig. 3). So despite the higher "sticker price" of college, the actual cost of educating each student is even greater. This subsidy comes mostly from endowment earnings and gifts in private colleges and universities, and from government appropriations in the public sector. Since the economic downturn, appropriations for public education have declined significantly, and private institutions have seen a decrease in their endowments and annual gifts. As a result, net tuition now covers a higher percentage of total costs in the public sector and at private liberal arts colleges than it did ten years ago.

While the average student in all sectors is subsidized (excluding for-profits, of course), it has been shown that the size of the subsidy is positively correlated with the selectivity of the institution.[13] The averages reported here therefore mask significant differences across institutions. Within the liberal arts sector, for example, the subsidy offered by highly selective institutions with large endowments significantly exceeds that at less selective liberal arts colleges. This link between an institution's wealth, subsidy, and selectivity is at the heart of Hoxby's (2009) analysis of the growing bifurcation between the "haves" and "have-nots" in higher education.

Looking at a Representative Liberal Arts College

As the costs of higher education have increased faster than inflation over the past decade and as family incomes across all quintiles have declined, how have these national trends affected the private liberal arts college sector? To address some of these issues, we created a representative liberal arts college (RLAC) by aggregating and averaging data from twelve institutions: Bryn Mawr, Colorado, Franklin & Marshall, Lafayette, Macalester, Pomona, Sewanee: The University of the South, Smith, Swarthmore, Vassar, Wheaton, and Williams. These institutions were chosen because their presidents or other senior administrators were panelists at The Future of the Liberal Arts College in America conference held in spring 2012.

RLAC's profile in 2009/10 looks like many liberal arts colleges. It has just under two thousand students and a small enrollment increase of approximately 5 percent between 2000/01 and 2009/10. RLAC's student/faculty ratio was 10.8 in 2009/10, and the fictional institution had a budget of $120.1 million. RLAC differs from the majority of liberal arts colleges in its selectivity and its endowment of more than $700 million (compared with the average endowment value of $324 million of 98 small [under 3,000] private institutions with a basic Carnegie classification of Arts & Science).

As was the case nationally with liberal arts colleges from 2000/01 to 2009/10, student charges (tuition and room and board) grew significantly—RLAC experienced a 60 percent increase. Given that family incomes declined in real terms for all quintiles over this time period (see fig. 2), paying tuition at RLAC required a larger percentage of household income in 2010 than it did in 2000.

The average cost per student at RLAC in 2009/10 was $60,201, and the average student charge (tuition plus room and board, or sticker price) was $49,025. Therefore, even students paying full tuition at RLAC received an average subsidy of more than $10,000 per year, mirroring the national data (see fig. 3). While the sticker price of RLAC increased by 60 percent, its financial aid budget more than doubled. The discount rate (the percentage of every tuition dollar given back in financial aid) at RLAC increased from 30 percent in 2000/01 to 37 percent in 2009/10. In addition, the percentage of students receiving aid increased from 56 percent to 60 percent.

The increased expenditure on financial aid over this period (more than 100%) is one explanation for the increase in RLAC's sticker price. But what are the other causes of the increase? First, cost per student, net of financial aid, increased by 42 percent. The increase in inflation, or the Consumer Price Index (CPI), over this same period was 24 percent. Why did costs increase above inflation? A key explanation is that labor costs for faculty increased by 40 percent. The fact that RLAC's costs increased at a faster rate than the CPI because of its labor costs is consistent with the analysis in the previous section: Higher education has a higher wage premium because it employs so many people with advanced degrees, not just faculty but also staff such as information technologists and other professionals.

Another explanation is that while costs continued to increase, revenue sources beyond tuition are limited. The major sources of revenue for liberal arts colleges are student charges (net of financial aid) and endowment earnings. During this period (2000/01 to 2009/10), RLAC's endowment barely kept up with inflation, so increases in student revenues were required to pay for the increased costs. Yet as mentioned above, the sticker price remained below the cost per student in 2010, so every student still received a subsidy. However, student charges covered a higher share of total expenses and grew from 72 percent to 81 percent of expenses per student during this period. This result is consistent with the national data presented in figure 3 showing that the percentage of costs covered by net tuition increased from 2000 to 2010.

Does RLAC accurately represent the liberal arts college sector? As we have shown, the trends of the averaged data for these twelve liberal arts colleges support the national data overviewed in the previous section. Tuition increased above inflation and family incomes. Costs also increased above inflation, largely driven by increases in the costs of highly skilled labor. Subsidies for full-pay students remained but were reduced. Yet despite these similarities with the national trends, RLAC has significant financial advantages that much of the liberal arts sector does not enjoy.

Most important, RLAC was fortunate to have an endowment of more than $700 million. This amount falls into the Platinum category, the highest of three categories as described by Lucie Lapovsky in a paper that compares three liberal arts colleges with significantly different levels of endowment per student, labeling them Platinum, Gold, and Silver.[14] Even though the endowment did not grow at the rate of inflation over this period, it provided an important source of revenue to support increases in financial aid and other expenditures in addition to tuition.

A related advantage of RLAC is that it enjoys a strong national reputation and is experiencing the growth in demand documented by Hoxby (2009).[15] Because of demand, RLAC can set its own price. It can also provide need-based financial aid for the educational purpose of socioeconomic diversity but does not need to significantly discount tuition to simply fill beds. Not only does RLAC have a greater endowment per student than the typical liberal arts college, but its net tuition per student is also greater, meaning there is significantly more to spend on instruction for each student. Despite these market advantages, RLAC must question if its financial model is sustainable. Because costs increased faster than inflation while family incomes did not even keep pace with inflation, and because it is highly unlikely that endowments will continue to increase at double-digit rates as they did before the downturn, the pressure to find ways to control costs is significant.

Responding to the Challenges

The data on American liberal arts colleges suggest that we are entering an era in which change is needed. Demand is up, in part because of increased economic returns to postsecondary schooling.[16] Costs are up, in part because of the increased cost of skilled labor and a variety of quality improvements. The actual price paid (net tuition) is up for many families relative to household income, as higher tuition has not been completely offset by higher financial aid in many cases, while household incomes have been stagnant or declining over the last decade.

Within liberal arts colleges, differing circumstances result in differing challenges. For well-endowed and selective colleges, large endowments per student, which have experienced significant volatility, create management issues as spending rules translate volatility in endowment returns to volatility in support for operating budgets. (Of course, schools with smaller endowments would be happy to have these problems in exchange for larger endowments.) However, the wealth of these institutions and demand from higher-income students, whose families have done relatively well over the last thirty years, have allowed those schools to charge higher tuition while protecting access for middle- and low-income students through financial aid. For liberal arts colleges with smaller endowments, slow growth and declining family incomes generally have put significant pressure on tuition revenues, as has discounting beyond need through merit-based financial aid, while they still face the pressures of increased costs for skilled labor.

Until now there have been limited incentives or pressures for liberal arts colleges to be more innovative about improving productivity and lowering costs. Many upper-income families have been willing to pay for additional programs and services that they perceive as valuable to their children, and schools have competed for those students by spending on services, thus pushing up costs. This has been particularly true among the most selective private colleges and universities, where 70 percent of students come from the top 20 percent of income distribution. While these highly selective colleges have greater resources to invest in productivity-increasing innovations, they have faced fewer pressures to do so.

Controlling Costs in the Years Ahead

Liberal arts colleges, particularly those not among the wealthiest, will face challenges because they must balance innovations and services with controlling costs. One challenge, of course, is that these schools attract students from different socioeconomic groups. While those at the top end are willing to pay for a variety of programs and experiences, families who are less well-off may be less willing or unable to afford these expenditures. If colleges and universities continue to meet the demands of their higher-income students for these programs, this puts pressure on financial aid budgets as they continue to support diverse student bodies.

Improving graduation rates as a means of controlling costs is one obvious possibility that has been receiving increasing attention, given that graduation rates at our public institutions are, on average, below 50 percent.[17] Changes that improve graduation rates without either eroding quality or increasing costs significantly could potentially reduce the costs of a college degree by large amounts. Streamlining the curriculum could reduce barriers to completing degree requirements and improve both graduation rates and time to graduation, but this may be viewed by some as reducing the quality of the academic experience.

Many liberal arts colleges already have significantly higher graduation rates than do public institutions, in fact justifying some of the higher costs. But there are still possibilities to pursue. For example, schools could add summer sessions, as Wesleyan University has recently done. One often overlooked cost of higher education is earnings foregone while in school, and a three-year rather than a four-year program would significantly reduce this cost. This assumes that the three-year degree does not involve just eliminating one academic year's worth of credits but instead allows students to earn those credits during the summers. A three-year program would increase savings but could significantly affect the educational experience, perhaps reducing the quality and value of the degree. Adding summer sessions would also make greater use of facilities, reducing capital costs. It is important to note that this would not necessarily save on labor, since additional faculty would be needed to teach these classes during the summer.

Attracting and retaining talented faculty is critical to maintaining excellence. While many colleges are trying to reduce costs by hiring more part-time and junior faculty,[18] there is increasing evidence that this approach reduces the quality of the educational experience. An alternative is to focus faculty efforts on activities that are critical to effectiveness. For example, any non-core activities undertaken by faculty that could be done at less cost by others or by using technology would free up faculty time for more productive activities. An example would be technologies that check prerequisites at the time of registration, freeing faculty time for more important advising or instructional activities.

There may also be opportunities to reallocate faculty time to higher productivity activities within the time currently allocated to teaching. Early evidence suggests that hybrid courses, involving some online materials as well as time in class with a faculty member, may be able to reduce costs while maintaining or improving learning outcomes.[19] It is unlikely that these hybrid courses will work across the curriculum, but they could be useful in some areas. For example, a hybrid course may be a better alternative than a large lecture class in some cases. Schools that pride themselves on having small, intimate seminars may find technology solutions to cost challenges less appealing, although their attractiveness will also depend on the current level of financial pressure, with those facing the greatest pressures most likely to experiment with new alternatives.

Other ways to reduce costs are more questionable. Asking faculty to teach more could reduce costs but would affect quality in both the short and long run. This would be similar to asking faculty to take a pay cut, reducing their compensation relative to other career opportunities. Colleges might also consider cutting back on expenditures for social functions, technology add-ons, counseling, internships, under-enrolled classes or programs, organic foods, or athletics. The problem with this strategy is that many families are willing to pay for programs or services that they deem valuable. This is particularly true at colleges and universities competing for students whose families are willing and able to pay for (perceived) quality.

Another possibility is allowing colleges and universities to "collude" in lowering costs. This would acknowledge that controlling costs is a prisoners' dilemma: while everyone might want to do it, doing so unilaterally can put an individual institution at a competitive disadvantage. Collusion, with all of its negative connotations, could be welfare-improving if it allowed cooperation on cost control in service of affordability and mission.[20] While colleges and universities might be able to agree on some expenditures to avoid or minimize (such as merit aid, climbing walls, or saunas), cutting others would be more problematic. Individual institutions would probably not be willing to commit to constraining their ability to make decisions about such things as average class size or teaching loads or number of languages taught.

One current risk is that the government will interfere more with policies if costs are not better managed. Price controls seem unlikely, but the government could start trying to tie support of one type or another to goals of access. President Obama made several policy proposals that move in this direction. Any such policy changes might involve unintended consequences: some incentives might actually align with established values, but not others.

It is important to understand that reducing financial aid does not reduce the cost of producing a year's worth of education. It simply changes the net price that students are asked to pay. In fact, cutting financial aid actually allows schools to spend more because it increases net tuition revenues, allowing increased expenditures. Constraining financial aid in many cases would be easier than controlling costs as a means of dealing with financial pressures, but such a shift risks alienating the public and reducing access for many students and families.

Virtually all of the highest-tuition colleges and universities in the United States offer significant need-based financial aid, so those students paying the full sticker price are most often from higher income families. Decisions at those schools to hold down tuition increases—the price students from higher-income families pay—and to compensate by reducing financial aid spending, would reduce access for talented students from low- and middle-income families. Holding down tuition while reducing financial aid is a transfer of financial assistance from one set of students (financial aid students) to another (full pay students). It does not reduce the costs of educating a student.

One consequence of declining availability of public financial support and increased tuition costs is that families will bear more of the cost of education. Because loans for many students are more than justified by the returns on higher education, it makes sense to facilitate more borrowing on the part of students and families, despite all the concerns about students graduating with excessive loan burdens. We should, however, encourage policy makers to increase income-contingent options for borrowers. Access to credit would help families with liquidity constraints that want to invest in higher education given the expected returns. Making loan repayment dependent on students' postcollege earnings would protect some people from excessive debt, since not everyone will make the expected return. Much work has been done devising income-contingent options, which suffer from adverse selection problems. Loan forgiveness for individuals who go into low-paying professions, similar to loan forgiveness options for public service, may be an effective strategy.[21]

While the public and private non-profit colleges and universities are struggling with issues of cost and access, the for-profit sector has become an important component of American higher education. We should pay more attention to them, both because they may be able to make a positive contribution to increasing access to education in America and because they may challenge how we have traditionally operated. Higher education has traditionally been in the public and non-profit sectors because of concerns that the private market would not supply these services in an optimal way.[22] While these concerns have attracted increased government oversight, the for-profits are also innovating, particularly in the use of technology, which may hold lessons for liberal arts colleges. Interestingly, a variety of selective private non-profit colleges and universities are entering the space of the for-profits both by partnering with them and by offering competing products and services.[23] The for-profits are going to test the definition of academic quality and what students and families want and are willing to pay for.

Conclusions

The United States has been at the forefront of higher education for over a century, with more than four thousand institutions meeting the needs of students and their families. The liberal arts colleges have been particularly successful in preparing students to meet the complex challenges of our rapidly changing world. Yet in today's economic climate, colleges themselves must face the challenges of rising costs resulting from high wages for a skilled labor force and from programs and services that have increased both the quality and expense of higher education. Even institutions that rely on endowment earnings and gifts have suffered during the recent recession. The escalation of costs, the rise in tuition, and the possibility of declining financial aid have all significantly increased the anxiety surrounding access to college on the part of students, families, and policy makers as well as of colleges and universities themselves as they work to fulfill their missions.

While the cost of a liberal arts college education is likely to increase at rates higher than those for other goods and services, tuition can not continue to exceed the growth in family incomes as has been the case over the past decade. To sustain progress, the leaders of liberal arts colleges must think creatively, continue to look for ways to control costs, and watch for new opportunities that reflect changing conditions. These realities hold important lessons for everyone who looks to the American system for leadership and fresh thinking about higher education and the superb advantages it offers to individuals and communities.

NOTES

1. Barack Obama, "Remarks by the President in State of the Union Address" (January 24, 2012), http://www.whitehouse.gov/the-press-office/2012/01/24/remarks-president-state-union-address.

2. President Obama's challenge to colleges and universities to slow tuition growth or risk losing taxpayer support is a good example. Public institutions have increased tuition precisely because of declining taxpayer support, as they attempt to protect quality. In other sectors, costs and tuition have gone up despite public support, as institutions compete for students by adding programs and services. It is this latter group to whom President Obama was issuing his challenge.

3. The liberal arts colleges included all participated in "The Future of the Liberal Arts College in America," the conference at Lafayette College on April 9–11, 2012, that sparked this book.

4. Seed Media Group, "Knowing Sooner," *Seed,* December 6, 2010.

5. "Trends in College Pricing," 2011 Report of the College Board, http://trends.collegeboard.org.

6. Examples include the creation of Yale-NUS, a liberal arts college in Singapore, and significant interest in liberal arts education in China, including the founding of Yuanpei College at Peking University.

7. William J. Hussar and Tabitha M. Bailey, *Projections of Education Statistics to 2020,* NCES, IES, U.S. Department of Education, September 21, 2011, http://nces.ed.gov/pubs2011/2011026.pdf.

8. Ron Haskins, Harry Holzer, and Robert Lerman, *Promoting Economic Mobility by Increasing Postsecondary Education,* May 2009, www.economicmobility.org.

9. Thomas Friedman, "New Rules," *New York Times,* Sept. 8, 2012, www.nytimes.com/2012/09/09/opinion/sunday/friedman-new-rules.html?emc=tnt&tntemail1=y.

10. Caroline M. Hoxby, "The Changing Selectivity of American Colleges," *Journal of Economic Perspectives* (American Economic Association) 23, no. 4 (2009): 95–118.

11. *The College Board, Annual Survey of Colleges.* NCES, Integrated Postsecondary Education Data System (IPEDS), 2012.

12. Jacob Goldstein, "Figuring Out the Real Price of College," Planet Money Blog, *NPR,* May 11, 2012, www.npr.org/blogs/money/2012/05/11/152499671/figuring-out-the-real-price-of-college.

13. Hoxby, "Changing Selectivity," 95–118; Gordon C. Winston, "Subsidies, Hierarchy and Peers: The Awkward Economics of Higher Education," *Journal of Economic Perspectives,* 13, no. 1 (1999): 13–36.

14. Lucie Lapovsky, "Tale of Three Campuses: A Comparison of Three Small Liberal Arts Colleges," Lapovsky Consulting, February 14, 2012, http://lapovsky.com.

15. Hoxby, "Changing Selectivity," 95–118.

16. Claudia Goldin and Lawrence Katz, *The Race between Education and Technology* (Cambridge, MA: Harvard University Press, 2008).

17. William G. Bowen, Matthew M. Chingos, and Michael S. McPherson, *Crossing the Fin-*

ish Line: Completing College at America's Public Universities (Princeton, NJ: Princeton University Press, 2009).

18. Ronald G. Ehrenberg and Ling Zhang, "Do Tenured and Tenure-Track Faculty Matter? *Journal of Human Resources* 40, no. 3 (Summer 2006): 647–65.

19. See William G. Bowen, Matthew M. Chingos, Kelly A. Lack, and Thomas I. Nygren, "Interactive Learning Online at Public Universities: Evidence from Randomized Trials," *Ithaka S + R*, Carnegie Mellon, May, 22 2012, www.sr.ithaka.org/research-publications/inter active-learning-online-public-universities-evidence-randomized-trials.

20. See Matthew Reed and Robert Shireman, "Time to Reexamine Institutional Cooperation of Financial Aid," *The Institute for College Access and Success*, June 2008, www.usc.edu/programs/cerpp/docs/Timetoreexamineinstitutionalcooperationonfinancialaid.pdf.

21. Bruce Chapman, "Income Contingent Loans for Higher Education: International Reforms," in *Handbook on the Economics of Education*, vol. 2, ed. Eric Hanushek and Finis Welch (Amsterdam: Elsevier, 2006).

22. Henry Hansmann, "The Role of Nonprofit Enterprise," *Yale Law Journal* 89 (April 1980): 835–98.

23. Nonprofit and public university involvement with Udacity, edX and Coursera are examples.

CHAPTER 4

Using Governance to Strengthen the Liberal Arts

Susan Frost
PRINCIPAL, SUSAN FROST CONSULTING

Shelly Weiss Storbeck
MANAGING PARTNER, STORBECK/PIMENTEL & ASSOCIATES LLC

Governance issues in higher education rarely make headline news, but that's exactly what happened in June 2012 when the University of Virginia's board of trustees abruptly forced the president to resign, then voted unanimously to reinstate her sixteen days later. While the main issues surrounding the unfortunate incident were complex, they are prevalent in most colleges and universities to some degree: rising pressures to cope with financial and technological changes, different styles of leadership, and multiple communication channels among board members and presidents.

If the dramatic events at the University of Virginia serve a broader purpose, however, it is to highlight the importance of good governance in determining the future of an institution. Clearly, the pivotal figure in how a college is governed is the president, because he or she sits between the faculty and the board, the two critical constituencies responsible for making strategic and tactical decisions. With that structure in mind, we devised a survey that looked at two key relationships on college campuses, particularly liberal arts colleges as opposed to research universities with larger administrative units: that of the board and the president, and that of the president and the faculty. Because our population was limited as described below, we consider this survey to be a pilot effort and anticipate that these findings will point the way to a fuller, more comprehensive project in the future.

Exploring Key Relationships

We conducted more than a dozen interviews with faculty members, presidents, and board members. We drew our population from colleges whose presidents served on the program of "The Future of the Liberal Arts College in America and Its Leadership Role in Education around the World," a conference supported by the Andrew W. Mellon Foundation in April 2012 to help leaders of colleges explore issues related to the future of the liberal arts. Of the colleges represented by presidents on the program, we chose twelve at random and invited either the president, the board chair, or a faculty member with leadership experience in the formal governance process to participate in a telephone interview. Since clearly no one wanted to go on record to talk about sensitive internal affairs, we promised confidentiality in terms of identifying the interviewee and the institution. Of the board members, we asked primarily about their relationships with their presidents; of the faculty, we asked about their relationships with their presidents; and of the presidents, we asked about their relationships with both board members and faculty.

We focused on two basic questions:

- What features and practices in the area of governance promote creativity and fresh thinking about the liberal arts?
- What inhibits productivity in these key relationships as institutional direction is determined?

Our goal was to explore the broad views of decision makers and collect specific examples of useful strategies as well. We asked not only for general views on what improved relationships between the board and the president, and the president and faculty, as well as what undermined these relationships, but also for specific recommendations of "best practices." We were pleased that our participants described a wealth of good ideas.

Two themes emerged from our interviews. First, the 2008 economic crisis affected governance in several positive ways that are still coming to the forefront. During the crisis, administrators, boards, and faculties came together over the need to ease tension between traditional management practices and immediate economic questions and to confront pressures created by major social, economic, global, and technological changes that are occurring faster than ever before. According to a recent survey of presidents conducted by *Inside Higher Ed* in 2012, these pressures include potential cuts in aid, rising tuition, increased competition for students, financial support from alumni, and budget shortfalls.[1] As a result of the crisis, board members and faculty expressed the hope that the form of collaboration forged during the economic crisis continues in the future.

Second, we see a growing culture clash as a younger generation of business and technology leaders, many of them successful entrepreneurs or venture investors, step into leadership positions on higher education boards. Although many of these young leaders have only a few years of experience governing a college or university, they feel strongly about how institutions should change and how that change should be managed. For the most part, they do not favor the collaborative, incremental approaches that are a hallmark of the academy, but they prefer to move quickly to apply strategies that worked in their business ventures. Meanwhile, faculty leaders are upholding traditional planning and governance processes—leading, we believe, to the kind of friction revealed in the University of Virginia case. In more and more cases, it falls to the president to seek a workable middle ground.

In addition, entrepreneurial leaders like these board members are making their own way into the presidential ranks, bringing business practices to higher education and often clashing head-on with more traditional faculty decision-making practices. The American Council on Education's five-year study on the "Pathway to the Presidency" has witnessed a steady increase of these "nontraditional" presidents noting that they now make up 20 percent of the total.[2]

Governance in the New Economic Era

The compelling need to confront the recession of the late 2000s brought governing groups together in new ways, replacing their previous forms of more isolated work with more action-oriented dynamics. Rather than going back to business as usual, most people we interviewed expressed the desire to build on the practices that carried them through the crisis and use them to govern and set strategic direction in the future. Three themes relate to the new dynamics of board governance: more open communication, with special efforts to reach faculty members who are not part of the formal governance process; more consistent engagement with the board in compelling, authentic work; and the use of collaborative projects that are limited in scope and time to set direction rather than focusing on developing a more traditional overall strategic plan.

During the crisis, the board and faculty both appreciated *more open communication* from the president and with each other, and many expressed the hope that the flow of information would continue. Board members noted that in the past, meetings were more structured, almost scripted, and designed not to encourage spontaneous discussion but to impart information. During the crisis, however, some presidents replaced this type of session with more open conversation and debate about strategies and practices focused on helping the college through the crisis. One faculty leader recognized that a "strong relationship between a president or a provost and a faculty can actually improve faculty governance." Another faculty leader advised her new president to communicate openly with everyone "until you are blue in the face." Echoing this view, an experienced president said that when he is "sick of saying the same thing over and over," he is still not sure he has explained an idea enough.

A third faculty member advised presidents to use both formal and informal structures to communicate with faculty: "I think the key to developing trust is to have direct conversations, interactions, and consultations that are very honest and transparent." Others agreed that leaders should help all members of the faculty—not just those who are part of the formal governance process—contribute to the conversation. "The governance structure excludes the faculty who sit on the sidelines and carp," said one faculty leader. "A president has to bend over backward to get those faculty voices heard."

Another faculty leader advised new presidents to allow time for relationships to build, pointing out that a president's success at selling an idea to faculty depends on how the faculty view the leader. These observations underscore the critical need to listen long and hard at first. In the words of one respondent: "If the president is well regarded by the faculty, has the personality to drive the agenda, seeks out time with faculty, and listens, then faculty will hear that person. Ultimately, listening is what binds an institution together."

One president acknowledged the validity of this viewpoint by describing how he created a shared governance plan that brought together a broad range of stakeholders. "The task forces of our board involve faculty, trustees, and administrators, so faculty are working far more closely with the board on key issues, and they are getting to know the board members," he said. "This has strengthened my relationship with the faculty because they have a better understanding of the dynamic between the president and the board."

The second finding, *engaging the board in authentic work,* can help the members become more deeply attached to the institution. During the crisis some boards set aside their routine, more formal ways of working and responded in ad hoc settings with the president and faculty. Perhaps as a result, several board members expressed dissatisfaction with being "managed by the administration." Board members, in the words of one president, are "hungry for strategy conversations." She went on to observe that managing the crisis required a new form of engagement that energized many board members, who now report that they want to deal with real issues and know what faculty are doing in their daily work. A board leader at a different institution said he particularly welcomed opportunities to visit labs and classes, saying that the visits "contributed to openness and transparency, and to board members' overall knowledge of college. Ultimately, this helps with fundraising as well."

The presidents we interviewed cautioned, however, that this different form of board engagement calls on them to define roles, clarify relationships, and "stay on top of the action." One president warned that open engagement should not be confused with casualness: "Board members have to remember that they are board members. There is no such thing as a casual conversation about the college or board business with faculty." Another president explained that while it is important to have board members engaged in talks about the future and strategy, the board's primary responsibility is fiduciary. The president must ensure that the board has the information it needs make important decisions.

An experienced president offered different advice: even when conditions are positive, be sure to gauge the quality of the board experience regularly, checking with members to see if the president is communicating consistently and providing timely information. Consistent communication might also allay less helpful approaches. According to a former board chair at another institution, a chair can either "breathe down the neck of the president or encourage fellow board members to back-channel, and neither are desired." An astute president looked deeper: "It is important to understand that board members have multiple roles at institutions and to cultivate those. Board members are your donor community. They need to be engaged in various levels and enjoy their interaction with the school. We occasionally have trustees who take things offline, and you need a strong alliance with the board chair to reel them in."

Addressing current issues with projects that are limited in time and scope is the third finding related to the new dynamics of board governance. Board members tend to prefer sharply focused projects over longer, vaguer processes traditionally used to produce a comprehensive strategic plan. Sometimes begun in a retreat setting, these focused projects produce a plan designed to take the institution forward in a few strategic areas instead of trying to cover the whole institution.

An experienced board chair observed that "finding ways to harness energy and focus on specific issues is a difficult challenge."

Faculty also described favorable experiences with a more targeted approach to planning. One faculty member advised presidents to bring together faculty and trustees who share expertise or interests in a strategic area and have them work together to offer suggestions. In his words: "Vibrant partnerships lead to a more vibrant community."

These types of collaborations and partnerships can lead to organic change that may prove to be more authentic and longer lasting. In a study that used the global city as a model for an organization that encourages change from the inside rather than from the top, Susan Frost and Rebecca Chopp were struck by the degree to which the global city comparison applied to higher education leaders and scholars.[3] Global cities are not a more complex form of the traditional cities. Rather than creating fixed structures that seem designed to dampen change (as in a more traditional city), "leaders find ways to engage individuals at all levels in shaping the city's practices and culture. We see signs that some U.S. universities are adopting the global city model in the metaphors and strategies currently being used in higher education. Permeable boundaries, partnerships, strategic sites, contextual and multi-disciplinary identities—these phrases all describe a fluid, organic orientation toward new conditions, as well as a more practical approach to solving problems."

Interviewees in this study echoed this approach when they talked of encouraging—at times even hurrying—natural change. They seemed to realize that jarring alterations usually fail to work in liberal arts colleges. Even when aspirations are large—and perhaps especially then—strategies for change worked best when they were grounded in current circumstances and made sense in the community.

The global city analysis underscored the idea that academic institutions have unique traits that are quite unlike those found in business and industry. In 1976 Karl Wieck, a leading theorist on organizations, described higher education organizations as "loosely coupled systems," that is, places where the actions of one part can have little effect on other parts—or they can trigger unpredictable responses one would not expect.[4] Because formal structures in colleges and universities are typically weak, new ideas and plans thrive when they grow from organic change rather than from imposed change in the structure.

Susan Frost saw this force at work during an eight-year study of research universities and the practices they used to flourish. Although some consider the elite institutions she studied to be tradition-bound, they routinely increased both their focus on clearly bounded strategic areas and their flexibility to act. Rather than changing incrementally or across the board, they created specific routes to their aspirations.[5]

Once a project with a clear objective is organized, according to the authors' experience, what seems to work best is to enlist committed people to design a plan, set an end date, and offer high-quality support. One strategy that has proven effective is to divide strategic work into three action categories: (1) strategic action for the campus to consider changes in policies or practices or improvements to the educational program; (2) strategic action for the board to take up that might include decisions about new facilities or about policies that relate to the college mission; and (3) tactical items that call for administrative action as part of the normal course of business, including campus practices that have raised questions but have not commanded action in the past, such as encouraging recycling on campus, altering parking policies in some ways, and changing security measures in residence halls. If special interest groups have tried and failed to get attention for items like these, those groups may use the strategic process to make a stronger case. Addressing the tactical items administratively and reporting on progress can clear the field for the authentic strategic work these targeted processes are designed to support.

One critical element of targeted strategic processes is the day-to-day support the administration can provide for the groups who are charged to design a plan. Experienced leaders know they cannot give a group a charge and expect the members to go off and accomplish the work. Such groups need help—from vice presidents who know the institution well, to support personnel who can schedule and staff the meetings, to advanced-level students who can gather data and organize details. When faculty members make up the group, it helps to structure the work more like an academic project than an administrative exercise. This can mean encouraging group members to tailor the charge before they begin, to respect the academic calendar by taking time off for exams and the opening of a new semester, and to engage graduate and undergraduate students to provide support.

When big issues need to be discussed, we agree with one board leader who advised presidents to discuss those questions over several board meetings, including one to debate the question but not to decide. Said one college president: "It is better to think about big questions over time than to force a major decision in a two-day process. Since board members are on campus only a few times a year, they can be out of sync with the action."

A Culture Clash

The second theme involves a culture clash among board members and institutions, and the data that we collected before the University of Virginia incident predicted that presidents will find this dynamic increasingly difficult to manage. Several of our respondents cited examples of, in most cases, younger persons who have been very successful entrepreneurs or venture investors becoming board members. Now these high-energy people are attaining positions of authority on boards of trustees. During the crisis, their natural approach was to apply the strategies that worked for them in business, and they are continuing in that vein. As one experienced board leader said, "After the financial crisis, some board members who are very successful in their careers wanted to shoot from the hip just to do something bold. They failed to understand how our usual ways of working have made us very stable. Our president worked out the macro issues in a white paper, showing what was possible and what was stupid to do."

Another board leader shared a similar perspective: "When there is a crisis, entrepreneurial board members want to apply what has worked for them. They need exposure to the different ways a college operates versus corporate or other nonprofit operations. You need people who are patient to serve on the board."

In their article comparing colleges to global cities, Frost and Chopp described how many colleges and universities began to resemble metropolises as leaders adopted business strategies to steer their increasingly complex institutions. "This approach appealed to leaders in 1983 when George Keller advocated it in his best seller, *Academic Strategy: The Management Revolution in Higher Education.* As the subtitle implied, Keller described a way to replace collegial forms of academic leadership with strategies and structures drawn from the business community." Frost and Chopp point out that "intentionally or not, those strategies and structures became the driving force of many institutions, while the intellectual vigor that should be the focal point of the academic community often remained deeper in the background."

As events at the University of Virginia show, this divergence between business and academic approaches, competitiveness and collegiality, can become a lightning rod on a campus. To ease or avoid such tensions, some presidents recommend organizing board conversations by separating questions about the future from those involving pressing current issues. As one president said, asking questions about the future offers an opportunity to educate the board about the broader issues in higher education. "Trustees are not well informed about higher education—they don't come from that world. Their experience comes from their undergraduate years and their love for the college, so the stakes are high for them personally. But they also need to have opportunities to study the larger issues." Along these same lines, a faculty member observed that bringing together faculty with trustees and leaders to think about the future of the college in grand, unrestrained ways can help all the parties work together to see both differences and commonalities. Even when individuals share such experiences, jarring episodes can occur—and we expect the frequency and intensity of these debates to continue.

Presidents and board leaders also advise using a few strategies to orient new board members. One president said: "On my mind a lot is how to create a shared understanding of the board's role, how the board sees its role, and how it wants to function. I believe that part of my job is not only to have a certain model in mind, but to have the board craft a role itself. My team and I strive to create an experience that moves the board members in a progression from education to engagement to leadership. Ultimately, I want to get the board to lead."

Although promoting deep understanding of a culture might seem more abstract than retaining habits that helped during a crisis, our respondents had some specific practices to share. One president advised her peers to resist "laying out your vision too soon to the community. Unlike medicine, where you are saving lives, in these settings there is no value to 'being first or right!' Get to know the place through informal ways. For instance, have small groups of faculty for meals at your home to prove you are not inhabiting a palace and to show you have a human side as well."

Another president counseled: "Never let the board set up their own chat room; all significant conversations about institutional direction need to take place in the board room, not as sidebars dominated by a few who prefer a less responsible mode of electronic discourse rather than facing colleagues and having a true exchange." According to another experienced leader: "Presidential failures don't come from people who weren't extremely bright or didn't have good ideas; these failures emanate from those who did not understand the culture of the institution or those for whom their human relationship skills were simply nonexistent."

Remember the power of the human touch. One board leader spoke about a retreat where, he recalled, "I was able to spend thirty minutes with a faculty member to learn more about what she was working on, and after this discussion I helped to sponsor the course she was teaching. This was incredibly important to her and to the value of the course. The course ended up being nationally acclaimed.

It allows me to say to the president that a course and a faculty member are things to watch. And that started out with a very informal meeting."

Leading Forward

Most of our president respondents told us that their colleges are out of crisis mode but that they expect to feel the effects of the economic downturn for years to come. Along with trustees and faculty leaders that we interviewed, they also expect to see changes in the way governance is handled in the future. Many of these stakeholders cited open communication, consistent engagement in authentic work, and a focus on targeted collaborative projects as strategies that worked during the crisis, leading to more productive decision making and outcomes.

As many boards experience a cultural shift with a new generation of entrepreneurs and venture investors joining their ranks, these strategies will become even more important as colleges continue to build on their traditional strengths while taking full advantage of new, and sometimes very different, opportunities. Ultimately, presidents make the difference where governance is concerned. Staying close to members of the board *and* members of the faculty is critical—as are so many other aspects of a president's complex role.

NOTES

1. Kenneth C. Green, Scott Jaschik, and Doug Lederman, *Presidential Perspectives: The 2011 Inside Higher Ed Survey of College and University Presidents*, Inside Higher Ed, 2011, www.inside highered.com/sites/default/archive/storage/files/SurveyBooklet.pdf.

2. Bryan Cook and Young Kim, *The American College President, 2012*, Washington, DC, American Council on Education.

3. Susan Frost and Rebecca Chopp, "The University as Global City: A New Way of Seeing Today's Academy," *Change* 34, no. 2 (March/April 2004): 44, www.susanfrostconsulting.com/ChangeFrostMA04.pdf.

4. Karl E. Weick, "Educational Organizations as Loosely Coupled Systems," *Administrative Science Quarterly* 21, no. 1 (March 1976): 1–19.

5. Susan Frost and Aimee Pozorski, "Chaos and the New Academy," www.susanfrostconsulting.com/FrostPozorskiChaos&NewAcademy.pdf.

CHAPTER 5

Orchestrating Shared Governance

Joanne V. Creighton
PRESIDENT EMERITUS AND PROFESSOR OF ENGLISH,
MOUNT HOLYOKE COLLEGE

Having served as president at three liberal arts colleges,[1] I have thought a lot about the relationship of the president to the board and to the faculty. Indeed, I believe that the president's success in large part will rise or fall on how skillfully he or she handles these relationships. The Janus-faced college president stands between the board and the faculty, is a member of both, is accountable to both, must speak the language of both, must be able to translate one to the other, and must help to facilitate communication and shared work while at the same time being the executive leader who sets and keeps the focus on a clear agenda for the institution.

In his various commentaries on boards, Dick Chait has helped those of us in the academy to be more aware of the various kinds of capital that trustees bring to the academic world: intellectual, reputational, political, and social, not to mention actual capital.[2] Typically incredibly generous with their time, energy, and money, they are essential to the very existence of our colleges.

When you think about it though, the board of trustees is a curious entity: a body of unpaid volunteers, many with no experience in higher education, who come to the campus typically three or four times a year and who are vested with considerable authority and responsibility for the welfare of the institution. The board is the "boss" of the president, yet most trustees do not have an in-depth understanding of the president's job or of the guilds of professionals who make up the intricately complex academic culture, nor do they have the time to learn all they would need to know. Part of the president's job is to help to educate the board and to ensure that important institutional information is synthesized and organized in such a way that the board can exercise strategic oversight of the effectiveness of president and of the institution. Of course, trustees will use their own professional judgment honed from other contexts as well, offering often valuable perspectives. This job of educating trustees is always a work in progress, because usually some trustees are cycling off and new members are cycling on to the board, so the composition and dynamics of the board keep changing.

Just as the president must try to explain the institution to the board, he or she must also try to explain the board to the campus—to the students and staff and to the faculty especially. Indeed, the president is the most important interface between the on-campus and off-campus constituencies. He or she must elucidate, negotiate, and reconcile what can sometimes seem like two cultures: that of academia and that of business—since so many trustees, in my experience, work in corporate America. What is valuable about this interface and educational for the president is that much is to be learned from both perspectives.

Faculty members have a great wealth of knowledge to impart to students and deeply held commitments to academic standards, but they can be naive about how their institution exists in a competitive world. So too, although many trustees have highly developed business acumen, they can be impatient and simplistic about how to get things done in an academic environment. The president tries to draw from the strengths of each while not being deterred by their limitations.

In this shared governance setting, an important issue has to do with jurisdictional boundaries and who is responsible for what. In truth, as president I try to maintain boundaries with the board and to blur them with the faculty, although I also try to draw them all together to shape the priorities of the institution.

In my view, under ideal circumstances the board hires the president, who hires the senior staff, who together with the president administer the institution with the board one step removed—receiving, reviewing, suggesting, approving, but not directly managing or micromanaging. Of course, in addition to its hiring and firing of the president, the board has responsibility for the fiscal integrity of the institution and ultimate oversight of all aspects of institutional functioning. But the expectation usually is that it will delegate leadership and management to the president. Many of us have worked with boards and senior administrators to develop "dashboards of leading indicators" and other mechanisms to keep the board focused on the big picture, strategic oversight, and priorities setting. However, some boards want a greater degree of engagement in managing the institution, and, especially in times of duress such as during the recent recession, some boards have pushed for more activist roles.

Certainly, engaging the talents and energies of the board in "generative" thinking, to borrow a term from Dick Chait, can be productive. In Chait's most recent work, he welcomes a blurring of boundaries between president and board:

Because we resolutely regard this as shared work, we cannot offer what the board-improvement field so often promises trustees and executives: a set of bright lines that neatly divide the board's work (policy, strategy, and governance) from the staff's (administration, implementation, and management).... Like copilots of commercial aircraft who typically take turns flying . . . trustees and executives can take turns initiating generative deliberations; one can lead and the other respond.[3]

I say, be careful what you wish for. Copiloting in higher education can be confusing and downright counterproductive. The board has plenty of consequential, engaging work to do without confusing its role with that of the president. A lot of time and energy can be spent feeding the generative appetite of the board. In my experience, trustees love brainstorming. Such sessions can be valuable in generating and refining ideas, but only up to a point. In truth, their visits are too brief, their knowledge of the intricacies of the executive work too thin. The president— who must be at the controls every day—sometimes needs to manage the board's expectations, to help them to appreciate the protocols of institutional governance, and to see that the generative energies of an academic institution don't reside only or even primarily in the trustees, but rather in the larger culture, especially in the faculty, who have an extremely important role in planning and governance.

Having long been a faculty member before crossing over to the "other" side, I try to blur the boundaries between "us" and "them," to insist that in governing the college, we are all in this together, with the faculty playing a central role. Shared governance is more than ideal; it is essential. The faculty has legislative power and responsibility for the curriculum and academic appointments. Its expertise is fundamental to any academic planning and valuable in most administrative arenas. A president ignores or underestimates the faculty's role at her peril. While formally the president is the "boss" of the faculty, in actuality, a president also serves with the consent of the governed, the faculty especially, whose latent power is considerable. They can and frequently do topple a president when their displeasure is aroused. To avoid that, a president should work to build trust and make the faculty full-fledged partners in advancing the college. To start to do that, the president should listen patiently to institutional stakeholders and learn all he or she can about the place before presuming to know anything.

They say a president should have "vision."[4] I say, beware of the college president who comes into office with a full-fledged vision, like Athena from the head of Zeus. Like Alexander Haig, the president can say, "I'm in charge," but with equally shaky credibility. So many others—faculty, students, staff, trustees, alumni—make up the fabric and generating energies of the institution, along with its accumulated history, customs, policies, and traditions. A vision cannot be simply imposed from without.

Rather, vision is the ability to *see* what is there and imagine what more might be there if an institution were to realize its unique genius and full potential. To acquire that kind of vision, the president should head and champion a collaborative strategic planning process designed to set a clear institutional agenda. He or she should invite campus dialogue with a positive approach. Starting with the proposition "We're in trouble—what should we cut?" is demoralizing and counterproductive. Rather, the initial inquiry should be "What are our strengths, our core purposes, and essential services? How do we enhance them?" Not only is listening key, but multiple opportunities for engagement are available. Mixed constituent groups can work. The president should gather, like a magpie, the best, most promising ideas from the incredible pool of smart, talented people who make up a college. I find that every comment, no matter how initially annoying, helps to refine and build a nuanced shared understanding.

The president should keep the focus on the big picture and higher purposes. People get mired in their own parochial viewpoints and problems; they need to be inspired by, and encouraged to take, the larger view. Planning at its best, even in the toughest economic environment, is an affirming process. Only after articulating and affirming the shared values and aspirations for the institution, should one address the problems and challenges that inhibit or prevent their realization. Problems should be addressed, and addressed squarely.

In order to do this, the president must be fearlessly candid and open with information. Put everything on the table. Have no sacred cows, no forbidden subjects. Present the unvarnished financial facts. Do not be afraid of emotional and heated discussions. Not everyone will be comfortable with this degree of transparency, nor will everyone trust that you are not hiding something. But eventually these doses of reality do, if one is patient and unrelenting enough, have the effect of winning over most people and drawing them into shared problem solving.

I am also a strong proponent of using drafts to communicate quickly and broadly with college constituencies. Drafts are wonderfully useful, allowing you to test out ideas without boxing yourself into the corner. ("What, you don't like this idea? That's okay; it's only a draft. How would you reframe the issue?") Drafts help you to have iterative, interactive processes, to stake out territory, and to get people used to ideas and invested in the building of consensus. At Mount Holyoke

I led two planning processes, and at each one we shared three public drafts before the final document was drawn up. The second drafts went to all 30,000 constituents, including alumnae, who were invited to send their comments. The final documents were unanimously approved by both faculty and the board— no small feat. They had been shaped, refined, and vetted by an extraordinary number of contributors. It is fair to say that the final plans were owned by the constituents of the institution and that indeed they also took ownership of the implementation.

If you can get everyone—faculty, trustees, students, alumni—on the same page in this way, you will experience the generative power of shared governance and will be propelled by the collective energy and aspiration of institutional stakeholders. It is then that you may well experience the exhilaration that comes with the extraordinary privilege of serving as president.

NOTES

1. Interim President, Wesleyan University, 1995–96; President, Mount Holyoke College, 1996–2010; Interim President, Haverford College, 2011–13.

2. Richard P. Chait, William P. Ryan, and Barbara E. Taylor, *Governance as Leadership: Reframing the Work of Nonprofit Boards* (Hoboken, NJ: John Wiley & Sons, 2005), 137–61.

3. Ibid., 95, 97.

4. Some ideas in this section were included in Joanne V. Creighton, "That Vision Thing," *Presidential Perspectives*, 2011–2012, Series 6, 1–4, www.aramarkhighed.com.

PART III / Knowledge, Learning, and New Technologies

CHAPTER 6

Breaking Barriers and Building Bridges in Teaching

David W. Oxtoby
PRESIDENT, POMONA COLLEGE

Interdisciplinary research, bringing together contributors from a range of fields to collaborate on broad problems or bringing a novel perspective to a traditional subject, is the hallmark of scholarship in the twenty-first century. A future breakthrough in molecular biology may rely on advanced techniques in statistics or computer science, while an analysis of political movements in China may be shaped by an understanding of the history of religious minorities in that country. The era in which advances in knowledge could be simply classified by traditional academic disciplines has passed. But why has interdisciplinary work had so much less impact overall on how we teach and learn? How can our colleges encourage the crossing of boundaries by our faculty and students, preparing our graduates for a world in which solutions to important problems require ideas from multiple sources? Answering these questions is critical for the future of liberal education in our institutions.

Structural and Cultural Impediments to Interdisciplinary Innovation

I spent the first twenty-six years of my career at a research university (University of Chicago) and have been, for the last nine years, at a liberal arts college (Pomona College). My experience in the research university world showed me the importance placed on interdisciplinary work in research and in graduate teaching. There was a flexibility that led to the formation of new research centers every year which brought together faculty members from a range of academic departments, almost always in response to external funding from grant agencies and foundations. New graduate programs were regularly created at Chicago in the form of degree-granting "committees" that gathered faculty members from across the university.

Of course, traditional departments persisted, but there was an openness to a variety of groupings both intellectually and in the allotment of space to faculty members and their research programs.

In coming to a smaller college, I expected such cross-departmental connections to become even easier. Given the smaller scale and the ease for faculty members to make connections across the entire institution, I thought surely barriers to starting and maintaining interdisciplinary experiments would be lowered. Instead, I was surprised to find that if anything the opposite was true. While some of what I say relates specifically to Pomona College, my contacts with faculty elsewhere suggests that most liberal arts colleges fall short of the ideal of those flexible interdisciplinary habits of mind that we seek, at least in principle, to convey to our students.

Why is this? First, the smaller scale of our colleges can actually reduce flexibility. If a single central person in a new interdisciplinary field is away on sabbatical, the entire program may suffer or be put on hold. While it is common at a large university for one or more members of a department to have space in another building, it is almost a matter of principle that everyone from a department should be housed together at a small institution.

Second, with this fixed, smaller number of faculty, it is simply harder to sustain a level of interdisciplinary work because the same individuals are doing it all. One faculty member in our politics department, for example, also plays critical roles in three interdisciplinary concentrations: public policy; environmental analysis; and science, technology, and society.

Third, the disciplines often can be bound up in the local politics of fighting for and retaining faculty positions, which can be threatened if new faculty members are brought in who cross disciplinary boundaries and can contribute to core teaching in more than one area. One small college I know has separate departments of Spanish, French, and Italian.

But the principal reason for this lack of interdisciplinary effort at many liberal arts colleges is that most faculty members become more traditional in mindset as they move from research to advanced teaching to core teaching. While novelty in research is rewarded, there are few incentives to change the way we teach; departmental curricula are agreed on collectively, and change can threaten that consensus. It is easier to move from the blackboard to PowerPoint (adapting to new technology) than to change the fundamental content of a course over time. There are, of course, some noteworthy exceptions to this lack of interdisciplinary teaching at the institutional level (St. John's College stands out here) and at the level of particular courses (courses in science for nonscientists tend to be especially open to cross-fertilization). But these are exceptions, not the general practice.

In courses offered to satisfy concentration requirements, a comparison of recent college catalogs with those from twenty or thirty years ago shows a growing number of choices but, paradoxically, often less flexibility than in the past. Instead of a structure of "core plus electives" within a concentration, there are now often a series of tracks within a field, with each track specified in great detail. Many new interdisciplinary concentrations that arose from student or faculty desires to connect disparate fields in creative ways have evolved to become just as prescriptive as the disciplinary fields against which they began in rebellion. Are colleges giving in to the push (from students and from society) to plan everything down to the smallest detail? Do we not trust our students to make good choices within a framework that includes a large degree of flexibility?

Interdisciplinary experiments at the introductory level seem even harder to undertake and to sustain. If the lifeblood of a department is its majors, then there is an incentive for every department to create a strong, stand-alone introductory course that will attract entering students and get them to commit to further study. But is this the best approach? Could we, for example, conceive of an introductory course that might integrate sociology and anthropology? Students coming from high schools where neither subject is taught might welcome a chance to encounter both fields and understand how they connect to and differ from each other. If a substantial number of students will be taking basic courses in biology, chemistry, and physics (as is true now in all our colleges), should we consider a one- or two-year program in which these different fields interweave with one another in a pedagogically valuable manner? Instead, while faculty and academic administrators recognize the value of interdisciplinary teaching and coursework, interdisciplinary courses often become confined to first-year seminar programs or core requirements created because we know they are good for our students. Yet departmental and disciplinary silos continue to dominate the curricular landscape.

There are, of course, exceptional models of curricular or programmatic interdisciplinary education. I would mention an example from my own neighbor in Claremont, Scripps College, where the interdisciplinary humanities core is a hallmark. That program's success and sustainability depend not only on continuing resources and careful faculty oversight but especially on the commitment and participation of the entire faculty. There are different models in other institutions.

Other structural and cultural impediments to interdisciplinary innovation remain just as strong as ever, in spite of many years of discussion and experimentation. As already discussed, interdisciplinary academic programs that burst forth from the clashing of disciplines can become, through the momentum of institutionalization, disciplines with their own professional associations, journals, jargon, and standards. Think of programs in media studies, cultural studies, or neuroscience, for example. Moreover, college-wide efforts to create interdisciplinary or transdisciplinary requirements or core courses can be thwarted by less-than-enthusiastic faculty members struggling against the demands of their home departments and majors. Interdisciplinary teaching and research is sometimes a tough fit with promotion and tenure review. And contrary to all that we read about the need for "creative and integrative thinkers" and the tyranny of disciplinarity, graduating with an interdisciplinary major presents additional challenges in the job market or in applying to graduate schools.

Emerging Areas of Opportunity

Despite all this, liberal arts colleges may have unique opportunities for interdisciplinary innovation. While small departments and faculties can be an obstacle, they can also foster a willingness to collaborate for the purpose of building critical mass. Consortial relationships between colleges create other possibilities. In Claremont, our consortium of five undergraduate colleges and two graduate institutions lends itself to just this type of collaboration and provides the structure for long-term viability and strength of interdisciplinary majors and departments. Intercollegiate departments and programs such as media studies, Africana studies, and environmental analysis are successful not only because they bring what would otherwise be a small number of faculty, courses, and students on separate campuses together, but because they are refreshed and enlivened by the different approaches and emphases on each campus. For example, the media studies faculty at Pomona focuses primarily on theory and analysis, but students take courses in media *production* at Pitzer College or Harvey Mudd College, where this is a faculty strength. A consortium also allows synergies to bubble to the surface through new majors that would not be supportable in a single college. For example, our faculty recently approved a new five-college undergraduate major in Late Antique and Medieval Studies to be housed in classical studies. It will draw on seventeen faculty members and forty-seven courses in history, religion, classics, archaeology, and art history and will offer language instruction in Arabic and Hebrew as well as Greek and Latin.

Perhaps another way around the challenges I have outlined is to foster interdisciplinary innovation focusing not so much on the programmatic level (by starting a new program or major or implementing a new requirement), but with an eye to the type of outcomes we hope our students will achieve, the kind of academic life we hope to enable for our faculty, or the habits of mind we hope to foster.

In recent years, colleges and universities in this country have been appropriately pushed both by society and by students and parents to justify the investments being made in the education of students. Some of this pressure is in the direction of more "practical" courses of study that are directly related to jobs students can move into right out of college. As liberal arts colleges, we stand for a broader and deeper form of education in which we prepare students for jobs that are rapidly changing and that may not even exist right now. But if these are our principles, we need to ensure that our product lives up to that promise.

For example, one of the goals of a liberal education is to teach students to engage with the "great problems," those that go beyond the limits of a single discipline and that are not subject to easy answers. If we are to bring such problems into our classrooms, we need to be prepared to move outside of our disciplinary comfort zone to bring other approaches into play. This can happen through team teaching or through individual faculty members being willing to take a chance and teach material from areas with which they are not fully conversant. Teachers need to learn from (and alongside) their own students. I am fortunate to have this experience in the environmental chemistry course I teach at Pomona, where the issue of climate change brings suggestions from the class that connect to engineering, economics, and political science as well as from the core areas of chemistry that I myself know best.

Successful interdisciplinary programs have been launched with a "problem-based" approach that seeks to teach and model integrated knowledge through interdisciplinary approaches to complex problems. For example, teams of students from across departments tackling the problem of global poverty would quickly understand the importance not only of economic analysis but also of cultural and historical awareness, understanding of religious worldviews, climate study, nutritional science, and more. A problem-based emphasis can involve individual courses or entire majors. Robert Sternberg, for example, argues that while problem solving may actually be impeded by the narrow disciplinary thinking encouraged by traditional curricular requirements and structures, approaches such as interdisciplinary problem-based learning foster the kind of creative, integrated knowledge educators hold as ideal.[1]

Another goal of liberal education is to teach students to become good citizens of the country and the world, people who can apply critical thinking skills to help society make wise policy decisions. Here also, our faculty members serve as models for their students (and learn from their students). Maintaining an openness to real-world applications of our disciplines and keeping up with current policy decisions in the news will not only enliven our classrooms but also challenge us to change our teaching continually. The risks associated with bringing the world into our classroom are more than compensated by the greater engagement of our students that can result.

Connecting the Disciplines through the Arts

Finally, I am interested in exploring another approach for fostering interdisciplinary learning and breaking down disciplinary silos on our campus. One of the core purposes of liberal education is to encourage the development of our students' creativity, which will serve them throughout their lives and their careers. This is done, not by specifically teaching courses on "creativity," "entrepreneurship," or "leadership," but by encouraging all students to develop their creative faculties through a range of courses outside their own comfort zones. I have argued elsewhere for the importance of integrating the creative and performing arts more centrally into the curriculum and for the value of creativity and experiential, or "embodied," learning to a liberal education.[2] Going even further, I would venture that a visible and robust arts program can be a bridge that connects disciplines in a meaningful way through thematic and practical experience in (art) making, design, conceptualization, and performance.

At Pomona College we are experiencing some of the possibilities of arts-focused initiatives through a new four-year program that we call "Elemental Arts." This initiative, funded by the Mellon Foundation, takes one of the four classical Greek elements as an annual theme and the inspiration for study and creative activity. In the first, year the element was water. While primary leadership comes from faculty in environmental analysis as well as theatre, dance, music, and studio art, the initiative also involves Pomona's Draper Center for Community Partnerships.

Throughout the year, the initiative on water featured symposia, film series, and lectures around the theme; theme-based arts programming such as a new play festival; dance performance, musical concerts, and arts exhibitions; and an arts-immersion course offered to first-year students. It also provided an organizational framework for connecting other happenings on campus, for example, lectures on the tsunami in Japan and water resources in the California desert. I am particularly proud of the community service emphasis of the elemental arts initiative. Pomona College students worked with young students from the Fremont Academy in the neighboring city of Pomona to write and perform a play based on Axolotl, the Mexican Water Monster. And finally, through the initiative we are able to challenge our students by offering grants which support student-initiated projects in the arts.

As with any interdisciplinary initiative, the question of sustainability arises. Long-term commitment of resources and leadership are essential, and faculty and students must receive professional and academic support and rewards for their efforts. Of course this is true of any endeavor we undertake in higher education, but some are more familiar or routine than others. A significant investment in the arts and a commitment to integrate arts experience, art-making, and creativity fully into the campus environment provide the foundation not only for vibrant and sustainable interdisciplinary work but also for the educational outcomes and goals of a liberal arts education.

Providing Sustainable Conditions for Interdisciplinary Teaching

Leaders of liberal arts colleges have a unique opportunity to model educational ideals not only through our curricular structures but also through our campus environments and the nature of our communities. While interdisciplinarity has been an educational ideal that has presented persistent challenges for decades, liberal arts colleges can take up those challenges with flexibility and nimbleness. Perhaps because interdisciplinarity resists the structures of institutions and traditions, it is always slightly out of our reach; it must be continually reinvented and rediscovered to retain its vibrancy and power. Liberal arts colleges may provide the best academic conditions for that invention and discovery.

Strong presidential leadership is necessary in order for liberal arts colleges to build the bridges necessary for sustainable interdisciplinary teaching. Key actions that I recommend for the future are:

1. Create *faculty incentives to foster interdisciplinary teaching.* These include encouraging team teaching (recognizing that this requires additional faculty resources), supporting out-of-term course development, and enabling cross-disciplinary concentrations to thrive without creating new departments. Recruit new faculty who are open to collaboration between traditional disciplines.

2. *Explore interdisciplinary partnerships with other colleges.* In cases with favorable geography, nearby institutions can share interdisciplinary courses or majors; in other cases, collaboration between faculty (and students) can take place during term breaks or using virtual methods of interaction.

3. *Recognize that the core goal of a college education is the development of creative capacities in our graduates.* The creative and performing arts can play a central role in fostering those capacities, encouraging students to see traditional issues in new ways and connecting faculty and students across the campus in novel initiatives.

NOTES

1. Robert J. Sternberg, "Interdisciplinary Problem-Based Learning: An Alternative to Traditional Majors and Minors," *Liberal Education* 94, no. 1 (2008): 12–17.

2. David W. Oxtoby, "The Place of the Arts in a Liberal Education," *Liberal Education* 98, no. 2 (2012): 36–41.

CHAPTER 7

Interdisciplinary Perspectives and the Liberal Arts

Wendy L. Hill
Provost and Dean of the Faculty, Lafayette College

At a presentation in 2008 at New York University's Steinhardt Institute for Higher Education Policy, William Durden, president of Dickinson College, suggested that the key to the future of liberal arts colleges "lies in embracing our past by offering a distinctively American higher education for the twenty-first century. Rather than apologizing or justifying those qualities that separate us from other institutions of higher learning, we must celebrate those unique characteristics." I couldn't agree more. Liberal arts colleges have every right to celebrate unapologetically the enduring value of their educational model. What they do is not just special but enviably unique, and enhancing these distinctive aspects is pivotal to their future. In this chapter I present some of the hallmarks of our academic mission that are cause not only to extol but also to affirm our leadership in higher education. I'll begin by briefly reviewing how teaching, learning, and research characterize liberal arts colleges and result in distinctive experiences for both students and faculty. I will then describe how interdisciplinary perspectives in many ways define liberal arts colleges and argue that the essential collaborative spirit required for such approaches is increasingly important to our institutions. I conclude by focusing on faculty and offering some suggestions for fostering interdisciplinarity and collaboration within our colleges. Both are key to optimizing our uniqueness and need to figure prominently in our efforts to provide an exceptional and distinctive education for the twenty-first century.

Teaching and Learning

Liberal arts colleges are not just smaller versions of research universities. Many things separate us from other types of institutions in higher education and justify the designation "distinctive."[1] One characteristic is how we teach. The pedagogies we employ are invariably student-centered. We are more likely to use "high impact" approaches and believe strongly that teaching is *not* a sideline for faculty.[2] Pedagogies of engagement are not exclusive to liberal arts colleges, but recent work has demonstrated that students are much more likely to experience these approaches at liberal arts colleges than at other types of institutions.[3] Vander-Stoep and colleagues defined six measures of good teaching that correlate with increased cognitive and motivational outcomes and found that these approaches are more common at liberal arts colleges.[4] Furthermore, liberal arts institutions practice pedagogies that require higher levels of academic rigor.[5]

Liberal arts colleges graduate curious, adaptable, and broadly educated students who become thoughtful leaders and engaged citizens. The broad student learning outcomes to which we aspire foster the holistic development of students. Foremost among these are to enhance critical thinking and problem solving, communicate clearly, be open to different people and ideas, and cultivate social responsibility.[6]

Not surprisingly, given the information revolution, the specific areas about which we teach have changed over the years in response to the fluid definition of what it means to be a broadly educated citizen. We have migrated from a small number of content areas to a vastly greater array of subjects, an intellectual panorama. The Center for Education Statistics codes more than ninety specific academic majors in the arts and sciences, a far cry from the seven *artes liberales*.

Of course, just learning about a discipline considered one of the liberal arts does not guarantee that it will be taught in a manner consistent with our mission. A "liberal arts state of mind" needs to be inculcated. A course, even one devoted to one of the original Quadrivium or Trivium, that only requires memorization of facts, falls short. A bona fide liberal arts course requires the fostering of exploration and curiosity. It is more a way of learning, a habit of mind, than pieces of information.[7]

Research

Our institutions believe the teacher-scholar model is fundamental to the intellectual vibrancy of our campuses. Our faculty members also contribute to the advancement of scholarship and artistic endeavors of the larger community. Research and teaching can seem to conflict, so is it really possible to maintain parallel emphases on both? The research by Astin and Chang (1995) demonstrates that our dual commitment to strong teaching and productive scholarship is another point of distinction. In their study, Astin and Chang measured the research orientation and the student development orientation of 212 colleges and universities to determine if any of them emphasize both research and teaching. From this analysis they identified eleven institutions (and only eleven) that effectuate both research and student development. Strikingly, *every one* of these institutions is a private liberal arts college.[8] They concluded that the selective residential liberal arts college comes closer than any other type of institution to achieving a balance between research and teaching students. Moreover, work by McCaughey demonstrates that scholars from selective liberal arts colleges, at least in the disciplines investigated, published at rates similar to the mean level of publishing by peers at research universities.[9] Hence, not only is the teaching of faculty at liberal arts colleges engaged and rigorous, but the scholarship is at high levels. The balance between teaching and research may at times feel precarious to faculty, but I would argue that research, properly proportioned, is essential to the academic vibrancy and intellectual distinctiveness of our campuses.

Astin and Chang's other findings also paint a picture of the distinctive teaching, learning, and research at selective liberal arts colleges. For example, they found that students attending liberal arts colleges were more likely to take interdisciplinary courses, to get engaged in their professors' research, and to conduct independent research. Compared to faculty at other types of institutions, faculty at liberal arts colleges more often team-teach and teach interdisciplinary courses. Faculty at liberal arts colleges interact across departmental or disciplinary lines more frequently than do faculty from all other types of institutions.[10]

Ruscio, as a result of extensive interviews, concluded that faculty at selective liberal arts colleges are less "taxonomically upstanding" than faculty at research universities.[11] He suggested that the research conducted by liberal arts faculty was more akin to Boyer's description of the scholarship of integration and not narrowly focused.[12] Just as we encourage students to expand their horizons, so too does it appear that liberal arts colleges foster a similar kind of exploration for faculty. It is interesting to note that faculty from research universities point to the bureaucracy involved in conducting research as a major impediment to redefining their scholarly interests.[13]

Scholarly productivity and effective teaching are interdependent, and faculty from liberal arts colleges often describe research as an investment in students.[14] To liberal arts faculty, the fusing of teaching and research is admirable and very much in keeping with our mission. Attempting to describe the merging of research and teaching led my neuroscience colleague at Davidson College, Julio Ramirez, to coin the word "terching."[15] Terching may be a somewhat awkward term, but the practice is anything but. It is a seamless and powerfully rewarding experience to both students and faculty.

As Ruscio points out, "The teacher-scholar model in a liberal arts college is not an adaptation of the research university approach to a constrained organizational setting. Instead, it is a model with virtues all its own, developed in a setting that affords advantages not available elsewhere."[16] I believe the teaching, learning, and research at liberal arts colleges is distinctive. They are also wonderfully intertwined, which leads to an environment that fosters exciting synergies. Interconnections are key to our continued excellence.

Interdisciplinarity and the Distinctiveness of Liberal Arts Colleges

The distinctive teaching-learning-research environment at liberal arts colleges uniquely positions our institutions to advance Gregorian's "unity of knowledge" and "commonwealth of learning." Rather than rely on the continued fragmentation of knowledge, clarions call for the application of relevant interdisciplinary approaches.[17]

Why is fostering interdisciplinarity the right approach for liberal arts colleges? First, it is consistent with our history and mission.[18] Indeed, it harks back to our founding tenets—what Huber and Hutchings (2004) identify as a capacity to see connections. Similarly, Cronon (1998) points out in his essay entitled "Only Connect . . ." (a reference to the directive from E. M. Forster's book *Howard's End*), that a liberally educated person means "being able to see connections that allow one to make sense of the world and act within it in creative ways."[19] And while I grant that Bodenbender (2003) sees enormous value in the disciplinary lens, he also posits that the liberal arts are necessarily interdisciplinary.[20]

Interdisciplinarity adjusts students and faculty from an emphasis—some have suggested an over-emphasis—on a specific major or disciplinary perspective. In fact, I would argue that the narrow vocationalism that Brann (2000) identified as an "illiberal tenet" is evident in what we might call "major-itis" in our students (even if the major is among the anointed "liberal arts" areas).[21] We should recall that our institutions were not founded on the principle that earning a baccalaureate degree required a major course of study. Major requirements were introduced at most of our institutions many decades after their founding. For example, at Lafayette College, founded in 1826, it was not until 1915 that students were required to major in a specific discipline as part of the requirements for graduation.

Similar curricular overhauls were taken at peer institutions, no doubt attempts to emulate the disciplinary focus of research universities.[22]

Interdisciplinarity is consistent and compatible with our history; however, these would not alone be warrants for interdisciplinarity. It is the validity of the educational approach that compels us to embrace this model. Interdisciplinary teaching promotes greater student engagement in learning, enhances the development of higher cognitive skills, fosters more creative thinking, increases sensitivity to ethical issues, and leads to greater tolerance for ambiguity.[23] Kezar and Lester (2009) conclude that collaborative and interdisciplinary research creates innovative and holistic knowledge.[24] Furthermore, as suggested by Newell (2007), interdisciplinarity is the bridge between the academy and the real world, therein empowering students to integrate disciplines to address complex problems.[25]

A liberal arts education depends upon a foundation of broad perspectives with interdisciplinary desires to develop connections. In contrast, Katz suggests that research universities are being "fractionalized" into research centers dominated by scholars committed to disciplinary approaches.[26] Granted, we will never have as broad a scope of activity or the same kind of depth as found at research universities, but our institutions' smaller size and greater interactions among faculty and students are advantages in the pursuit of interdisciplinary connections and innovations.

Fostering Interdisciplinarity and Collaboration

While it may be obvious, it should be highlighted: faculty members are key to interdisciplinarity. Institutions need to ensure that structures and processes are in place to support interdisciplinary approaches, but faculty engage in and realize the efforts.[27] Inevitably, whenever an initiative that relies on faculty participation is proposed, it needs to be tied to the faculty reward structure of the institution, that is, tenure and promotion as well as merit pay. However, in the end, the quality of our faculty will determine the quality of our interdisciplinary accomplishments.

We should examine our hiring practices and, as suggested by Ferrall (2011), move from a reliance on passive search procedures to actively recruiting faculty.[28] Pursuing applicants who can make topical connections as well as those with collaborative and interdisciplinary interests should figure prominently in searches. This may be hard because, as the quip goes, earning a Ph.D. is learning more and more about less and less. It could be that an inherently collaborative scholar has been constrained by the disciplinary approaches of graduate school. There is evidence that some graduate programs are embracing new approaches to initiatives designed to produce interdisciplinary scholars, but there is ample evidence that the research universities still build disciplinary silos.[29] Nevertheless, we need to move our interdisciplinary goals into the fore of our faculty recruitment procedures.

Once hired, faculty members are often confronted with rampant skepticism suggesting that interdisciplinarity is a peril to tenure. Blog sites and other venues are rife with advice to new faculty about how they should avoid interdisciplinary pursuits and only take on these interests *after* receiving tenure. Interdisciplinarity is viewed as just too risky. Where are the role models for interdisciplinary teacher-scholars? I heard Cathy Trower's lively parody at the 2008 meeting of the American Association of Colleges and Universities during which she satirized interdisciplinary faculty pursuing tenure as being Alice in Wonderland, with standards constantly changing and characters as strange as the Mad Hatter and Cheshire Cat.[30] Carp (2008) similarly suggests that trying to achieve tenure as an interdisciplinary faculty member is like being Blanche DuBois in Tennessee Williams' *A Street Car Named Desire*. Not only does Blanche have to "rely on the kindness of strangers," but Carp points out that she suffered horribly.[31] It would seem hopeless to even the most courageous of faculty.

I would like to offer a better role model, Hermione Granger, the profoundly potent protagonist of J. K. Rowling's *Harry Potter* series. Granger's ability to navigate successfully between the wizarding world of Hogwarts and the human (muggle) world mimics the crossroads traveled by interdisciplinary faculty. (Please don't take this to mean that an interdisciplinary scholar has to rely on magic!) Why is Hermione successful? Yes, she is smart, confident, and resourceful. But, perhaps just as important, she has clearly articulated goals—do well on the wizarding exams, conjure up a *Homenum Rovelio* spell, make a polyjuice potion, defeat the evil Valdemort. Similarly, we need to provide clear goals and processes for interdisciplinary scholars so that they can be as successful as Hermione.

One of the approaches we have pursued at Lafayette College in supporting interdisciplinarity is using memoranda of understanding (MOU) to be explicit about responsibilities and expectations as well as to provide greater clarity regarding the tenure and promotion process. MOUs have been helpful, especially in outlining teaching responsibilities, scholarship evaluation, and service commitments. One of the most cited impediments for pursuing interdisciplinarity for faculty at liberal arts colleges, a concern about the impact on a department of teaching courses "outside" the department,[32] can be lessened by detailing in an MOU the timeline and responsibilities for course offerings. We are also using MOUs as a way for tenured faculty to redefine their roles. This seems to help provide clear connections across disciplines and support interdisciplinarity for faculty at all ranks. Gregorian and Trower suggest that sabbatical support in another department also fosters collaboration and interdisciplinarity.[33]

Institutions have been generally obsessed with individualistic work versus collaborative successes.[34] This restrictive focus needs to be loosened in order to enable and support interdisciplinary work. Questions about contribution are fair, but there are certainly projects where it is difficult (some might even say impossible) to delineate where one person's contribution ended and another's began. This should not be an impediment to gaining tenure and being promoted.

Fairweather (1993) presents evidence that the salary reward system may be different at liberal arts colleges than at other institutions.[35] It seems to me these results reflect institutional interest in recognizing both teaching and scholarship in addition to service. In concept, interdisciplinarity warrants consideration in merit pay. There are as many merit pay systems as there are colleges, so I recognize how complex it will be institution-to-institution to develop a pay formula with interdisciplinarity as a new variable. Nevertheless, if interdisciplinarity is essential to our educational model, then it should be weighed during determinations of salaries.

Although the factors discussed so far seem important, Wergin (2011) has demonstrated that faculty members are influenced by a relatively small number of motives not captured by the attention paid to the "reward structures" at an institution. According to Wergin, "We are much better off when we focus on what makes people want to get up and come to work in the morning." He offers four motivating factors (autonomy, community, recognition, and efficacy), which are significant intrinsic rewards for faculty.[36] I would argue that these motivations are likely engendered by engaging in interdisciplinary teaching and research. As a consequence, interdisciplinarity, along with attendant collaborations, will be personal incentives for individual faculty and, collectively, important for the greater campus community.[37]

Gregorian called for a reform in higher education where we "reconstruct the unity and value of knowledge" because "the complexity of the world requires us to have a better understanding of the relationships and connections between all fields that intersect and overlap."[38] Liberal arts colleges are already doing this, but we strive to contribute even more. By harking back to our past and continuing to embrace interdisciplinary teaching, learning, and research we will enhance our leadership role in education.

Embracing and Fostering Interdisciplinary Approaches

Liberal arts colleges need to better capitalize on our unique teaching-learning-research environment to help advance a more comprehensive understanding of the complex world in which we live. Toward this end, interdisciplinary approaches should be embraced and fostered. Interdisciplinary perspectives in many ways define liberal arts colleges and have been shown to enhance student engagement and learning. The essential collaborative spirit required for interdisciplinarity is increasingly important to our institutions, and furthering this approach is consistent with compelling intrinsic values. Realizing these connections will have attendant advantages to our educational communities and to advancing our exceptional and distinctive kind of education for the twenty-first century.

We need to move our interdisciplinary objectives into the fore of our faculty recruitment procedures and shift from a reliance on passive search procedures to more actively recruit faculty personnel with collaborative and interdisciplinary interests. Furthermore, institutions should ensure that structures and processes are in place to support interdisciplinary approaches by faculty and students: foremost among these for faculty are clear expectations and procedures for tenure, promotion, and salary considerations for the interdisciplinary teacher-scholar. These systems need to demonstrate, with confidence and conviction, the critical value of interdisciplinarity to the institution and its core mission.

NOTES

1. William G. Durden, "Reclaiming the Distinctiveness of American Higher Education," *Liberal Education*, 93, no. 2 (2007): 40–45; S. Koblik and S. Graubard, eds., *Distinctively American: The Residential Liberal Arts Colleges* (New Brunswick, NJ: Transaction Publishers, 2000); Paul D. Umbach and George D. Kuh, "Student Experiences with Diversity at Liberal Arts Colleges: Another Claim for Distinctiveness," *Journal of Higher Education* 77, no. 1 (2006): 169–92.

2. George D. Kuh, *High-Impact Educational Practices: What They Are, Who Has Access to Them, and Why They Matter* (Washington, DC: Association of American Colleges & Universities, 2008); Alexander W. Astin and Mitchell J. Chang, "Colleges That Emphasize Research and Teaching: Can You Have Your Cake and Eat It," *Change* 27 (1995): 44–49; Earl J. McGrath, *The Graduate School and the Decline of Liberal Education* (New York: Institute of Higher Education, 1959).

3. Ernest T. Pascarella, Gregory C. Wolniak, Tricia A. D. Seifert, Ty M. Cruce, and Charles F.

Blaich, *ASHE Higher Education Report Special Issue: Liberal Arts Colleges and Liberal Arts Education: New Evidence on Impacts* 31, no. 3 (2005): 1–148.

4. Scott VanderStoep, Kathleen S. Wise, and Charles Blaich, "Student Engagement in Liberal Arts Colleges: Academic Rigor, Quality Teaching, Diversity, and Institutional Change," in Handbook of Engaged Scholarship: Vol. I, Institutional Change: Contemporary Landscapes, Future Directions, ed. H. E. Fitzgerald, C. Burack, and S. D. Seifer (East Lansing: Michigan State University Press, 2010), 131–47.

5. Paul D. Umbach and Matthew R. Wawrzynski, "Faculty Do Matter: The Role of College Faculty in Student Learning and Engagement," *Research in Higher Education* 46, no. 2 (2005): 153–84.

6. Durden, "Reclaiming the Distinctiveness of American Higher Education," 40–45; Victor E. Ferrall Jr., *Liberal Arts at the Brink* (Cambridge, MA: Harvard University Press, 2011); Michele T. Myers, "Preparing Students for an Uncertain Future," *Liberal Education* 87, no. 3 (2001): 22–25; Martha C. Nussbaum, *Cultivating Humanity: A Classical Defense of Reform in Liberal Education* (Cambridge, MA: Harvard University Press, 1997).

7. Carol Geary Schneider, "Practicing Liberal Education: Formative Themes in the Reinvention of Liberal Learning," *Liberal Education* 90, no. 2 (2004): 6–11.

8. The 11 colleges scoring high on both research and teaching were Bard, Bryn Mawr, Carlton, Colorado, Harvey-Mudd, Occidental, Pitzer, Smith, Swarthmore, Wheaton, and Williams.

9. Robert A. McCaughey, *Scholars and Teachers: The Faculties of Select Liberal Arts Colleges and Their Place in American Higher Learning* (New York: Barnard College, 1994), and "Scholars and Teachers Revisited: In Continued Defense of College Faculty Who Publish. Liberal Arts Colleges in American Higher Education: Challenges and Opportunities," *ACLS Occasional Paper* 59 (2006): 88–97.

10. Astin and Chang, "Colleges That Emphasize Research and Teaching," 44–49.

11. Kenneth P. Ruscio, "The Distinctive Scholarship of the Selective Liberal Arts Colleges," *Journal of Higher Education* 58, no. 2 (1987): 205–22, and "Response: Faculty Scholarship in Liberal Arts Colleges," *Liberal Arts Colleges in American Higher Education: Challenges and Opportunities ACLS Occasional Paper*, 59 (2005): 113–19.

12. Ernest L. Boyer, "Scholarship Reconsidered: Priorities of the Professoriate," *The Carnegie Foundation for the Advancement of Teaching* (1990). Lisa R. Lattuca, *Creating Interdisciplinarity: Interdisciplinary Research and Teaching Among College and University Faculty* (Nashville, TN: Vanderbilt University Press, 2008). Lattuca provides a description about why some propose that the scholarship of integration should not be considered separately from Boyer's scholarship of discovery.

13. Lattuca, *Creating Interdisciplinarity.*

14. McCaughey, "Scholars and Teachers Revisited," 88–97; Ruscio, "Response: Faculty Scholarship in Liberal Arts Colleges," 113–19.

15. Jeanne Narum, "Interview with Julio Ramirez: Distinguished Teacher Scholars," *Project Kaleidoscope* (2004), www.pkal.org/documents/JulioRamirezDTS.cfm.

16. Ruscio, "Response: Faculty Scholarship in Liberal Arts Colleges," 113–19.

17. Vartan Gregorian, "Colleges Must Reconstruct the Unity of Knowledge," *Chronicle of Higher Education* 50, no. 39 (2004): B12. There are numerous definitions of interdisciplinarity, but the kinds of approaches on which I focus fall generally under Klein and Newell's (2007) definition of interdisciplinarity as "a process of answering a question, solving a problem, or addressing a topic that is too broad or complex to be dealt with adequately by a single discipline. Interdisciplinary approaches draw on disciplinary perspectives and integrate their insights through construction of a more comprehensive perspective." This definition covers

both teaching and research. See Julie Thompson Klein and William H. Newell, "Advancing Interdisciplinary Studies," in *Handbook of the Undergraduate Curriculum: A Comprehensive Guide to Purposes, Structures, Practices, and Change,* ed. Jerry G. Gaff and James L. Ratcliff (San Francisco: Jossey-Bass, 1997), 393–415.

18. Diana Rhoten, Veronica Boix Mansilla, Marc Chun, and Julie Thompson Klein, "Interdisciplinary Education at Liberal Arts Institutions," *Teagle Foundation White Paper* (2006).

19. Mary Taylor Huber and Pat Hutchings, *Integrative Learning: Mapping the Terrain.* (Washington, DC: Association of American Colleges and Universities, 2004);

William Cronon, "Only Connect . . .": The Goals of a Liberal Education," *American Scholar* 67, no. 4 (1998): 73–81.

20. Brian Bodenbender, "Facing the About: Why Disciplines Are Essential to the Liberal Arts," *LiberalArtsOnline* 3, no. 10 (2003), www.liberalarts.wabash.edu/lao-3-10-discipline-crit -think.

21. Eva T. H. Brann, "The American College as *the* Place for Liberal Learning," in *Distinctively American: The Residential Liberal Arts Colleges,* ed. S. Koblik and S. Graubard (New Brunswick, NJ: Transaction Publishers, 2000), 151–71.

22. Earl J. McGrath, *The Graduate School and the Decline of Liberal Education* (New York: Institute of Higher Education, 1959).

23. Julie Thompson Klein, *Creating Interdisciplinary Campus Cultures* (San Francisco: Jossey Bass and the Association of American Colleges and Universities, 2010). AF Repko, "Assessing Interdisciplinary Learning Outcomes," *Academic Exchange Quarterly,* 12 (2008): 171–78.

24. Adrianna J. Kezar and Jaime Lester, *Organizing Higher Education for Collaboration: A Guide for Campus Leaders* (San Francisco: Jossey-Bass Press, 2009).

25. William H. Newell, "The Role of Interdisciplinary Studies in the Liberal Arts," *LiberalArtsOnline,* 7, no. 1 (2007), www.liberalarts.wabash.edu/lao-7-1-interdisciplinary-ed/.

26. Stanley N. Katz, "Liberal Education on the Ropes," *Chronicle of Higher Education* 51, no. 30 (2005): B6.

27. A wider range of institutional approaches that support interdisciplinary and collaborative teaching and research are presented in Susan Elrod and Mary J. S. Roth, *Leadership for Interdisciplinary Learning: A Practical Guide to Mobilizing, Implementing, and Sustaining Campus Efforts* (Washington, DC: Association of American Colleges and Universities, 2012), 55; S. H. Frost, P. Jean, D. Teodorescu, and A. Brown, "Research at the Crossroads: How Intellectual Initiatives across Disciplines Evolve," *Review of Higher Education* 27, no. 4 (2011): 461–79; Klein, *Creating Interdisciplinary Campus Cultures*); and Kezar and Lester, *Organizing Higher Education for Collaboration.*

28. Ferrall Jr., *Liberal Arts at the Brink.*

29. National Academy of Sciences, *Facilitating Interdisciplinary Research* (Washington, DC: National Academies Press, 2004). Cathy Ann Trower, *Success on the Tenure Track: Five Keys to Faculty Job Satisfaction* (Baltimore: Johns Hopkins University Press, 2012); Katz, "Liberal Education on the Ropes," B6.

30. Also described in Ella Powers, "Alice's Adventures in Tenureland," *Inside Higher Ed,* January 28, 2008, www.insidehighered.com/news/2008/01/28/aacu.

31. Richard Carp, "Relying on the Kindness of Strangers: CEDD's Report on Hiring, Tenure, Promotion in IDS," *Association for Integrative Studies Newsletter* 30 (2008): 1–6; Klein, *Creating Interdisciplinary Campus Cultures.*

32. Lattuca, *Creating Interdisciplinarity.*

33. Gregorian, "Colleges Must Reconstruct the Unity of Knowledge," B12; Trower, *Success on the Tenure Track.*

34. Kezar and Lester, *Organizing Higher Education for Collaboration.*

35. James S. Fairweather, "Faculty Rewards Reconsidered: The Nature of Tradeoffs," *Change* 25, no. 4 (1993): 44–47.

36. Jon Wergin, "Beyond Carrots: What Really Motivates Faculty," *Liberal Education* 87, no. 1 (2011): 50–53.

37. Michael Nelson, "Faculty and Community in the Liberal Arts College (with Observations on Research and Teaching)," *PS: Political Science and Politics*, 27, no. 1 (1994): 73–76.

38. Gregorian, "Colleges Must Reconstruct the Unity of Knowledge," B12.

CHAPTER 8

Technology in Education

Revolution or Evolution?

Adam F. Falk

PRESIDENT, WILLIAMS COLLEGE

It seems you can't pick up a newspaper or magazine—*The New York Times* education section, *Chronicle of Higher Education, EDUCAUSE Review*—without encountering the passionate assertion that information technology has changed everything about our students and how we must educate them. Streaming video. Chat rooms. Laptops. iPods. Course management systems. iPads. The list goes on, and it will continue to go on, as a seemingly endless stream of new technologies emerges.

There's no doubt that all this technology is fun and interesting, and it presents new and innovative ways to do the work of preparing young women and men to engage the world as educated and thoughtful adults. But there are those who would make a stronger statement: that these new technologies have changed, or will soon change, the very fundamentals of a liberal arts education. Even at a place as seemingly secure as Williams, with our 219 years of history and our enduring metaphor of a faculty member on one end of a log and a student on the other, I hear concerns about our coming obsolescence in the face of the computer and Internet revolutions. Will Williams still matter? Will a liberal arts education offered in the mountains of rural New England become irrelevant to the tweeting students of the twenty-first century? Too slow, too stodgy, too boring? Do we at Williams, and at all liberal arts colleges, need to become something completely different if we are to survive?

My response to this question is unambiguous: notwithstanding the very real changes that technology has brought, the core fundamentals of education, both the education we offer at Williams and education as a larger practice, remain intact. Moreover, we should fiercely resist the reflexive conclusion that because our students come to Williams with different modes of encountering and absorbing information (multitasking, multimedia, instant access, short attention spans) we must become like them if we are to reach them and educate them. Rather, I believe our task to be the opposite: to understand both the advantages and the deficits that this new world of continuous information flow provides and use the brief opportunity of students' time in college to reinforce the capacity and disposition for slow, reflective, and difficult engagement with ideas. In fact, our students are, more than ever, hungry for just this sort of experience.

Earlier Forms of Distance and Self-Paced Education

Our current situation is hardly novel. The invention of the printing press might have been thought to presage the end of the university ("Why bring all these students to Oxford when we can just send them all the books by horseman? That would be much cheaper and more efficient, and they could study at their leisure at home, when most convenient.") But no such thing occurred. Quite the contrary, of course. And there are more recent examples of times when innovative uses of technology didn't end education as we know it. I offer three from my own experience.

When I was seven years old, my favorite Saturday morning activity was to get up early and watch reruns of *Gilligan's Island*. But if I got up too early (in those days when there were only four channels), I had to put up with the tedium of both the *Farm Report* and *Sunrise Semester,* which ran at 6 a.m. on CBS. *Sunrise Semester,* which lasted from 1957 to 1982, was New York University's first experiment in distance education. Real courses were offered, with NYU faculty broadcasting from a studio in New York. According to the NYU website, the first course offered was "Comparative Literature 10: From Stendhal to Hemingway," taught by Prof. Floyd Zulli. Students could receive college credit by paying $75. Some 700 applied, 177 completed the course, and 120,000 followed the courses on television without signing up.[1] (Incidentally, these numbers are similar to those for "Machine Learning," offered in the spring of 2012 by a Stanford professor under the auspices of Udacity.)

Sunrise Semester was a great success. It ran for a quarter of a century, won an Emmy Award, and was viewed by millions of people. It began in 1957, at the dawn of the modern era in which television sets became ubiquitous in American homes. Certainly, the pioneers of *Sunrise Semester* must have entertained the idea that with access to the best lectures for every student in every home, the days of the expensive residential college would soon be at an end. But why did this exciting new technology of television not have this effect? Because, of course, college education isn't simply about the most efficient or most engaging means of transmitting information—it's about the creation and nurturing of a community of students, studying and learning together, in a particular kind of social and physical environment.

However, we do sometimes learn things on our own. When I was a freshman in high school, I was bored in my regular mathematics class, and my teacher gave me what was called a "programmed" book on probability and statistics. The book had a series of foldout pages. On each page was a discussion of a concept, and on the foldout flap was a series of questions. The answers were on the back of the flap. You were meant to go on to the next page only when you'd answered the questions correctly. The whole thing was very engaging and very effective. It was the only formal course in probability that I ever took, and it served me well through a professional career in theoretical physics. Working in an entirely self-directed way, I really learned the material, and I loved it. In the book's rigor and its appeal, I imagine it was the equal of any self-paced text available for the iPad today.

This was a very efficient and cost-effective way to learn probability, but the world of mathematics teaching was never taken over by programmed textbooks. We didn't do away with all the math classes, hand the students these books, and send them to the library. These independent methods always had their place, of course, but why wasn't education transformed when the day came that programmed texts could be produced cheaply? I would maintain that it is because even the best students cannot learn everything on their own, no matter how good the materials. It is more fun, and far more effective, to learn as part of a community of students, supported by real human interactions.

Finally, when I was in college, I taught calculus by mail for Duke University's Talent Identification Program (TIP). My student, Jane, was in the ninth grade and had no opportunity to learn calculus in her high school. I sent her the text and the problem sets. She sent the worked problems back to me every week, and I would correct them and return them to her. We handled exams the same way. Jane did marvelously, earning a 5 on the AP calculus BC exam (and an 800 on the SAT math test, back when that meant something). Jane was a brilliant kid for sure, and TIP Math by Mail was just what she needed in a school that couldn't meet her needs. Yet once again, the existence of high-quality distance education programs more than a quarter of a century ago didn't keep schools and parents from thinking that the more expensive option of offering calculus in the classroom was actually the best way to enrich the math curricula. Today, almost all good American high schools offer calculus.

The point of these anecdotes is that, in very real ways, effective (and cost-effective) technologies to support distance education and self-paced learning have been with us for many decades. Printing, television, and the postal service are remarkable tools. And in fact, they have been used since their inventions to enhance and deepen education. What none of them has done is change the fundamental fact that at its heart, education is a social activity that takes its highest form within a real community of students and faculty. Neither books nor video nor chat rooms have made colleges obsolete.

A Recent Case Study in Distance Education

Nonetheless, many argue that our present moment differs from all those that have come before. Perhaps they are right. Perhaps the new tools of information technology provide something deeper than just new modes of content delivery. Perhaps our students are so accustomed to online interaction that the virtual communities erected within modern course management systems are all that they need to be connected to their fellow students. Perhaps their brains really are wired differently now.

Personally, I doubt it. But even if some or all of this has happened, and we really have entered a Brave New World, I would argue that some simple, interrelated principles remain:

1. Education is still as much about human interaction as about delivering content. More so, in fact.
2. New technology is expensive, especially technology on the cutting (or bleeding) edge, and immediate obsolescence is a perpetual danger.
3. The introduction of technology does not generally drive down overall costs; in fact, it's likely to increase them.

Johns Hopkins University's Advanced Academic Programs (AAP) are professional master's programs in a variety of fields, offered largely by part-time faculty who work in the relevant professions. About half of its two thousand students are in a variety of programs in biotechnology, many of them working in the biotech industry hub in Montgomery County. Initially, AAP offered these courses extensively and successfully in a modern glass-and-steel facility in the heart of "DNA Alley." One could not imagine a better location, and the programs, which were of high quality and high relevance to the target audience, flourished.

And yet, by 2005 it became clear that there were good reasons to consider offering some of these courses, and perhaps entire degrees, online. Certainly, the combined brand of Johns Hopkins and biotechnology was a powerful and global one, and there were excellent opportunities to offer these courses to students outside the Washington area. These programs generated net revenue, so extending their reach was desirable. Moreover, the lives of local students, forced to battle Beltway traffic while balancing demanding jobs and family responsibilities, presented challenges that could be met by presenting the courses in an asynchronous and nonlocal format—online, using a course management system. Even today, a significant majority of these online learners actually live within fifty miles of that glass-and-steel building, which turns out to be an entirely typical phenomenon.

In the days when much of this was new, AAP faculty were concerned to demonstrate that the delivery of courses online was the equivalent of what was referred to as "on-site." So they did a controlled study with the offerings in bioinformatics. A faculty member who was to teach online needed first to have taught the same course in the conventional classroom. The content of the online and on-site courses was identical, and students were given the same final exams. Both student satisfaction and student learning outcomes were assessed and compared.[2]

The study showed that an online course is every bit as effective as an on-site course— even, perhaps, slightly more so. But this happy outcome is the direct result of a material investment in the online course that is no less than the investment in teaching on site. A core component of the online course, both educationally and in terms of student satisfaction, is the extensive interaction between the faculty member and the students, both in moderated chat rooms and on an individual basis. Sustaining such virtual conversations at a high level is enormously time consuming for the professor. As a consequence, the student-faculty ratio in the online course must be approximately the same as (or even lower than) in the conventional course. There are no simple economies of scale in teaching online if it's to be done well. Similarly, the preparation time for faculty who teach on line is higher than for those who teach face-to-face. Although the preparation is by far the heaviest the first time the course is taught, online courses must be updated as much as on-site courses, and faculty turnover is just as common. It's no easier to "package" online courses so they may be taught by "anyone" than it is for face-to-face education.

Despite the lack of savings of money or faculty time in teaching on line, there were great benefits to AAP and its students in adopting this model. By 2010, half the enrollments in AAP's biotechnology program were in online courses. The spatial and temporal flexibility afforded by online delivery was of critical value both to the local population of working adults and to developing a global student body. And although they were not inexpensive to deliver, the courses were educationally successful because, among other reasons, they made it a core priority to create and nurture a virtual community of deeply engaged students. The critical importance of this aspect of the online courses was clear in student satisfaction surveys and in interviews.

Lessons for Liberal Arts Colleges

So what are the lessons in all this for Williams and other liberal arts colleges? Our core mission is to educate students; our defining structure, a personal, intimate, collaborative environment. Young women and men come to us because they want to be in a place where they will know the faculty and their fellow students, and the community will know them. We know, and they know, that for the great majority of them, this is the sort of education that will prepare them best to be purposeful in their lives and effective in the world. The great potential of the new technologies is not to upend these core values but to allow us to fulfill our existing educational mission more effectively, especially by giving us new strategies to transcend our limitations of scale and location.

In particular, distance education holds the promise, if thoughtfully deployed, of extending our curricula into areas not covered by our relatively small faculties. In our new multi-polar world, there are many more languages that students will want to learn than we can possibly offer in our classrooms. French, Spanish, German, Russian, Japanese, and Chinese simply are not enough anymore. Internet-based instruction could be a vital solution to this challenge. In a similar vein, efficient, high-quality, low-cost videoconferencing technologies can bring our students into truly meaningful collaborative contact with students around the world, enhancing the traditional international dimensions of our curriculum, such as study abroad and courses on global topics, with substantive virtual experiences. (At Williams we have a long-standing relationship with the American University of Cairo by which we use videoconferencing to teach a course jointly each year. During the Arab Spring of 2011, this was a powerful educational experience for our students.) New technologies will certainly bring richer multimedia teaching materials, even if they won't be any cheaper than conventional textbooks. Some of those materials may even allow colleges to change, in exciting ways, the very modes of instruction. Colleges may even find that computerized, programmed delivery of some standard elementary topics becomes of such high quality that some modest efficiencies can be realized while maintaining educational standards.[3]

Educational innovation comes in many forms, and not all of them rely primarily on integrated circuits. One of the most exciting and highly anticipated projects on the Williams campus is the new library we are building. This facility will bring together our extensive book collections in the humanities and social sciences, our wonderful rare book library, and a new Center for Media Initiatives and will surround them with dedicated spaces for interdisciplinary and group work. It will create a vibrant academic hub that will excite students' passions, nurture their curiosity, and above all else, bring them together in shared space, not cyberspace. Academic work *has* changed over the years: it is more collaborative, more disciplinarily fluid, and more eclectic in its sources and methods. A modern library is no longer simply a box for books and carrels; rather, it is the crossroads of the campus both physically and metaphorically, where students and faculty meet, and where technologies both new and old come into conversation. Great academic architecture brings people into contact with each other, with tools, and with ideas. Information technology is surely a part of this story, and our new library will support it as never before, but it is only one strand among many in the tapestry we are weaving at Williams.

But are students now so fundamentally different that they can only learn, or learn best, via the new modalities embedded in our current technological revolutions? There is no question that a teenager raised in a world of Wikipedia and ubiquitous multimedia stimulation doesn't encounter the world or have the same relationship to information as did today's college leaders when we were that age. But it simply doesn't follow that the only education that will seem relevant to these students, the only education that they will absorb and embrace, is one that foregrounds the most disjunctive and hyperkinetic features of the modern world. Speeding along the Information Superhighway can be cognitively exhausting, and for many students it is ultimately unsatisfying. If their experiences before college have not encouraged them to slow down and think carefully about a coherent set of information rather than surf a relentless wave of disconnected facts, then college is certainly the time to start. This deeper connection to ideas, I am convinced, is what they are really hungry for.

Educational innovation need not involve semiconductors. At Williams, we offer some courses in a tutorial format wherein a faculty member facilitates a weekly discussion with two students in which the students alternately critique each other's work and defend their own over the course of a semester. We made significant investments to deepen this program in the last decade, to make tutorials available to students early in their careers, to extend the model to the sciences, and to provide the opportunity for any student who seeks it. Tutorials are now offered in almost every department; most students graduate from Williams having taken a tutorial, and many take more than one. The expansion of this program required an investment in people that seemed to some critics to represent a retrograde commitment to a pedagogy of the past, during an era of great technological advances. After all, tutorials represent a deeply personal, interactive, and challenging mode of learning, with no particular emphasis on technological sophistication. Yet student satisfaction with the tutorial program is by far the highest of any part of our formal curriculum; student learning in tutorials is the deepest as well. We consider this program one of our great successes, a hallmark of a Williams College education, and an expression of our fundamental and enduring educational values.

On all of our campuses, the inexorable march of technological progress will continue to present both terrific opportunities and substantial challenges. We must seek to seize the one while navigating the other. The truest promise of the new information technologies is to deepen our work with students, to strengthen our forms of pedagogy, and to enhance the connectedness of the educational experience. At its best, technology allows us to fulfill our purposes more completely. But we must guard scrupulously against the dangers of distraction, faddishness, and apocalyptic anxiety, with their great capacity to dissipate our precious resources of time and money. Technology is no panacea for the cost of a high-quality college education, and college leaders must resist pressures to say that it is.

We must resist, too, the powerful temptation to follow every trend that our peers seem to be pursuing. For example, we should contemplate the expense of putting courses on line only if doing so clearly serves our institution's own particular mission; we should not make such commitments simply for fear of being perceived as not on the cutting edge. By the same token, large-scale investments in any specific technology, including iPods, iPads, or high-definition videoconferencing, are certain to be an expensive waste if they are not grounded thoroughly in larger educational initiatives that are faculty-centered and pedagogically motivated. My one recommendation to us all is to be guided firmly by the principle that technology must be deployed as a tool in the service of our educational mission, never the other way around.

I have spent decades asking alumni, old and young, what mattered most to them in their college educations. Fundamentally, the answer has never changed. Students and alumni point to a small number of critical relationships with individual faculty members who taught them something deep and important, faculty who mentored them in theses and research, faculty who helped them personally, faculty who woke them from their slumbers. Upon reflection, alumni express little preference for those who were, in their time, the flashiest or the closest to the cutting edge.

Bringing faculty and students together and giving them the space and time to interact is what we at liberal arts colleges do best. That is our core purpose. Technological evolution will make it possible to do this better in all sorts of important ways. But if the printing press and television did not cause a revolution to bring us down, the iPad and the Internet will not do so either.

NOTES

1. New York University Presents 175 Facts about NYU, www.nyu.edu/library/bobst/research/arch/175/pages/sunrise.htm.

2. A thorough discussion of this controlled experiment is given by Kristina Obom and Patrick Cummings, the directors of the program, in "Comparison of Online and Onsite Bioinformatics Instruction for a Fully Online Bioinformatics Master's Program," *Journal of Microbiology & Biology Education* (May 2007): 22–27.

3. I would insist on the word "modest" to describe the potential savings from computerized delivery of elementary material, even though many students would take these courses. In terms of faculty time, which is the most significant cost driver in liberal arts colleges, teaching large introductory courses is by far the most efficient thing we do. There are no more than a few dozen such courses at a typical liberal arts college. Assuming (unrealistically) that they could be taught on line at no cost and with equal quality, and (equally unrealistically) that all faculty teaching time could be recaptured as budgetary savings, and given the usual teaching loads, one could hope to see a reduction of no more than about 10 faculty FTE. This would amount to a savings of about one million dollars, a significant number, but at less than one percent of a typical college's budget hardly a game-changer for our economic model. And realistically, one would expect savings to be far lower, if realized at all.

CHAPTER 9

You Can Run, but You Can't Hide

Kevin M. Guthrie
PRESIDENT, ITHAKA

Colleges and universities have survived numerous calamities over the centuries—civil wars and world wars, industrial revolutions, and depressions—and have remained remarkably strong and vibrant. Seventy (82%) of the eighty-five institutions of all kinds established by 1520 that continue to exist in recognizable form are colleges or universities.[1] Although colleges are criticized for being slow moving and impervious to change, they have evolved as necessary and have adapted effectively to their changing environment. In contrast to most of the criticism we read in the popular media today, these institutions certainly seem to have done some things right!

We must also recognize that the Internet and networked technologies have unleashed a set of forces on education such as have never been experienced before. No one knows what impact these forces will have on the traditional liberal arts college, but it would be unwise to pretend that it will not be momentous. Furthermore, the fact that these forces are sweeping over education during a time of economic hardship is likely to accelerate the pace of change. The question is whether colleges can continue to evolve fast enough to succeed in a more dynamically competitive environment.

The recent well-publicized efforts to provide massively open online courses for free or at very low cost is a harbinger of things to come. It does not matter if the current efforts have a working business model or are truly effective; what matters is that by engaging tens of thousands of students simultaneously, they demonstrate what is made possible by such courses. Even if these enterprises do not succeed, projects with some of their attributes will. By understanding the primary forces that make these innovations possible, leaders of higher education institutions may be able to develop strategies to take advantage of them.

The fundamental driver of these changes is that information can be stored in digital form and transmitted over networks, both cabled and wireless. Increasingly, one can stay connected to these networks all over the world and in the most remote locales. Aside from the mind-bending speed of this development, to say that it is transformative is not a hyperbole. Not only does this movement to digitally store and transmit content profoundly undermine an economy that was predicated on storage and distribution of physical objects, but it also makes possible new kinds of social interaction that used to be limited by time and geographic proximity. For content like books, journals, video, and audio, proximity to storehouses of objects has far less value once this content is in digital form and available on the network. For more interactive communications, we are at an early stage in the development of technology-enabled social communities. These social networks offer new kinds of interaction that often serve as an effective complement to face-to-face communication and sometimes even as a substitute for those interactions. Together, these innovations are poised to disrupt the normal processes of teaching and learning at higher education institutions.

Sharing Information *Is* the Mission

Higher education institutions have thrived through many other periods of technological innovation. What makes this one so different is that the technology involved is truly at the core of these institutions' mission and primary activities: creating and disseminating information and knowledge. Not only have the technologies and processes that they rely on been stable for centuries, but much of what they do has been insulated from certain commercial forces. There is a reason that the academy has conventionally been called the Ivory Tower. But the development of the Internet has led to a networked information marketplace where all of the services are used and shared across domains. As William G. Bowen said in his Romanes Lecture in 2000, referring to the impact of digital technologies on higher education:

> I use "digitization" to mean the electronic assembling, disassembling, and transmitting of the basic elements of intellectual capital. These include words, sounds, pictures, and data. The ability to take these sources apart, send them easily over distances, and reconstruct them renders the walls around universities far more porous. Once those walls are pierced in this way—that is to say, once both the basic materials and the fruits of the work of academic institutions are easily gathered and sent—the very currency of the university becomes

dramatically more accessible, and these institutions find themselves drawn increasingly into the realm of commerce.[2]

Equally important, the world of commerce now penetrates the university. The tools of research and teaching are not walled off from the consumer world. Services like Google are used both for academic research and for a search to find the nearest coffee shop. Amazon is used to purchase books that once would have been exclusively provided by the academic library or university bookstore. And Facebook is used to find colleagues who are interested in similar areas of study. The academic enterprise is not shielded from the economic and technological forces operating at massive scale on the web. There is no escaping them.

Five Forces Acting on the Consumer Web

So what are the forces operating on the commercial web, and how do they shape the enterprises that operate in their midst? I offer five broad categories, but I make no assertion that this is a comprehensive or exhaustive list or that it is supported by extensive research or data. It is a product of my own observations. The five forces are: (1) today's added value is tomorrow's commodity; (2) services that can go to the cloud, will go to the cloud; (3) read-write capabilities lead to two-sided markets; (4) the network enables many-to-many interactions; and (5) everything users do leaves a trail, leading to data analytics. What will it mean when these forces press against the traditional bundle of activities associated with teaching and learning in a college context?

Today's Added Value Is Tomorrow's Commodity

Thomas Hobbes wrote that life in the state of nature is "nasty, brutish and short,"[3] and so it is with the life cycle of products on the web. When a new innovation is created, it can grow extremely rapidly. If it is profitable, competitors will emerge quickly, since the barriers to entry to develop a web-based service are generally low. New entrants often identify the most profitable component of a service and focus specifically on that aspect, thereby creating a wedge that often "unbundles" the overall product. This unbundling force has had its most dramatic impact on industries like newspaper publishing.

This unrelenting force demands that services constantly innovate and even reinvent themselves as their profitable services become commodities and they have to develop new services that add special value. I call this "moving up the value stack," and all services on the web must face it. Netflix offers a case in point. No sooner had it developed a fantastically successful service warehousing and distributing DVDs (forcing Blockbuster into bankruptcy) than it found that it had to offer a web-streaming service to compete with video-on-demand services offered by cable companies.

Services That Can Go to the Cloud, Will Go to the Cloud

The low cost of transmitting data on the web, combined with the economies of scale that prevail for technology-based services, means that if a service can be standardized and offered from a remote networked location, it is likely that it will be. The economic drivers are compelling not only for hardware infrastructure (e.g., Amazon S3) but also for software-based services (e.g., Salesforce.com). JSTOR represents a kind of cloud-based service in the sense that libraries rely on this not-for-profit enterprise to store, preserve, and provide access to the digitized versions of older journals. The reasons behind this migration of locally provided services to centralized services are well articulated by Nicholas Carr in *The Big Switch: Rewiring the World, from Edison to Google*.[4] Carr compares the fundamentals of the computer industry with the power industry and traces the migration of electric power supply from being locally provided to being provided centrally as a utility.

Read-Write Capabilities Lead to Two-sided Markets

One aspect of the web that distinguishes it from other major media innovations is that it supports both reading and writing. Anyone with access to the web is simultaneously a consumer and a producer. It is not a unidirectional broadcast medium like television, radio, movies, or magazines. The incredibly successful massive-scale enterprises on the web (e.g., eBay, Wikipedia, Facebook, Twitter) serve as marketplaces where consumers *and* producers meet to trade products or information. These two-sided markets can grow to offer extraordinary depth as well as breadth, whether it be finding tiny niche communities of collectors on eBay or locating a $.99 app in the Apple App Store that can measure the speed of a ball going down a hill for a seventh grader's science project. Almost anything can be found in this storehouse of seemingly unlimited inventory.

The Network Enables Many-to-Many Interactions

One can argue that each of the first three forces has earlier precedents in the pre-web world. Economies of scale exist in many businesses. Audio and video cassette players supported "reading" and "writing," and two-sided markets have existed in many contexts. The most deeply revolutionary aspect of the web is the way it enables people to communicate with many other people simultaneously. Mass broadcast media supported one channel communicating with many, but never has there been the capacity for many people to communicate with many other people on a limitless number of direct channels. Everyone is a broadcaster or a publisher and a consumer at the same time. Services taking advantage of this new capacity are the most innovative in the sense that they are offering a truly new capability, as opposed to making a preexisting capacity better, faster, or cheaper. New companies like Facebook, Twitter, and LinkedIn tap into this new area of opportunity.

Everything Users Do Leaves a Trail, Leading to Data Analytics

When you have a telephone conversation, unless it is recorded, it is gone except for what is remembered by its participants. The default condition is obsolescence. When you send an e-mail, what you have communicated is recorded unless it is deleted. The default condition is persistence. The same is true for interactions over the web. Your actions—your clickstreams—are tracked by web servers when you visit sites, click on links and buttons, and interact with websites. These can be saved into databases and files that can be later mined for patterns of activity or other diagnostic information. This ability to track usage logs, mine them, and conduct strategic analysis is creating an entirely new industry. Google uses this kind of analysis to continuously improve its search results by following the actions of its users to help it determine which search terms yield the most successful results. Other sites mine usage data to help identify things that might interest you (so-called recommender systems). The most successful web-based companies have made and are making enormous investments in data mining and analysis of user activity to improve and sell their products.

The Higher Education Context

If you accept that higher education now coexists on the same network as the consumer web, then these forces will have an impact on the traditional services provided by higher education institutions. This is true of a variety of activities that take place on campus, such as administrative services like admissions or academic services like publishing. It is also true for teaching and learning.

Today's Value, Tomorrow's Commodity

A teaching faculty member offers a bundle of services in teaching a course. What comprises this bundle? He or she usually develops the course syllabus and assigns readings, delivers some number of lectures, usually (but not always) leads a smaller discussion group, assigns papers and projects, gives tests, grades papers and tests, and communicates with students about the logistics or substantive content of the class. Some of these are relatively straightforward and are consistent from semester to semester (e.g., the lecture); and some of them, such as leading a class discussion or grading a paper, are unique to the specific students participating at a particular point in time. In large introductory courses, one professor's set of lectures will cover quite similar content to another professor's set of lectures, although of course some professors will be better at delivering the materials, leading to a more engaged experience for students.

The forces of the web described above have the tendency to disaggregate bundled services and drive a wedge between those services that are commodities and those that are of higher value. If the success of the bundle depends on one or two components subsidizing the other components, a difficult situation can arise if competitors successfully develop low-cost services that attract customers or users from the profitable service. A commercial example of this unbundling phenomenon is the newspaper industry, where the web systematically disaggregated profitable services such as classified ads from the newspaper bundle.

One of the "profitable" services in the teacher's bundle is the lecture. If a class is taught year after year, the lecture costs little for the teacher in terms of his or her time, and yet it comprises a major part of what the student pays for in taking a course. For classes with relatively consistent content across institutions, one can argue that it is like a commodity. The response that appears to be emerging in the web marketplace is that the lecture is indeed a commodity, and this has led to the concept of "flipping the lecture," where lectures are recorded digitally and can be watched by the student anytime, anywhere. Courses that are little more than a series of lectures are likely to find it difficult to compete with massively open online courses, because the experience of watching a lecture on line is not sufficiently different from attending it in person as one of 300 students—not to mention that the competitive provider has the potential to attract a superstar teacher/lecturer to deliver a great lecture to any student, anywhere in the world.

Services That Can Go to the Cloud, Will Go to the Cloud

Those services that are relatively consistent across institutions are likely to be provided by a central provider. In the early days, there will be resistance to allowing a large-scale third party to provide such services because higher education institutions will consider their needs unique, or they will want to defend student privacy or a similar local interest. But the economics of these cloud services are so compelling that it will become difficult to resist. So we see more and more colleges relying on Gmail for e-mail or Blackboard for course management systems. In the context of teaching, it is likely that platforms are going to emerge that will provide a suite of services to support interactive and adaptive learning. The most appealing of these services will provide feedback to students and faculty in real time and will adapt to support each student's specific needs. What remains to be seen is whether such systems can successfully provide sufficient standardization to be economically beneficial while also being able to customize the system to meet individual faculty needs and desires. Customization is going to be critical, especially in the near term, if these systems are going to be widely adopted.

Read-Write Capabilities Lead to Two-Sided Markets

Just as every web user is both a consumer and a producer of content, so is every teacher both a consumer of course materials and a producer. Successful platforms will plug into this capability to make it easy for faculty to find elements of other faculty members' courses that they can incorporate into their own, and vice versa. Furthermore, at an institutional level, the web will cause some institutions to emerge as net producers of courses, while other institutions will emerge as net consumers of courses. This will enable smaller schools to offer courses in more subjects and disciplines. A key issue will be what local value is added by a school that is a net consumer of courses provided by faculty housed at other institutions. What will prevent students from bypassing the local intermediary and taking the courses directly from the highly regarded remote institution?

The Network Enables Many-to-Many Interactions

This revolutionary aspect of the web has perhaps the most inertia preventing its adoption in the higher education context. Many, if not most, people would argue that face-to-face social interaction, with all of its many benefits, cannot be duplicated virtually. Of course, many aspects of this statement are undoubtedly true. But it is also the case that social networking applications like Facebook and Twitter have drawn people together and have helped them to maintain relationships over time and distance that were impossible in a non-networked world. These interactions may not be a complete substitute for face-to-face interaction, but they can often be a powerful complement. What remains to be seen is whether technology-enabled social activity can lead to peer discussions and interaction that rival what happens in a discussion section of a classroom. As many university presidents tell their incoming freshmen year in and year out, "You will learn more from each other than you will from your professors." Admittedly, this includes many interactions that occur outside of the classroom and are part of the process of growing up in a residential college, but it also applies to the discussion in a classroom. Watch carefully as the technology that supports peer-to-peer interactions becomes more facile and sophisticated; the nature of web-based discussion may prove sufficiently engaging to serve as an acceptable substitute for many students.

Everything Users Do Leaves a Trail, Leading to Data Analytics

In the new adaptive learning systems that are beginning to emerge, such as Carnegie Mellon's OLI courses or Pearson's MyLab, every activity of the student can and will be tracked. The tracking of users' actions will first be used to customize the learning track to provide the student with feedback on how he or she is doing; it will also be used to provide feedback to the teacher to understand how the students are doing both as individuals and as a group. And finally, these usage logs can be used in the aggregate to continuously improve the system. When combined with performance on quizzes and tests and other measures of how the students mastered the material, massive amounts of usage data could show which of the system's interventions were more or less successful and which tracks through the material were optimal, given a student's progress to a certain point. If a single company or a small number of companies came to dominate the provision of this kind of a base platform in the way that Google now dominates search, it could prove to be a very powerful and self-reinforcing position. In addition to the control of these data potentially leading to monopoly control, these data are also extremely important to research into how people learn and what helps them to learn better. We have the opportunity to measure learning progress and learning outcomes in a way that was impossible in face-to-face teaching and learning. Who is going to control those data? What does this development mean for teaching and learning?

Lessons for Academic Leaders

Higher education is now facing the same forces that are influencing web consumer services. My hope is that this description might serve as a framework to help higher education leaders develop strategies to address the changing environment. A valuable exercise would be to bring together senior leadership to discuss how each of the five forces affects the administrative and academic services of the college. For example, given that services that can go to the cloud will go to the cloud, leaders should determine what administrative services on a college campus can be reliably outsourced. On the academic side, leaders should consider how to enhance course offerings on campus, given access to a more efficient global network where all faculty members are both consumers and producers of courses and course content. Similar evaluations of the impact of the five forces on the administrative services and academic offerings of the college can be conducted.

A more ambitious step would be to develop a strategic plan for information technology for the campus. The IT strategy must address more than just administrative services for e-mail or a course management system; it must also assess the new opportunities for education technologies to influence the academic enterprise. This planning process should include key administrative and academic officers and should start with an objective assessment of the current costs and levels of satisfaction for various uses of information technology. Areas of comparative advantage for the college, with an emphasis on services that depend on the most defensible local capabilities and assets, should be identified and prioritized. With such a baseline assessment in place, consideration can then be given to the most compelling opportunities for investment.

In a rapidly changing environment, some resources will need to be reserved for investment in experiments and novel approaches and for faculty and staff development. A senior leader such as the CIO or chief academic officer should be empowered to invest in these new opportunities and to oversee and evaluate their implementation. This person needs to be a respected champion on campus who is sensitive to local factors and circumstances, who has a strong understanding of the impact and potential of new technologies, and who is knowledgeable about how new approaches are being implemented successfully at other institutions. In other words, there needs to be institutional commitment to the systematic and iterative integration of these new technologies into the operations of the college.

Pursuing such strategic change will require strong and careful leadership. There is understandable and justifiable resistance to moving too quickly. The new technologies and the network environment have been with us for little more than a decade, while the fundamental and successful approaches to teaching and learning have been with us for more than a century. It would be unwise to pursue blindly the paths of Internet companies in their infancy, many of which will not still be in existence a few years from now. But evidence is growing that there are opportunities to employ new technologies and new platforms in ways that can conceivably lower costs while attaining comparable learning outcomes.[5] We need our best educators and educational institutions to embrace these technologies in smart ways so that we can educate the most students possible as effectively and economically as possible. To dismiss these technologies without assessing them to determine what works and what doesn't is inconsistent with the best traditions of the academy to improve on the past through careful research and open intellectual engagement.

The cost of higher education has been increasing at an unacceptably fast pace over the last several decades. If the mission of colleges is to be an engine of opportunity in a society where someone from any socioeconomic class has a chance to get the best education, colleges will have to arrest the staggering growth in tuition costs. If colleges are unable to take advantage of the opportunity that technology offers to do more with less, they risk becoming institutions populated only with the children of the wealthy. And that may be the best that they can hope for. More draconian scenarios portend a period of intense competition for full-paying students and the financial failure of many institutions as students pursue other options for postsecondary education. My hope is that leaders of today's liberal arts colleges can put in place the strategic plans and processes to make the best and most effective use of these new technologies and lead us to a time where more students, not fewer, have an opportunity to get a great liberal education.

NOTES

The chapter's title refers to "He can run, but he can't hide," a quote attributed to Joe Louis on the eve of his fight with Billy Conn, June 9, 1946.

1 Clark Kerr, *Users of the University* (Cambridge, MA: Harvard University Press, 1982), 152.

2. William G. Bowen, *At a Slight Angle to the Universe: The University in a Digitized, Commercialized Age* (Princeton, NJ: Princeton University Press, 2000), 5.

3. Thomas Hobbes, *Leviathan*, 1651.

4. Nicholas Carr, *The Big Switch: Rewiring the World, from Edison to Google* (New York: W. W. Norton, 2009).

5. See William G. Bowen, Matthew M. Chingos, Kelly A. Lack, and Thomas I. Nygren, *Interactive Learning Online at Public Universities: Evidence from Randomized Trials* (New York: ITHAKA S+R, 2012).

CHAPTER 10

Technology, Learning, and Campus Culture

Daniel R. Porterfield

PRESIDENT, FRANKLIN & MARSHALL COLLEGE

In his final Sunday sermon on March 31, 1968, "Remaining Awake through a Great Revolution," Martin Luther King Jr. said, "Through our scientific and technological genius we've made of this world a neighborhood. And now through our moral and ethical commitment we must make of it a brotherhood."[1] Of course, forty-four years ago even Dr. King could not have imagined the densely interconnected global neighborhood we would create through inventions like the Internet, digitized content, search engines, massive social media platforms, massive online open courses (MOOCs), GPS systems, and proliferating smartphones. Nor could anyone have forecasted the revolutionary applications of mushrooming digital capacities in fields ranging from finance to physics, from education to entertainment, from commerce to law enforcement, and from health care to warfare. What Dr. King saw, however, was prophetic for our time—the need to "remain awake" to our shared humanity and basic needs, because astounding inventions and discoveries do not necessarily lead to progress in human relations and may exacerbate current problems or create new ones.

Even as we revel in the benefits of the digital revolution, which are legion, we must attend to potential dark sides. For example, it is discomfiting that companies, law enforcement agencies, and governments covertly watch and preserve histories of our web browsing. No one knows how the next decade of enhanced computational capacity will affect labor trends, international finance, medical care, or developing economies. Will the digital divide worsen or take new forms?[2] How will cyber-terrorism unfold? Are we ready for quantum leaps in the uses of artificial intelligence, "Big Data," and designer genomes?

Then there is the reality that new technologies become "persuasive," in that using changes the user, and not always for the better. We all know people who have become addicted to e-mail culture or who use Facebook to compulsively "egocast." We all recognize that it is easier to surf the Web than to study, and to cut and paste ideas rather than create new ones. At a deeper level, the social critic Jaron Lanier argues that the Internet has evolved to create tools and frameworks that limit individual consciousness and "tend to pull us into life patterns that gradually degrade the ways in which each of us exist as an individual."[3] Reminding us that social media is still in its early stages, MIT Professor Sherry Turkle and others argue that heavy use of social media weakens people's ability to interact authentically and may make us more transactional, guarded, superficial, reactive, and lonely in our relationships.[4] Adolfo Nicholas, S.J., the superior general of the Jesuits, decries what he calls "the globalization of superficiality" perpetuated by technologies that are "shaping the interior worlds of so many . . . , limiting the fullness of their flourishing as human persons and limiting their responses to a world in need of healing, intellectually, morally and spiritually."[5] Such concerns are not without precedent; in general, societies tend to create and apply new breakthrough technologies before developing shared intellectual and ethical frameworks for understanding the implications of the changes.

The Campus as a Greenhouse for Technology

Of course, the academy actively takes part in our twenty-first-century digital revolution. Our campuses are greenhouses for technology. We create and sustain technological cultures. We have made extraordinary discoveries about phenomena like the genome, the earth, and the cosmos. If the West has experienced a Kuhnian paradigm shift in the uses of digital technology and the kinds of research questions advanced computational technology now allows us to address, then American higher education has been both a driver and a beneficiary. Looking forward, some see enormous promise for democratizing education. K–12 schools and higher education of all types are exploring both blended online-classroom learning, which has the goal of improving student outcomes.[6] Many colleges and universities are now experimenting with MOOCs, both to expand access to knowledge and, perhaps, to create new efficiencies or revenue sources.[7] Hopeful visionaries like Douglas Thomas and John Seely Brown argue that new information technologies may help us create a revolutionary "culture of learning" to empower individuals to become active creators and curators of knowledge and not simply consumers.[8]

How do we make sense of the pace, scope, directions, and meanings of the digital technology revolution? Surely it is not enough to simply adopt the stances of the technophile or the technophobe, for, in the words of Shakespeare, "The web of life is of a mingled yarn, good and ill together."[9] We in higher education must strive for the longer and deeper views. While it is a reality that each institution must show purpose in determining which business decisions related to information technology and online learning make most sense right now, the higher education community cannot neglect the larger unfolding societal and humanistic questions. Like the huge, multifaceted issues of globalization and global climate change, the digital revolution demands our sustained engagement and best thinking.

Using the Liberal Arts to Engage Major Issues of Technology

Because of our relatively small sizes, strong faculty/student mentoring relationships, vibrant campus cultures, intellectual traditions, and shared humanistic values, liberal arts colleges may be uniquely positioned to provide sorely needed intellectual leadership in framing the big questions about technology, community, and humanity. While such considerations do not easily lend themselves to a detailed action agenda, there are a few steps we can take confidently right now.

First, and most importantly, we can intensify our efforts to engage the major issues and questions. From seminars to special lectures, from cross-disciplinary colloquia to senior theses, we should explore any and all aspects of the "good and ill" histories of technology and today's unfolding digital revolution. This type of theme requires holistic thought and multidisciplinary perspectives. For example, advancing knowledge about the effects of social media on children will require insights from fields including psychology, neuroscience, philosophy, social science, and computer science. Such topics play to the intellectual strengths of liberal arts colleges, whose closely situated faculty come together more easily for research, colloquia, team teaching, and problem solving.

Clearly, the rise of the MOOC is a trend that the liberal arts sector must grapple with, even as we assert the value of mind-on-mind, active learning. We must acknowledge that potential of MOOCs to advance values we share—broad access to knowledge and education—along with perceptions of their failings—passive learning, the lack of faculty-student mentoring, and their tendency to convey information rather than help students learn to create knowledge. The growth of MOOCs could lead to a lowering of standards about what constitutes a meaningful and liberating college education; it no doubt will be necessary for higher education and societal leaders to interrogate both the purported value of MOOCs, and the financial interests of those who provide them.

This is not to say that liberal arts colleges can or should shy away from using technology to enhance learning. At Franklin & Marshall College, we have begun to engage digital technology questions in new ways. In recent years, we have created a computer science major, worked with other institutions in a Bryn Mawr College project on blended learning in the curriculum,[10] and secured Howard Hughes Medical Institute funding to allow undergraduates to conduct and apply new research on disabling genetic conditions among Amish children.[11]

As technology continues to develop, our intellectual tradition of unbounded inquiry and critical thought may be the greatest resource we offer society. This strength seems especially valuable at a time when most digital technology users participate in systems that force us to give away our personal information and privacy. Consider the brave new world of digital culture for which we receive no bills—from Facebook and Twitter to Pinterest and Instagram to YouTube, Gmail, and Google—except that we actually do pay steep prices with our data. Most of the digital networks in which we participate own all the information we enter or post and then track our usages precisely, thus providing their "free" services because they make money selling our records or using them for targeted advertising.[12] It should give everyone pause to remember that virtually every click or keystroke we make is being used or stored for data mining. Smartphones now function as tracking devices recording our digital fingerprints and our actual footprints.[13] This dimension of technological "progress" warrants the independent critical evaluation that American higher education was built to provide.

Second, we should purposefully evaluate our students' experiences with digital technology and help them with difficulties. The priority we place on teaching undergraduates gives us rich experiential knowledge of the borderlands where emerging adults live with and within protean technology platforms. A few facts for context:

- Today's college students report that they spend twelve hours per day engaged with some type of media, and 9.5 hours are spent with tech gadgets of some sort.[14]
- Among tomorrow's college students, 95 percent of teens age 12 to 17 go on line, and 80 percent use social media sites.[15] Leading social media companies are competing to see how best to involve younger children in online activities like games, chatting, and photo sharing.[16]
- By 2016, ten billion mobile Internet devices will exist globally, or 1.4 devices per person. Smartphone traffic will be about fifty times today's size.[17]

These findings paint a clear picture: If the new technological cultures are water, our students are fish. They work, study, read, learn, search, shop, flirt, befriend, love, play, hurt, and heal with and within our now mobile technologies. They form identities, have fun, and make meaning with and through them for both "good and ill." For example, many students enjoy being connected to networks of friends and family from many stages of their lives. But sometimes these linkages lead students to rely too heavily on parents. Moreover, resources like Facebook can create digital shadows that trail behind in new stages of development. As a result, it can be hard to shed one's skin and develop one's identity; consistency looks better and need not be explained.

Then there's the power of self-expression that online culture allows. Each student can now become an independent publisher and curator of culture, potentially communicating with millions through social media. And yet, when we present ourselves within the categories and options those platforms provide, identity becomes a prefabricated commodity, and a numbing sameness prevails. Does it influence young adult development, intellectually and personally, to grow up presenting one's self, and being presented by others, though de-individualizing forms of mass media? Do we need to find new ways to teach our students to become creators of knowledge and designers of their own knowledge platforms?

And then there are the questions of day-to-day emotional wellness. Wired adolescents now must perpetually enact and perform their social identities. There seems to be more performance anxiety, more peer pressure, more body image obsession, more harassment, more stalking, and more identity thefts. We need to better understand how and why some students internalize criticism and attacks on them made online. Many young people multitask compulsively, privilege fast thought over deep thought, and feel the anxiety of perpetually falling further behind others. Through smartphone apps, many students spend hours in game cultures, which can be relaxing but also can become obsessive and addictive, empty and yet another way of being subjected to online surveillance. All of these trends need to be evaluated in dialogue and partnership with students. While we cannot reverse the changes of our age, we can try to understand the digital revolution's impacts on the young and empower our students to make free and informed choices about technology. At Franklin & Marshall College, we have asked our senior associate dean for planning and analysis of student outcomes to coordinate our efforts to assess technology uses and experience across all student groups.

Third, to counterbalance the growth of online cultures and their early impacts on the young, all of us who work at liberal arts colleges should reinvest in the communities and physical spaces of our campuses. While this point may seem obvious, we should not neglect the extraordinary power of an engaging four-year college experience defined by intellectual richness, a supportive community, and ample opportunities for all students to create distinct, enduring meaning. By gathering diverse learners of all ages and by giving those students, faculty, staff, and alumni the finest campus environments for ideas and relationships, we help our students create and embrace life outside of virtual worlds and cyber-communities. Our libraries and seminar rooms, our dance studios and dining halls, our spaces for sport and places for prayer, and our quadrangles and residence halls let people find themselves and each other in glorious individuality.

Over several decades and administrations, Franklin & Marshall College has made a sustained commitment to developing the power of place. In the 1990s, President Richard Kneedler, the faculty, and the trustees created new campus venues for the performing arts. In the 2000s, President John Fry and Dean of the College Kent Trachte led the faculty and the students in pioneering work to transform a traditional residence life approach into a new system in which all students belong for all four years in one of five College Houses that foster intellectual life, faculty relationships, and student leadership in managing their distinct house traditions and governments. Now in the early 2010s, Franklin & Marshall is creating a still more vibrant campus community by increasing financial aid by more than 50 percent, expanding student recruitment nationally and internationally, sponsoring a dynamic weekly lecture series during a "common hour" when classes and meetings cannot be held, planning a new sport and recreation precinct adjacent to campus, and, led by the faculty, reviewing and renewing our curriculum. I offer these details not only because they speak to specific ways that liberal arts colleges can and do respond to the rise of virtual communities and digital culture, but also to make the larger point that institutional excellence in doing so requires coherent visions and strategies across the decades.

Finally, as student-centered educators, we should collaborate in order to frame and act on these questions together. Perhaps it is time to form a new study group of liberal arts colleges and to collaborate across campuses about how best to maximize the "good" of digital technology and minimize the "ill." There are at least four questions we might consider together:

1. Do we believe we have a special responsibility to shape the future by preparing students to be critical thinkers about digital technology?
2. Are we deploying our resources most effectively?
3. Are there new resources and new knowledge that can help liberal arts colleges, if we collaborate?
4. What do we owe the world?

These are not minor questions, for they require us to talk about competitive pressures and core values, practical factors, and our enduring aims. We must remain awake and in dialogue during a great digital revolution. Where are these changes taking society and humanity, especially the young? What are we gaining, what are we losing, what real choices do we face, and how can liberal arts colleges make a signal contribution to students and to civilization?

If today's digital revolution presents real if unclear opportunities and threats and may reshape our relationships and even aspects of our humanity, we can take heart in knowing that such concerns in fact are not entirely new. As T. S. Eliot wrote more than seventy-five years ago in "Choruses from the Rock":

> The endless cycle of idea and action,
> Endless invention, endless experiment,
> Brings knowledge of motion, but not of stillness;
> Knowledge of speech, but not of silence;
> Knowledge of words, and ignorance of the Word . . .
> Where is the Life we have lost in living?
> Where is the wisdom we have lost in knowledge?
> Where is the knowledge we have lost in information?[18]

The act, fact, and form of the poem—its very existence—serve as an inspiration: In times of uncertain change, the intellectual and artistic traditions of the Enlightenment, and of the liberal arts college, contain the resources to discern, preserve, and adapt in the service of humanity.

NOTES

1. James M. Washington, ed., *A Testament of Hope: The Essential Writings and Speeches of Martin Luther King, Jr.* (New York: HarperOne, 1990), 269.

2. Matt Richtel, "Wasting Time Is New Divide in Digital Era," *New York Times*, May 29, 2012.

3. "These unfortunate designs are more oriented toward treating people as relays in a global brain. Deemphasizing personhood and the intrinsic value of an individual's unique internal experience in creativity leads to all sorts of maladies" (Jaron Lanier, *You Are Not a Gadget* [New York: Vintage Books, 2010], 14–15).

4. Sherry Turkle, *Alone Together: Why We Expect More from Technology and Less from Each Other* (New York: Basic Books, 2011).

5. "One can cut-and-paste without the need to think critically or write accurately or come to one's own careful conclusions. When beautiful images from the merchants of consumer dreams flood one's computer screens, or when the ugly or unpleasant sounds of the world can be shut out by one's MP3 music player, then one's vision, one's perception of reality, one's desiring can also remain shallow. When one can become friends so quickly and so painlessly with mere acquaintances or total strangers on one's social networks—and if one can so easily

unfriend another without the hard work of encounter or, if need be, confrontation and then reconciliation—then relationships can also become superficial. . . . People lose the ability to engage with reality. That is a process of dehumanization that may be gradual and silent, but very real. People are losing their mental home, their culture, their points of reference" (Adolfo Nicolas, S.J. "Depth, Universality, and Learned Ministry: Challenges to Jesuit Higher Education Today," keynote address at Networking Jesuit Higher Education: Shaping the Future for a Humane, Just, Sustainable Globe, Mexico City, April 22–24, 2010).

6. Tina Barsegian, "Three Trends That Define the Future of Teaching and Learning," Mind/Shift: How we will learn, KQED, February 5, 2011, http://blogs.kqed.org/mindshift/2011/02/three-trends-that-define-the-future-of-teaching-and-learning/.

7. Laura Pappano, "The Year of the MOOC," *New York Times,* November 2, 2012, www.nytimes.com/2012/11/04/education/edlife/massive-open-online-courses-are-multiplying-at-a-rapid-pace.html?pagewanted=all.

8. "The new culture of learning actually comprises two elements. The first is a massive information network that provides almost unlimited accesses and resources to learn about anything. The second is a bounded and structured environment that allows for unlimited agency to build and experiment with things within those boundaries. It is the combination of the two and the interplay between them that makes the new culture of learning so powerful" (Douglas Thomas and John Seely Brown, *A New Culture of Learning: Cultivating the Imagination in a World of Constant Change* [CreateSpace, 2011], 19).

9. *All's Well That Ends Well,* 4.3.69.

10. Steve Kolowich, "Online Learning and Liberal Arts Colleges," *Inside Higher Ed,* June 29, 2012, www.insidehighered.com/news/2012/06/29/liberal-arts-college-explore-uses-blended-online-learning.

11. Jason Klinger, "$1.4 Million HHMI Grant Bolsters F&M's Investment in Health of Community," *F&M News,* May 24, 2012, www.fandm.edu/for-news-media/press-releases/article/1-4-million-hhmi-grant-bolsters-f-m-s-investment-in-health-of-community-1.

12. Chris Hoffman, "You Are the Product, Not the Client: The Personal Data Economy Explained," *Makeuseof,* July 16, 2012, www.makeuseof.com/tag/product-client-personal-data-economy-explained/; David Goldman, "Why Your Facebook ID Is Marketers' Holy Grail," *CNN Money,* December 13, 2010, http://money.cnn.com/2010/12/13/technology/facebook_id_privacy/index.htm

13. Peter Mass and Megha Rajagopalan, "That's No Phone. That's My Tracker," *New York Times,* July 13, 2012.

14. "College Students Spend 12 Hours/Day with Media, Gadgets," November 2009, www.marketingcharts.com/television/college-students-spend-12-hoursday-with-media-gadgets-11195/.

15. "How American Teens Navigate the New World of Digital Citizenship," *Pew Internet,* November 2011, http://pewinternet.org/Reports/2011/Teens-and-social-media/Summary/Findings.aspx.

16. K. J. Dell'Antonia, "How Can Facebook Safely Add Under-13s?" *New York Times,* June 5, 2012.

17. "Cisco Visual Networking Index: Global Mobile Data Traffic Forecast Update, 2011–2016," Cisco White Paper, February 14, 2012, 3.

18. *The Collected Poems of T. S. Eliot* (New York: Harcourt Brace Jovanovich, 1991), 147.

PART IV / Collaboration and Partnerships

CHAPTER 11

The Future of Liberal Arts Colleges Begins with Collaboration

Eugene M. Tobin

PROGRAM OFFICER, THE ANDREW W. MELLON FOUNDATION

Most commentaries about the future of liberal arts colleges begin and end with a narrative of decline. This one will not.

"The American university of 1900," historian Laurence Veysey famously observed, "was all but unrecognizable in comparison with the college of 1860."[1] The new emphasis on research, the rise of professional education, and the recognition, particularly among leading public institutions, that universities have a social purpose and obligation to advance knowledge to the widest spectrum of society, underscored the nature of the change. A century earlier, David Starr Jordan, the founding president of Stanford, characterized the liberal arts college as "antiquated, belated, arrested, [and] starved." With time, he predicted, "the college will disappear, in fact, if not in name. The best will become universities, the others will return to their place as academies"[2] and remain, in Richard Hofstadter's ungenerous words, "precarious, little, denomination-ridden, poverty-stricken" institutions of "dubious educational standards."[3]

In 1950 the nation's private and public higher education sectors enjoyed an almost even split of undergraduate enrollment. Liberal arts colleges represented approximately 40 percent of all institutions of higher education. Following the explosive growth of the public university and community college sectors that began in the 1960s, the liberal arts colleges' share fell to 25 percent of all institutions in 1970, and the decline in the share of student enrollments was even greater, falling from 25 percent of undergraduate enrollments in the mid-1950s to 8 percent by the early 1970s, to between 3 and 4 percent today.[4]

No segment of American higher education has had more epitaphs written about it than has the liberal arts college sector. More than forty years ago, James Axtell published an essay in which he scolded historians for writing premature obituaries of liberal arts colleges. "The obituary they wrote," he observed, "reads something like this":

> Dateline Washington, 2 July 1862. The American Liberal Arts College died to-day after a prolonged illness. It was 226 years old. Born on the salty backwashes of the Charles River . . . shortly after the Massachusetts Bay Colony was founded, the scion of Puritan Reform and Renaissance Civility grew to sturdy usefulness in the colonial years by overseeing America's leaders prior to their war for independence. When the new nation emerged, however, demanding a larger, more expert citizenry, The College was unable to overcome its aristo-cratic origins . . . In the 1820s, when Jacksonian Democracy was urging needed reforms on American Institutions, The College's role in society contracted into a stance of pugnacious conservatism. . . . Today, after a recent cardiac arrest, its heart stopped on the floor of the House of Representatives, just as the roll call for Justin Morrill's Land-Grant Act had ended.[5]

A decade ago, Paul Neely, a prominent journalist and a Williams College trustee, compared the top tier of liberal arts colleges to high-end passenger trains in the late 1940s. "They performed exceptionally well, but people began to use automo-biles and planes more often. Eventually, the best passenger trains suffered not just because of direct competition but because they were isolated . . . and it did not mean as much to be the best when they were almost the only trains."[6] More re-cently, in his sprightly retrospective *Liberal Arts at the Brink,* Victor Ferrall, pres-ident emeritus of Beloit College, mused that a better title might have been "Liberal Arts Colleges: Why I Love Them and Why They Can't be Saved." Later, Ferrall admits that a more optimistic title would be "Liberal Arts Colleges: Before It Is Too Late, Get Your Act Together and Make Common Cause to Save Yourselves, Because No One Else Is Going to Do It."[7]

The Enduring Strengths of Liberal Arts Colleges

No one disagrees that there are challenges galore—distressed business models, shifting demographics, an overheated competitive environment, shrinking market demand, unsustainable increases in financial aid, demands for pre-professional programs, antiquated shared governance systems, a debilitating ambiguity about mission, and many more—that contribute to a simplistic, exaggerated rhetoric of crisis. In spite of over two hundred years of angst about their imminent demise and periodic reports documenting their disappearance and transformation, liberal arts colleges remain a valued, respected, influential segment of American higher education. Commentators praise their success in preparing future PhDs for careers in the sciences; for their emphases on critical thinking, oral and written communication, and visual and quantitative literacy; for developing their students' capacities for compassion, curiosity, empathy, humility, and innovation; and for the fact that their graduates have distinguished themselves in almost every field of human endeavor. No other sector of higher education has been as successful in creating opportunities for undergraduate research across the curriculum, in encouraging close relationships between students and faculty, and in inculcating a commitment to life-long learning. Liberal arts colleges represent the poetry in American higher education, but in an increasingly market-driven, utilitarian society, students and their families frequently ask questions that sound like those of the late Secretary of Defense Robert McNamara: "Where is your data? Give me something I can put in the computer. Don't give me your poetry."[8]

Prospective students, their families, and policy makers want to know why colleges cannot spend less and maintain quality without raising their prices. These concerns are particularly troubling for liberal arts colleges because they are so labor-intensive. Enrichments of students' educational experiences over the past thirty years—more faculty, more staff, more financial aid, newer facilities, expanding curricula, and more student services—have all been drivers of increasing cost and have depended, for the most part, on growing income streams from tuition, endowment income, and fundraising—none of which are likely to be as reliable in the future, at least not at past levels. When Woodrow Wilson served as the president of Princeton University, he had a great line describing his tumultuous fights to abolish the undergraduate eating clubs. "The trouble," he said, "is that the sideshows in American life have swallowed up the circus, and we in the main tent do not know what is going on."[9] One can make a convincing argument that the liberal arts college sector is a case study of how higher education has grown by adding new things without taking old things away. We are terrific at addition but subtraction has never had much of a following on our campuses. So what is a college to do?

Traditional responses for addressing the periodic economic downturns that buffet higher education, including calls to increase enrollment; reduce time-to-degree; implement across-the-board reductions; make more intensive, year-round use of facilities; and find new revenue streams through professional degree and certificate programs are primarily designed to restore financial equilibrium. A number of liberal arts colleges have been forced to address such cost drivers as student-faculty ratios, teaching loads, faculty research subsidies, student services, and financial aid. Even though there is growing awareness that the systemic challenges facing liberal arts colleges cannot be met solely by cost reductions and revenue enhancements, the sense of urgency and the receptivity to change vary widely across the sector, roughly in proportion to reputation and resources.

The Inward Focus of Liberal Arts Colleges

There is, however, another more intuitive explanation for why change does not come easily. Liberal arts colleges are among the most idealized and least understood institutions in American higher education. The sociologist Burton Clark called them the romantic and mysterious element in our educational system. In The Distinctive College, his elegant case studies of Antioch, Reed, and Swarthmore, Clark identified an array of conditions encompassing crisis, leadership, unique practices, programmatic distinctiveness, and a readiness for change as the centerpieces of his narratives. But Clark was not merely writing ethnographic histories. His goal was to capture the shared beliefs, attitudes, and values that produce a distinctive organizational saga, what he described as "a historically based . . . embellished understanding . . . located somewhere between ideology and religion . . . that turns an organization into a community, even a cult." In its benign state, Clark explained, an organizational saga creates an "unparalleled means of unity" that provides believers with "a deep emotional engagement." This intense pride, loyalty, and sense of being unique makes the leaders of liberal arts colleges behave, in Clark's words, "as if they knew a beautiful secret that no one else could ever share."[10] Every institution relies on deeply committed believers who internalize the organizational mission so that it becomes an unconscious part of their individual motivation. At the darker end of the spectrum, Clark acknowledged, organizational sagas can engage their supporters so intensely as to "produce a striking distortion, with the organization becoming the only reality [and] the outside world becoming illusion."[11] This can create a feeling "that there are really two worlds—the small blessed one of the lucky few and the large routine one of the rest."[12] Such a vision has never been a prescription for success, but it captures the conflicting sentiments of exclusivity and isolation that continue to pervade liberal arts colleges both within their own sector and in their relationships, or lack thereof, with other educational and cultural institutions.

Clark concluded *The Distinctive College* with the observation that an organizational saga can "be invaluable in maintaining viability in a competitive market."[13]

College leaders understand competition, but their organizational cultures and educational programs naturally focus inward. Until I left a college presidency and joined the Mellon Foundation, I did not fully appreciate how many colleges and universities really do see themselves as "unique"—and as "truly unique" when it comes to fundable ideas.[14] With some notable exceptions, liberal arts colleges seldom look for connections with other institutions; they feel comfortable competing for strategic advantage in terms of students, faculty, academic distinction, fundraising, and grants in the belief that all relevant expertise and experience can be found on one's own campus.[15] Even among liberal arts colleges' most exemplary consortia, a combination of financial and political constraints often militate against a consortium's attainment of its full potential. This is particularly true when the stakeholders of signature programs are threatened by the prospect of cooperation.

The Power of Cooperation and Collaboration

This remarkable degree of self-absorption persists despite the fact that colleges and universities do many of the same things, especially in the realm of teaching and learning. Colleges take on "self-contained and distinctive cultures," as Ray Bacchetti observes, "so that all institutional problems are local and all the resources needed to solve them are, by definition, close at hand."[16] Little energy or thought is given to the experience of others. Few lessons are learned that might inform or enhance the chances of success; rarely do colleges and universities build on the work of their peers, and seldom do they engage in comparative study, except when they are benchmarking their progress against one another.[17] Not surprisingly, there is even less formal interaction between liberal arts colleges and research universities, and this deeply ingrained mutual disregard, bordering on denial, speaks volumes about the organizational limitations of our highly compartmentalized higher education system.

Liberal arts colleges and research universities consistently portray their missions as occupying mutually exclusive, at times antithetical, positions with respect to teaching and research, but the reality is more nuanced. When private research universities of all sizes infuse undergraduate curricula with a strong foundation in liberal education and flagship public universities allocate scarce resources to honors colleges to create small classes, they are emulating the liberal arts college. Concomitantly, when liberal arts colleges allocate a significant percentage of their instructional budgets to support student-faculty research, frequent sabbaticals, and reduced teaching loads, they are acknowledging the growing connections between teaching and scholarship. Many liberal arts college faculty members produce excellent research, just as many research university faculty members provide good teaching and excellent research into what contributes to good teaching.[18] In such circumstances, familiarity has inspired competition, but for most institutions collaboration remains a more distant horizon.

This is unfortunate because at the undergraduate level, in spite of their obvious (and celebrated) differences in mission and in the scale of resources devoted to the creation of new knowledge, liberal arts colleges and research universities should have a mutual interest in resisting specialization, in sustaining their commitments to general education, in demonstrating that teaching and research are integrally linked, and in controlling costs. Research universities have the resources and infrastructure that would enable liberal arts colleges to expand their curricular offerings and provide their faculties with interesting scholarly opportunities, and liberal arts colleges have much to share with their university colleagues about getting undergraduates involved in research. More fundamentally, if research universities wish to embrace undergraduate education as a time for discovering intellectual passions and balancing private interests and the public good—what Andrew Delbanco calls the "college idea"—liberal arts colleges have much to share about how best to integrate social values and civic engagement.[19] Another incentive for the research universities is the opportunity to recruit liberal arts college students into their graduate programs. Liberal arts colleges and research universities are directly connected by their mutual interest in the preparation and development of future faculty and in the goal of continuing to diversify the professoriate. This underdeveloped partnership is as important for the purposes of improving undergraduate teaching as it is for the potential changes in graduate school training that may better prepare aspiring scholars for successful careers at liberal arts colleges.

None of this will happen on a noticeable scale until collaboration becomes a first response rather than an afterthought. Colleges have shared administrative services for years, particularly in such areas as insurance, energy, telecommunications, purchasing, registrar functions, catering, and technical support. More recently, college admission programs have cooperated in organizing recruiting for international students. But with the exception of a few long-standing regional consortia, academic collaboration has proven much more challenging. Amid the tug and pull of cultural, disciplinary, pedagogical, and financial pressures, colleges face a constant stream of self-imposed expectations: to educate global citizens, to enable students and faculty to cross disciplinary boundaries through a variety of diverse curricular offerings, to pursue opportunities for undergraduate research, and to integrate digital technology and cross-disciplinary methodologies into a problem-based curriculum. The pressure to add new programs is unrelenting, as are the curricular deficits and inflexibility that exist at many liberal arts colleges.

Here are six academic areas that cry out for potential collaboration across the liberal arts college sector and between liberal arts colleges and research universities. Liberal arts colleges need and aspire to:

- Internationalize their curricula, teach the less commonly taught languages, and invigorate or create new programs in critical geopolitical areas such as Latin America, the Middle East and North Africa, and South and East Asia.
- Explore intellectual themes that connect departments and disciplines without creating new majors or adding new faculty.
- Provide undergraduate research opportunities for students outside the sciences.
- Support the integration of the digital humanities into teaching and scholarship.
- Use digital technology to create new teaching resources such as virtual labs and create truly interactive learning platforms for use in introductory courses in subjects such as statistics and mathematics.
- Create arts-based campus cultures that embrace the making of art as an integral component of the life of the mind and a complementary means of connecting different bodies of knowledge.

Each of these curricular areas (and many others) would benefit from multi-institutional partnerships that develop hybrid courses (a combination of face-to-face, online, and machine-guided approaches); increase access to specialized curricular offerings; and inspire joint faculty institutes, strategic use of postdoctoral fellowships, shared faculty appointments, and artistic residencies. Virtual departments should be created in fields where course-sharing arrangements enhance faculty development and student learning, while controlling (if not reducing) costs, and encouraging collegial relations. At a time when liberal arts colleges are trying to complement the scale and intimacy of their social, pedagogical, and organizational strengths with the curricular breadth and opportunities of a larger institution, collaboration among liberal arts colleges and research universities must become a more prominent practice.

Seeing Beyond the Campus Gates

Higher education leaders who leave the academy for careers as foundation officers occupy an unusual niche in American higher education. In many ways their common goal, as Don Randel has noted, "is to listen for other people's good ideas and then try to find the resources with which to help them realize those ideas," much as they did as college and university presidents, provosts, and deans.[20] This requires careful listening, a willingness to think structurally and systematically, and the patience and modesty to let others embrace good ideas as their own, whatever their origin.

The opportunity to sit on the funder's side of the philanthropic table offers a rare opportunity to hear the presentation of the most creative ideas revealed in ways that even their most prescient advocates cannot always see because of their total immersion with their own institutions. When many of these ideas appear in various forms again and again, even a casual listener must wonder why virtually identical requests are presented as unique and distinctive. This is one reason that some of us in the foundation world are so adamant, even Cassandra-like, about wishing that more liberal arts college leaders could see beyond their campus gates, even as we admire their single-minded intensity and focus. The similarities and connections that link so many college, university, and foundation conversations are remarkable because their collective institutional insights cry out for cooperation even as their eloquent, passionate, sophisticated and dedicated champions appear inexplicably disconnected from one another.

This is particularly true when it comes to the subject of change. Sociologist Neil Smelser argues that higher education's "distinctive moral embeddedness," as personified by its three historic roles—teaching, the creation of knowledge, and service to society—generates high expectations, strong moral reactions, and crisis rhetoric that "does not welcome contingent, conditional, and qualified assessments."[21] In recent years I have occasionally felt like the smug businessman in Mike Nichols' 1967 film *The Graduate*, touting a magical panacea—not plastics but collaboration—and the reactions of presidents, provosts, and deans always remind me of Dustin Hoffman's character Benjamin, who is, in the words of one reviewer, "staring blankly into space through his goggles" at the bottom of his family's swimming pool.[22]

There are good reasons why college presidents respond politely and cautiously to such calls. Collaboration is hard work; it is time-consuming, organizationally complicated, potentially distracting, and politically fractious—and even when it works, faculties remain skeptical. Collaboration lacks the heroic exceptionalism that serves as the foundation of so many organizational sagas. When it comes to foundation grants, collaboration may feel like a consolation prize. Collaboration is neither a panacea nor a silver bullet, but it is the most underutilized resource in the liberal arts college toolbox.

NOTES

I would like to acknowledge the generous contributions and assistance of William G. Bowen, Philip E. Lewis, James L. Shulman, Mary Patterson McPherson, Rebecca Chopp, Daniel Weiss, Susan Frost, and Olivia Smith.

1. Laurence Veysey, *The Emergence of the American University* (Chicago: University of Chicago Press, 1965), 1, 338. A number of scholars, notably Roger Geiger and John Thelin, strongly disagree with Veysey's thesis that the modern American research university had taken a mature form by 1910.

2. Leon B. Richardson, *A Study of the Liberal College: A Report to the President of Dartmouth College* (Hanover, NH, 1924), 15, as quoted in Frederick Rudolph, *The American College and University: A History* (1962; repr., Athens: University of Georgia Press, 1990), 443.

3. Richard Hofstadter and Walter P. Metzger, *The Development of Academic Freedom in the United States* (New York: Columbia University Press, 1955), 223.

4. U.S. Department of Education, National Center for Education Statistics, *120 Years of American Education: A Statistical Portrait* (Washington, DC: U.S. Department of Education, 1993), table 23, Historical Summary of Higher Education Statistics, 1869–70 to 1989–90, http:// nces.ed.gov/pubs93/93442.pdf. At the same time, the nation's public colleges and universities were experiencing their own transformation. By 1980, 78 percent of the nation's students were attending public colleges and universities—42 percent at four-year institutions, 36 percent at two-year colleges—and the distribution within the public sector had undergone its own significant change. Back in 1960, 50 percent of public enrollments were concentrated in flagship universities (and other graduate-level institutions). Within twenty years, 75 percent of public-sector enrollments were based in open-admission community colleges and in less selective comprehensive institutions. See Clark Kerr, "The American Mixture of Higher Education in Perspective: Four Dimensions," *Higher Education* 19, no.1 (1990): 1–19, esp. p. 1; American Council on Education, *Fact Book on Higher Education, 1986–1987* (New York: Macmillan, 1987), 57.

5. James Axtell, "The Death of the Liberal Arts College," *History of Education Quarterly* 11, no. 4 (Winter 1971): 339.

6. Paul Neely, "The Threats to Liberal Arts Colleges," in *Distinctively American: The Residential Liberal Arts College*, ed. Steven Koblik and Stephen R. Graubard (New Brunswick, NJ: Transaction Publishers, 2000), 39.

7. Victor Ferrall, *Liberal Arts at the Brink* (Cambridge, MA: Harvard University Press), xii.

8. Quoted in Mark H. Lytle, *America's Uncivil Wars: The Sixties Era from Elvis to the Fall of Richard Nixon* (New York: Oxford University Press, 2006), 105.

9. Woodrow Wilson, "What Is College For?" *Scribner's Magazine*, November 1909, 576, quoted in Edwin E. Slosson, *Great American Universities* (New York: Macmillan, 1910), 506.

10. Burton R. Clark, *The Distinctive College: Antioch, Reed and Swarthmore* (Chicago: Aldine Publishing Company, 1970), 235.

11. Burton R. Clark, "The Organizational Saga in Higher Education," *Administrative Science Quarterly* 17, no. 2 (June 1972): 179.

12. Burton R. Clark, "Belief and Loyalty in College Organization," *Journal of Higher Education* 42, no. 6 (June 1971): 511.

13. Clark, *Distinctive College*, 262.

14. Ray Bacchetti and Thomas Ehrlich, "Reconnecting Colleges and Foundations," *Chronicle of Higher Education*, November 17, 2006, http://chronicle.com/article/Reconnecting-CollegesF/17545/.

15. Ray Bacchetti and Thomas Ehrlich, eds., *Reconnecting Education and Foundations: Turning Good Intentions into Educational Capital* (New York: John Wiley & Sons, 2006), 257.

16. Ibid., 263–64.

17. Ibid., 264–65.

18. I am grateful to Christopher Welna, president of the Associated Colleges of the Midwest for this important insight.

19. Andrew Delbanco, *College: What It Was, Is, and Should Be* (Princeton, NJ: Princeton University Press, 2012), 9–35.

20. Don M. Randel, "One Way to Think about Philanthropy," in *Under the Baobab: Essays to Honour Stuart Saunders on his Eightieth Birthday, The Elephant and the Obelisk, I, a Special Series and an Imprint of the African Yearbook of Rhetoric* (Cape Town: Africa Rhetoric Publishing, 2011), 78.

21. Neil J. Smelser, "Dynamics of American Universities," *Research & Occasional Paper Series*, Center for Studies in Higher Education, University of California, Berkeley (February 2012), http://cshe.berkeley.edu/publications/docs/ROPS.Smelser.DynamicsUniversities.2.14.2012 .pdf.

22. Stephen Holden, "What's That You Say Now, Mrs. Robinson?," *New York Times*, February 9, 1997.

CHAPTER 12

The College without Walls

Partnerships at Home and Abroad

Carol T. Christ
PRESIDENT, SMITH COLLEGE

The residential college has traditionally been a *locus amoenus,* an idealized place, bounded in its very nature, almost a kind of pastoral. An intentional community, in Rebecca Chopp's phrase, it seeks to model a democratic society for the purpose of developing both citizenship and leadership. As borders have become more open in the larger world, however, they have also become so in our colleges.

In an important sense, such outreach has deep roots in our histories. Many liberal arts colleges have aspired to develop an ethic of community service and leadership in our students from our earliest decades; it shapes our mission. Similarly, study abroad has a long history on our campuses; we have been pioneers in its development. In this new century, we are increasing the range of such opportunities and making them even more central to the design of the education we offer.

But increasingly we are moving in new directions—both on our own and in partnership with other colleges and universities. In this chapter I will describe two—pre-professional opportunities and collaboration with other institutions of higher learning.

Combining the Academic, the Professional, and the Practical in New Ways

We are gradually coming to recognize that the opposition between the liberal arts and professional education is a false one. The term *liberal arts* suggests to many of us a historical stability extending back several centuries. Yet any history of the American college curriculum shows that the idea of a stable central core constituting the liberal arts is a myth. In 1754 a prospectus for the new King's College, later to become Columbia University, announced that the course of study would include surveying, navigation, geography, history, husbandry, commerce, government, meteorology, natural history, and natural philosophy. When Thomas Jefferson reorganized the curriculum of the College of William and Mary in 1779, he abolished professorships of divinity and oriental languages and added professorships in public administration, modern languages, medical sciences, natural history, natural philosophy, national and international law, and fine arts.[1] These lists show us several interesting things. First, they demonstrate that ideas changed about what subjects constituted the liberal arts. Secondly, they show that the liberal arts have always included branches of study that we think of as professional. Educators were asking not *whether* to mix the academic, the practical, and the professional, but *how* to do so.

At Smith we have recently developed two programs designed to integrate the academic, the professional, and the practical in new ways: concentrations, as we call them, and global engagement seminars. Our program of concentrations took inspiration from the engineering program we launched at Smith in 2000. In their senior year, all engineering majors must complete a senior design project. Working in teams of three to four students on a yearlong project set by a commercial, government, not-for-profit, or research partner (for example, General Electric, Ford Motor Company, the Northampton Department of Public Works, MIT Lincoln Laboratory, the Natural Resources Conservation Service), the students develop a design solution to a problem the company is currently addressing. Recent projects have included a desktop computer that can withstand tropical conditions, a mobile hazardous materials treatment, utility redesign for a street in Northampton, a box elevator to minimize ergonomic risk, and a culvert design for the restoration of the Weir Creek Salt Marsh in Dennis, Massachusetts. The students work with a mentor from the partner organization and make a presentation of their solution to company representatives at the end of the term.

Although this kind of capstone project is fairly common in engineering programs, it is rare in liberal arts curricula. The example of the engineering curriculum had a stimulating effect on faculty from other areas, and we began considering ways in which the college might leverage its investment in internships (Smith provides every undergraduate with a paid internship at some time during her four years) to create a program of concentrations that would provide students similar opportunities to apply their academic work to problems in pre-professional, practical, or multidisciplinary areas. The first concentration we created was in Museum Studies, where students were required to complete a gateway course, two internships, and a capstone project. Students in this concentration have held internships in all kinds of museums all over the world; recent capstone projects have involved designing a children's museum exhibit, creating a collaborative youth project and exhibition, conserving two Japanese scrolls, and assessing museums' use of new wave social media. We now have a dozen concentrations, including Archives, Bio-mathematical Sciences, Book Studies, Global Financial Institutions, and Sustainable Foods.

Global engagement seminars also create an academic context for internships. Two faculty members from different departments bring a seminar-sized group of students to a place outside of the United States that is the subject of their study. After a month-long seminar, the students complete a two-month internship. In the first year of this program, we held global engagement seminars in Jerusalem, focusing on the complex history and politics of the city, and in Costa Rica, focusing on the politics and science of sustainability, particularly in regard to eco-tourism. The students who participated in this pilot program found it transformative, for they learned about the cultures they visited not only in the classroom but through work. They had to inhabit a subject position within the culture, understanding vividly in Costa Rica the tension between the experience of a visitor and the ways in which tourism was changing Costa Rican culture and society, and understanding in Jerusalem, as one student put it, how it felt to live in the midst of an intractable conflict.

Other liberal arts colleges and universities are developing similar programs as we seek to provide more experiences for our students that help them link the academic, the practical, and the professional in new ways.

Collaborating with Other Institutions of Higher Learning

Partnerships between and among institutions of higher education offer an even more profound opportunity for change. In the new economic environment for higher education in which we anticipate constrained growth in our traditional revenue sources—tuition increases, state support, growth in investment income— it is imperative to find new ways of reducing costs. Partnerships offer one of the most powerful ways to achieve this. None of us can do everything, nor can we afford to do so. In this environment, partnerships will become increasingly important to our colleges; indeed they will become essential.

Smith College is a member of the Five College Consortium that also includes Amherst College, Hampshire College, Mount Holyoke College, and the University of Massachusetts Amherst. We are geographically close; only ten miles separate the campuses most distant from each other. We are different kinds of institutions— four private liberal arts colleges and the flagship R-1 campus of a state university system. The original four partners helped to create the fifth, Hampshire College, both as an experiment in higher education and as a college that would depend for some of its resources and programs on the other four.

The consortium began formally as a library partnership, and our shared library system remains one of its most important advantages. We now share an electronic catalogue and a print depository, we coordinate our book purchase, and we increasingly share electronic resources. The Five College Library gives our students and faculty access to a far richer and deeper collection than any of us could afford on our own. Particularly in an environment in which we all struggle with the steeply escalating costs of information and library resources, so many of which are now electronic, collaboration is essential. It both controls costs and enriches program. We are challenged, however, by the subscription policies of many for-profit publishers of scholarly journals, who will only allow individual institutional subscriptions, providing no recognition for small consortia like ours. It is critical for us to tackle this pricing issue.

Early in its history, the consortium developed a cross-registration system whereby any student can enroll in any class at any campus, provided that he or she meets the prerequisite requirements. No money changes hands in this system; the traffic across it is free. Approximately six thousand students take courses each year at a campus other than their home campus. The traffic is not equal across the system. Hampshire, by design, sends more students to other campuses than any of the partners; the University of Massachusetts and Smith receive the most cross-registration enrollments; Amherst is also a net importer. Despite these imbalances in cross-registration, there has never been any pressure to charge sending campuses. We all see freedom of movement as a core value and benefit of the consortium. Because each institution experiences the worth of the consortium in multiple ways, we have never tried to balance payments in any particular aspect of our partnership.

Each institution pays an assessment to the consortium, which supports the small executive staff, aspects of the library system, a high-speed fiber optic network, transportation subsidies, and some Five College programs. Some aspects of the assessment are based on use; if three campuses share an administrative position, for example, its cost is split among the three. In addition, the shares are not equally apportioned. Hampshire pays less; the University of Massachusetts more.

The success of cross registration has been motivating increasing collaboration in academic programming. We have two Five College departments, Astronomy and Dance; two Five College majors, Film and Architecture; and fifteen Five College certificate programs, including four area studies programs, two ethnic studies programs, International Relations, Logic, and Coastal and Marine Sciences. Many departments that are formally separate work closely across the Five Colleges, coordinating areas of specialty in hiring and engaging in faculty seminars and joint projects. The membership of the University of Massachusetts in the consortium is particularly valuable to the four liberal arts colleges because it provides access to research programs and equipment, particularly in the sciences, that extend opportunities for faculty and students. Faculty members from the four colleges in the consortium occasionally participate on dissertation committees or teach graduate courses; some even supervise PhD dissertations.

Increasingly, we are extending our academic partnership to recognize areas of strength on the different campuses and shaping our hiring accordingly. For example, Amherst is becoming recognized as the lead campus for Russian, Smith for Korean, and Hampshire for film production. We are coordinating upper division electives in areas with fewer majors. Smith and Mount Holyoke, for example, are coordinating their upper division electives in Physics, transporting students between the campuses by bus, thus providing them a wider range of elective choices and a larger intellectual community.

We are increasingly making joint faculty appointments. There are now forty of these across the Five Colleges; Smith has twelve of these on a faculty of about 280. The joint appointments are structured in two ways—as a split appointment between two campuses, or as a split appointment between one campus and two or more partner campuses. In the case of the former, teaching and service responsibilities are split between the two partners; in the case of the latter, typically half of the candidate's teaching and service is done at the home campus, the other half among the other partners. Both kinds of appointments designate a home campus, which has the lead responsibility for tenure and promotion, although the other campus or campuses always have an important voice. For each appointment, a contract is drawn up at the point of hire in order to specify responsibilities both in appointment and in teaching matters.

We are developing particularly rich collaborations in the area of languages. The Five College Center for the Study of World Languages, currently located at the University of Massachusetts Amherst, offers guided independent study with a native-speaking conversation partner for two-skill language acquisition (listening and speaking) and mentored instruction in four-skill language acquisition (listening, speaking, reading, and writing) in less commonly taught languages such as Colloquial Arabic, Hindi, Pashto, Persian, Swahili, Turkish, Urdu, Uzbek, and Yoruba, for which students at any of the Five Colleges can register. In addition, we are increasingly trying to make movement among the campuses for subsequent years of language study a seamless experience for students by coordinating language curriculum across the colleges. Thus, a student who begins Arabic at Smith, for example, can move easily into second-year Arabic at Mount Holyoke or Amherst. This coordination is particularly important in languages in which all campuses do not teach the more advanced levels of the language.

We are developing a new collaboration between the university and the undergraduate colleges in regard to five-year master's degrees (completion of a master's degree with only one year's study after the bachelor's). In this new set of programs, students are accepted as undergraduates into selected University of Massachusetts Amherst master's programs. They take some of their master's work through cross registration while enrolled in their undergraduate college and then complete their master's work in a single year at the University of Massachusetts. Such joint programs approved by Smith include Architecture, Landscape Architecture, Sustainability Science, Public Policy, Neuroscience and Behavior, Statistics, and Linguistics. In a world in which a master's degree is an increasing advantage, this program allows students to reduce the time required for a bachelors and a master's degree by one year.

We all believe that technology can greatly enhance our academic collaboration, but we have not yet figured out specifically how. Even though our campuses are only a half hour's bus ride apart (on a free bus system), the bus schedule can seem an impediment to many students, making coordination with classes on their home campus challenging. We are experimenting with blended courses, combining face-to-face with web-transmitted classwork. A great advantage of shared faculty appointments is that the faculty member may travel, rather than the students.

The fiber optic network joining our campuses—the consortium's most ambitious project in the last decade—is fundamental to using technology to enhance our collaboration. We have not taken nearly enough advantage of its potential.

We also have significant opportunities for cost reduction in the area of administration. Currently we share a number of programs. We do joint purchasing through a statewide higher education purchasing consortium (which began as a Five College program over forty years ago and now has almost one hundred members). We have a Five College compliance and risk management program, which includes a four-college captive insurance company (the University of Massachusetts cannot participate because of its status as a state institution). Hampshire, Mount Holyoke, and Smith share a police department; Amherst, Mount Holyoke, and Smith share management of rental properties.

One of the lessons we have learned in the area of administrative collaboration is that not all partnerships require five partners. We have two-campus, three-campus, four-campus, and five-campus collaborations. Mount Holyoke and Smith share a director of employer relations in their career services department; Hampshire contracts with Mount Holyoke to provide environmental health and safety services; Mount Holyoke and Amherst share a grant accountant; the University of Massachusetts provides student health services for Amherst and Hampshire.

There are more opportunities for administrative collaboration, but progress has had surprising challenges. The small scale and face-to-face contact that we value in our curriculum is part of our administrative culture as well, although the benefits are harder to define. In attempts to create more administrative partnerships, we have encountered not only predictable human resources issues but cultural resistance, even when financial benefits are clear.

That the shared service revolution, which has been so important a cost saver in business, has largely bypassed the academy is puzzling because it provides an obvious opportunity for economies of scale. Although we rightfully argue the benefits of relatively low student/teacher ratios, the student/staff ratios of our campuses are often much lower. (At Smith they are, respectively, 9/1 and 3/1). A college is not an efficient scale for the provision of many administrative services—payroll, accounting, grants management, human resources, and information technology support, to give just a few examples. The provision of such services to a larger set of clients, whether though a consortial arrangement or an external provider, seems to me one of the best opportunities to reduce cost without reducing educational quality.

In the spring of 2011, Accenture, a management consulting firm, gave a one-day workshop for the presidents and business officers of liberal arts colleges to explore opportunities for administrative collaboration through shared services. Accenture had successfully designed shared service programs for large universities such as Yale and the University of Michigan. The workshop explored the question of the opportunities and challenges for such an approach among liberal arts colleges. We came to the conclusion that outsourcing probably represented a more efficient model than collaboration, but that the barriers to such an initiative were principally cultural. The economic savings result from the reorganization of work in which jobs are restructured or eliminated. Such a process is challenging in any organization; it is particularly so in small communities.

This brings me to a critical point about partnerships: they depend upon the trust and communication developed through human relationships. In the Five Colleges, officers with the same jobs—presidents or chancellors, provosts, vice presidents in principal areas of responsibility, directors of information technology or libraries—meet regularly and frequently, in most cases once a month. The kinds of relationships that develop over time with frequent meetings are essential to developing strong collaborations. Because institutions always have somewhat different plans and priorities, projects inevitably hit rough spots, and it takes trust and good communication to move beyond them.

Matching Partnerships with Goals

Higher education will increasingly depend upon partnerships of many kinds. An important part of any planning process should be the identification of partners, whether they are internal or external. Such partnerships can be multiple, in pursuit of different purposes. Four are most critical:

- Recruitment and enrollment partnerships
- Academic and research partnerships that extend the depth and range of programs to which students and faculty have access
- Library partnerships that reduce cost and increase collections and electronic resources
- Administrative partnerships that offer more efficient delivery of administrative services

I have not discussed recruitment partnerships, designed to increase access and promote diversity, or enrollment partnerships, designed to facilitate students' movements from institution to institution, because they have not been a major feature of the Five College Consortium. However, in an educational environment in which students increasingly attend multiple institutions in the course of earning their undergraduate degrees, liberal arts colleges should give more attention to enrollment partnerships, particularly with community colleges, to help students and their families reduce the cost of a higher education. Furthermore, institutions can profit from partnerships with the many fine not-for-profits who identify and mentor talented students from areas and populations that have not traditionally had high rates of attending college.

In operational partnerships, whether they are academic or administrative, colleges should not assume that one size fits all, that the same partner or set of partners is the right fit for every area and opportunity. We may achieve some efficiencies through outsourcing; the increasing movement of colleges and universities to Gmail is a good example. We may achieve others through large consortia like the Massachusetts Higher Education Purchasing Consortium. Other partnerships—in academic areas, for example—may work best with a small number of closely located institutions. We must size partnerships right, matching their scale to the results we hope to achieve. The Five Colleges have a t-shirt that we give to retiring presidents that says "COOPERATION IS AN UNNATURAL ACT." We have to make it natural to meet the challenges our institutions will face in the twenty-first century.

I conclude with the following recommendations:

- Seek ways of linking the academic, the practical, and the professional, creating greater integration between internships and classroom work.
- Seek library partnerships through which your institution can coordinate acquisitions and share electronic resources.
- Seek academic partnerships that at once enrich the academic program and save resources. Cross-registration and shared faculty appointments are particularly promising options to explore.
- Seek administrative partnerships and explore shared services to achieve more efficient delivery of administrative services.
- Develop transfer partnerships with community colleges to reduce the cost of the degree and facilitate student mobility.

NOTES

1. Frederick Rudolf, *The American College and University: A History* (1962; repr. Athens: University of Georgia Press, 1990), 31, 41.

CHAPTER 13

The Networked College— Local, Global, Virtual

Jane Dammen McAuliffe
PRESIDENT EMERITUS, BRYN MAWR COLLEGE

A wonderfully evocative photograph of Bryn Mawr College that dates from its earliest days presents a graceful, bell-towered building standing alone at the center of a cleared field. Viewing the photo today, we automatically populate that empty field with all that has been added, the beloved campus created by the vision and vigor of those who preceded us. We cherish this campus because its boundaries embrace our living community, one with deep roots in the past and a strong thrust toward the future. Liberal arts colleges have historically drawn much of their energy and effectiveness from their campus communities, gatherings of learners bound by intensive, continuous, collaborative processes of reflection, analysis, and discovery. On our campuses, faculty and students energize each other, tackle critical questions, and experiment with new ideas. We believe that educating by such methods creates the kind of adaptable, innovative, forward-thinking graduates who become leaders in all walks of life, who understand themselves as citizens of neighborhoods, nations, and even the world, engaging throughout their lives with those who hold new and differing perspectives.

Liberal arts communities, however, have not always reflected the demographic diversity of American society or drawn the best and brightest from less advantaged groups into their campus conversations. They have encouraged relatively little international participation, as important as some of our international alumnae/i have been. Prizing reflection over action, liberal arts communities have sometimes become protective nests—too inward looking, too sheltered, too sequestered.

In this century, those of us who love and lead liberal arts colleges are beginning to reimagine our institutions. The emphasis on community remains, but how we structure and populate these communities is changing. The very concept of community now has dimensions, both local and global, that move us far beyond our campus boundaries. Our daily lives, our neighborhoods, and our professions have been globalized. What we do locally both shapes and is shaped by what happens elsewhere. Community no longer presumes proximity. Technology and travel make it possible to build communities that transcend shared space.

Contemporary challenges call us to engage our institutions and our students with issues, groups, and activities that reach well beyond our borders. These challenges require us, as small institutions with limited resources, to expand our influence, to multiply our impact within our local areas, on national and international levels, and within the ever-widening world of virtual networks.

Local, Regional and National Networks

As Bryn Mawr College celebrated its 125th anniversary last year, we recalled with pride the significant milestones in the college's history, including two that point to our deeply rooted local and regional connections. In 1915, Bryn Mawr opened the nation's first university-affiliated school of social work.[1] From its beginning, the academic program sent students into surrounding communities, fostered a culture of intellectually productive fieldwork, and placed community engagement at the center of Bryn Mawr's institutional culture.

Six years later, the college began to offer an innovative summer program for female factory workers. College students and women in industrial workshops were brought together in a mutually enriching educational endeavor. As with the School of Social Work, this unusual and innovative program drew upon our Quaker-founded[2] values of social justice and civic betterment and reinforced an emphasis on local and regional civic engagement that links directly to the high levels of community-action work that characterizes our student body today. Today more than 70 percent of Bryn Mawr students volunteer in the greater Philadelphia region. Some work with schools and local nonprofits; others do community-based research for course credit as part of our Praxis Program.

In the following decades, regional academic linkages strengthened our long-standing connections to Haverford College and Swarthmore College as well as to the University of Pennsylvania. Termed the "Quaker Consortium," this network expands our academic offerings exponentially, allowing Bryn Mawr students access to over five thousand courses each year. It also opens undergraduate research opportunities for our students through the connections that faculty members at all four institutions have developed with local historical societies, corporate laboratories, and area museums.

These local and regional extensions of our campus community redounded to our benefit more recently as the college inaugurated an innovative multidisciplinary program called 360°. Gathering a group of students and faculty for a semester's multicourse exploration of a particular theme or topic, several 360° course clusters have incorporated community-based learning that builds on established connections. For example, a forthcoming cluster entitled "Women in Walled Communities" will include classwork at a correctional facility in Philadelphia.

Like other liberal arts colleges, Bryn Mawr has devoted considerable recruitment effort to diversifying its student body in the last several decades, threading out admissions networks through a much broader swath of American society and beyond. Mirroring the demographic shifts that the United States will undergo in the first half of the twenty-first century, Bryn Mawr is already becoming the "college of the future." Thirty-one percent of our current students are U.S. women of color; 16 percent are foreign nationals, and 18 percent are the first in their families to attend a four-year college. Our ability to extend our recruitment reach so effectively has required creating connections in communities across the country from which Bryn Mawr had not traditionally drawn students. The results are a much enriched campus experience for our students and an alumnae body that more truly represents the vast variety of American life.

Growing Our Global Networks

Barred from graduate work in the United States, a young woman named Martha Carey Thomas boarded a ship and sailed for Europe. After studies in Germany and Switzerland, she returned to this country in 1883 with a PhD awarded *summa cum laude* from the University of Zurich. Two years later she began her thirty-seven-year tenure as dean and then president of Bryn Mawr College, bringing to those positions an intellectual horizon far broader than that acquired solely through American models of education.[3] From its earliest days, therefore, Bryn Mawr enrolled international students and attracted faculty from Europe and beyond. A prominent example was Emmy Noether, who taught at Bryn Mawr in the 1930s. Lauded by Albert Einstein as the most "creative" and "significant" female mathematician who ever lived, she remains a notable name and was recently profiled in *The New York Times*.[4] Fleeing Nazi persecution, Noether moved in 1933 from the University of Göttingen to Bryn Mawr, where she was warmly welcomed.

We can even count institution-building among our early achievements in internationalization. By the end of the nineteenth century, a young student who returned to Japan from Bryn Mawr had founded Tsuda College, the first private college for women in Japan and an institution with which Bryn Mawr remains closely connected.[5]

This early sense of international awareness and connection eases the way for Bryn Mawr's current internationalization efforts. A persistent alumnae sense of the college as "very international" reflects the outsized influence that foreign students and faculty had on the lives of earlier graduates. It captures the awareness that prominent graduate disciplines like classical and Near Eastern archaeology regularly took Bryn Mawr students overseas for extended periods. It acknowledges our unusually broad range of language offerings, both ancient and modern, and it points to the college's long history of study abroad, initially in support of language study but now extending far beyond that focus. This legacy of international connections, when added to this century's accelerated globalization, positions Bryn Mawr to extend our campus networks across the globe.

In her recent book *Not for Profit: Why Democracy Needs the Humanities,* Martha Nussbaum makes a stirring argument for multicultural education and experience as indispensable for living in a pluralistic democracy.[6] As the importance of national boundaries diminishes, higher education has begun to rapidly reorganize itself on a global scale. More and more students, at both graduate and undergraduate levels, choose to study in other countries. Faculty members are now recruited irrespective of nationality. The most influential university rankings have ceased to be nationally focused but have become globe spanning. Excellent institutions around the world now compete for students, faculty, and research dollars.

All of this combines to compel Bryn Mawr's current focus on increased internationalization, but as an evolution not a revolution. One form of that evolution is building international networks on several fronts simultaneously—faculty to faculty, student to student, institution to institution—work that must be done strategically but also with an openness to serendipity. Auditing our current assets has been an indispensable first step, and we did this by posting a simple interactive world map on our website to display faculty research links, study-abroad sites, countries from which we draw students, and places where our graduates now live. Appointing faculty and administrative leaders who focus primary attention on building international networks has been another step forward. Alumnae connections are a great help, and to facilitate this, Bryn Mawr has just instituted an International Council of alumnae/i and parents that meets semiannually in Asia and Europe. Finding colleagues who are equally engaged in internationalization on their own campuses is yet another important asset. Through appointments to several commissions, boards, working groups and panels, I have been fortunate to interact with national and international leaders in this area.[7]

Networks multiply and flourish when they foster mutually beneficial partnerships. Here are a few examples of where Bryn Mawr's expanded international networks are beginning to bear fruit. We are working with a university in the Middle East to enhance the preparation of their students for graduate study in science (a Bryn Mawr strength). The work benefits Bryn Mawr by creating new connections for our science faculty and students as well as offering them opportunities for international experiences. At a women's college in India, we are developing a program that engages faculty and students in issues of educational reform through participatory classrooms. If the funding that we have sought for this program is approved, it will include co-teaching courses using IT, having cohorts of students from both schools engage with schools in Delhi and Philadelphia, and conducting comparative research that illuminates both situations. In the summer of 2012, we launched an innovative international summer program in partnership with a university in Singapore and another in China. Courses will be co-taught on the campus in China by faculty from different countries to students from different countries, focusing on issues of environment, globalization, and media.[8]

In the longer term, we envision various modes of faculty and student exchange with institutional partners, as well as the development of bi-national student cohorts who travel back-and-forth together. We hope that some of these connections can lead to collaborative certificates, degree programs, research centers—all of which can emerge from the cumulative understanding that comes from long-term commitment.[9]

Aligning Internationalization with the Mission of a Women's College

Many voices have been raised in recent years to name the distinctive moral challenge of the twenty-first century: the systemic oppression and brutalization that women across the globe continue to suffer. In a recent book, Kwame Anthony Appiah argues that moral revolutions can happen—and happen fast—when acting in accustomed ways is seen not only as immoral but also as dishonorable.[10] He bases his argument on the examples of dueling, foot binding, and slavery, then points to a practice like honor killing to say that its eradication could follow the same pattern. Almost every major problem in the world—extreme poverty, environmental degradation, human trafficking, sexual abuse, and forced labor—falls disproportionately on women. A powerful convergence of research and field experience is emerging that insists that solutions to these problems can only happen by addressing the moral dilemma of gender inequity by educating, empowering, and enabling women everywhere to lead lives of dignity and consequence. These issues are connected closely with Bryn Mawr's founding mission.

To that end, Bryn Mawr has joined with the other "Sister colleges" (Barnard, Mount Holyoke, Radcliffe, Smith, Vassar, and Wellesley) to create a partnership with the U.S. Department of State designated as the Women in Public Service Project (WPSP) and launched in December 2011.[11] WPSP seeks to build a generation of women leaders who will invest in their countries and communities, provide leadership in their governments, and change the way global solutions are conceived and constructed. Bryn Mawr and its partners envision a world in which political and civic leadership is at least 50 percent female by 2050. In consultation with an institute planning committee, WPSP has created a signature public service training curriculum offered at annual WPSP summer institutes, hosted by Wellesley College in 2012, by Bryn Mawr College in 2013, and by Smith and Mount Holyoke Colleges together in 2014. WPSP has also created a website and social media presence that is already being used to build a network of women in public service and that will serve as the foundation for a mentorship program.

As we link institutional internationalization to women's advancement, Bryn Mawr has reached out to women's colleges, both established and recently founded, in East and South Asia, in the Middle East, and in Africa.[12] In many parts of the world, growing collaboration between such institutions of higher education and governmental and nongovernmental organizations is also fostering a global engagement with women's education and empowerment. At Bryn Mawr, we see the present moment as one in which we can increase significantly the proportion of women whose lives are secure, healthy, self-confident, and meaningful. We can do this by understanding internationalization not just in terms of institutional but also of social advancement; by listening carefully and honoring the assets of different communities; by letting the inevitable challenges and comparisons of global engagement lead us to deeper understandings; by educating a generation of young women and men to understand that no one advances if we do not all advance together.

This is a process that must be globally collaborative, a statement that echoes the insights of Emily Greene Balch, a member of Bryn Mawr's first graduating class and the 1946 recipient of the Nobel Peace Prize. Balch operated from a foundational belief that the peaceful coexistence of nations was not enough. For Balch, peace, prosperity, and social well-being came not from isolation but rather from international interaction and the creation of communities of open-minded individuals across national boundaries.[13]

Creating Virtual Networks

Several years ago, while I was Dean of Arts and Sciences at Georgetown University, I sat in the back of a recently constructed telepresence classroom. Georgetown had just opened a small campus in Doha, Qatar; and this seminar room in Washington, D.C., along with its mirror image in Doha, was the university's first transnational teaching space. The visual and sound qualities of the setup were so good that it felt like those of us in the two locations were sharing a single room.

It was mid-semester in a political science course that gathered about ten D.C. students and an equal number of Doha students three times a week. In the pre-class moments as the students were gathering, I witnessed the following incident: a Qatari student walked into the Doha room, tossed his knapsack on the table, and, looking at the screen where the D.C. group was assembled, said, "Hey, Jack, how was the party last night?" Responding from D.C., Jack replied, "Hey, Muhammad, it was awesome. You should have been there." I felt a slight shock in that exchange and knew I was witnessing a game changer.

Telepresence connections of that quality are currently prohibitive for most liberal arts colleges, both in hardware cost and in bandwidth, but I doubt that will be the case forever. In the meantime, many of our students and faculty are already using Skype for international outreach with a frequency that makes this technology feel commonplace. One of our faculty members recently taught a course on multivariate statistics that he teleconferenced with colleagues and students at the University of Fribourg in Switzerland. In the fall of 2012, we will offer a freshman seminar that does the same with a local high school in Philadelphia; and in the spring of 2013, a class in urban planning will connect with a similar class at a university in Hamburg, Germany. For several years, language classes have been enriching the conversational opportunities available to students by using Skype to span the globe.

In association with Haverford and Swarthmore, Bryn Mawr is involved in a project through our Tri-Co (tri-college) Digital Humanities Initiative to increase the number of courses that have interactive video sessions with classes at overseas institutions. Over the next few years, we will also explore other networked platforms, from wikis to social media, for course collaboration. These may work their way into single class sessions, into entire courses team-taught by Bryn Mawr and partner faculty members for students at both institutions, and even into the trading of a Bryn Mawr course for one from a partner.

In an effort to try this myself, I ran a Skype seminar in spring 2012 with the presidents of women's colleges in Saudi Arabia, Japan, and India. At a preset time, each president gathered a group of students in her office and I did the same. After an initial exchange of greetings and introductions, we launched into a conversation about women's education and leadership and watched with delight as our students quickly took it over.

Fostering Global Dialogue

Today's liberal arts colleges are being asked to rethink the communities we create. The emphasis on community remains, but how we structure and populate these communities is changing. The advancement of human knowledge depends on creating intellectual communities that span the globe, that draw in different perspectives, different expertise. The conversations and communities into which we draw our students, correspondingly, must contain viewpoints from different social classes, different nations.[14]

Whether our goal is producing globally competent graduates, tackling pressing social issues, or undertaking cutting-edge science, we must see our work not only as providing new content in our classrooms but also as moving ourselves and our students into external networks of action and discovery. We must see dialogue and application as critical to student learning and faculty scholarship and as requiring us to provide settings that foster interaction beyond our campuses. We must also reflect on the role our institutions play in national, and increasingly international, systems of higher education. These are key new elements of liberal arts community building for the twenty-first century. We continue to operate through community, but we are extending what that community is.

Ultimately, Bryn Mawr recognizes that these activities will transform us as an institution in much the same way we ask our students to change. We will not be a campus-contained institution, but a broadly networked one. We fully expect courses to change when they are co-taught across national borders or embedded in community organizations; we expect research projects to shift direction through collaboration and multiple perspectives. We will not forsake our belief in the power of small-scale, intensive intellectual community for learning and discovery, but we will now pursue this through close partnership with a small set of like-minded institutions and organizations spread far and wide beyond our campus.

This, in turn, enables us to give a twenty-first-century vitality to much of what is core about Bryn Mawr. Women now account for 51 percent of tertiary enrollments worldwide. This milestone, reached only a few years ago, is the result of four decades in which new female matriculation outpaced male. This figure averages the even higher percentages found in countries like ours with lower averages in others. Nevertheless, nearly all nations have dramatically increased the numbers of young women attending colleges and universities, and nations as diverse as Saudi Arabia, China, Greece, and Mexico are now all above 50 percent.

We are at a watershed moment in women's higher education. Gender parity in numbers does not necessarily equal gender equity in rights and opportunities, but it constitutes an important platform for advancing such equity. This demographic shift opens space for a truly global dialogue among young women who will become leaders in their nations. Women's voices are likely to shift classroom cultures. Increasing numbers of educated young women are likely to change nations—and ultimately, the world.

Bryn Mawr, its sister institutions, and several coeducational colleges in the United States were founded on such beliefs well over a century ago. The going has not always been easy, but the progress has been undeniable. The opportunity that now stands in front of us will bring our institutions and women students into dialogue with like-minded institutions and aspiring young women around the world. It is for such reasons that Bryn Mawr is developing multiple platforms for its students and faculty to interact with those at colleges and universities beyond our borders. Ultimately, I believe that connecting women students with their counterparts around the world will create an unstoppable force for women's advancement. We have the opportunity to graduate women who will be future leaders and who will bring a broadened sense of women's empowerment to whatever profession they have chosen, at the same time that we directly tackle some of the most pressing gender issues of our times. This is as consistent with Bryn Mawr's long-standing mission as anything I can conceive.

A Practical Postscript

While I have used Bryn Mawr College as an example of how a small liberal arts college can begin to evolve into a more internationalized institution, much of the process could be duplicated by others. An audit of existing resources is a good first step. Most liberal arts colleges are already embedded in networks of international connections through faculty, alumnae/i, study-abroad sites, and the students we draw from around the world. Formalizing some of these connections by creating an international council of alumnae/i and parents builds a corps of institutional advocates and ambassadors in strategic locations across the globe. An additional step focuses on leadership. Most presidents will need to recruit faculty and administrative support for this work. The development of close connections with far-flung institutions, in particular, requires dedicated attention and experience as well as more time than most presidents can allocate.

The cultivation of such global partnerships, which for some colleges could be a further stage of internationalization, does not usually proceed in a strategically sequenced fashion. There is more serendipity involved than one might at first imagine. Clearly, a college can initiate contact with institutions for whom it identifies some affinity, but quite often a college may find itself the recipient of overtures from institutions it had not initially targeted. Exploration of such connections, however they are generated, will usually lead to a formal, but rather general, memorandum of understanding. From that point on, mutual institutional creativity will likely generate both expected and unanticipated forms of engagement.

In Bryn Mawr's experience, the rapid internationalization of our student body has been a function of both institutional decisions and global forces. Like most highly selective colleges, Bryn Mawr has long recruited and welcomed international students. Several years ago, however, we decided to uncouple our financial aid decisions from citizenship status. In other words, we award financial aid to domestic and international students on an equal basis. The impact of this decision, linked with a rapid increase in the global flow of students, is currently transforming our campus community. The inevitable result for Bryn Mawr and its peers of this and other processes of internationalization will be the eventual emergence of a new kind of college. We might call this globalized, networked, multicultural institution a "world liberal arts college."

NOTES

1. Helen Lefkowitz Horowitz, *The Power and the Passion of M. Carey Thomas* (New York: Alfred A. Knopf, 1994), 380–81.

2. For a short account of Bryn Mawr's Quaker history, see Eric Pumroy, "Bryn Mawr College," in *Founded by Friends: The Quaker Heritage of Fifteen American Colleges and Universities,* ed. John W. Olive Jr., Charles L. Cherry, and Caroline L. Cherry (Lanham, MD: Scarecrow Press, 2007), 147–62.

3. The friendship and financial backing of philanthropist Mary Garrett was a key support

for Thomas in the early period of her presidency. Garrett also made the endowment gift to establish the Johns Hopkins School of Medicine with the proviso that women be admitted to the school on the same terms as men. See Kathleen Waters Sander, *Mary Elizabeth Garrett: Society and Philanthropy in the Gilded Age* (Baltimore: Johns Hopkins University Press, 2008).

4. Natalie Angier, "The Mighty Mathematician You've Never Heard of," *New York Times,* March 26, 2012, www.nytimes.com/2012/03/27/science/emmy-noether-the-most-significant-mathematician-youve-never-heard-of.html?pagewanted=all.

5. For the fascinating story of Ume Tsuda, sent by the Meiji government to the United States at age seven and without her parents to be educated and returned to Japan, see Ume Tsuda, *The Attic Letters: Ume Tsuda's Correspondence to Her American Mother,* Yoshiko Furuki, editor-in-chief, and Mary Althaus, Yasuko Hirata, Tamiko Ichimata, Masako Iino, Akiko Iwahara, and Akiko Ueda, eds. (New York/Tokyo: Weatherhill, 1991).

6. Martha C. Nussbaum, *Not For Profit: Why Democracy Needs the Humanities* (Princeton, NJ: Princeton University Press, 2010), 91.

7. Examples include the UK/US Study Group, which produced *Higher Education and Collaboration in a Global Context: Building a Global Civil Society,* July 2009, initially as a private report to Prime Minister Gordon Brown, see http://globalhighered.wordpress.com/2009/07/29/higher-education-and-collaboration-in-a-global-context/; ACE Commission on Internationalization and Global Engagement from 2010 to 2013; UK-US Higher Education Policy Forum, 20–21 October 2011, St. George's House, Windsor Castle; ACE's Blue Ribbon Panel on Global Engagement, *Strength through Global Leadership and Engagement,* www.acenet.edu/AM/Template.cfm?Section=Programs_and_Services&ContentID=43034.

8. Susan Buck Sutton and Daniel Obst, eds., *Developing Strategic International Partnerships: Models for Initiating and Sustaining Innovative Institutional Linkages* (New York: Institute for International Education, 2011).

9. Sources on internationalization that I have found helpful include Hans de Wit, *Internationalization of Higher Education in the United States of America and Europe: A Historical, Comparative, and Conceptual* Analysis (Westport, CT: Greenwood Press, 2002); Charles T. Clotfelter, ed., *American Universities in a Global Market* (Chicago: University of Chicago Press, 2010); Philip G. Altbach, Liz Reisberg, and Laura E. Rumbley, *Trends in Global Higher Education: Tracking an Academic Revolution* (Rotterdam: Sense Publishers for UNESCO Publishing, 2010).

10. Kwame Anthony Appiah, *The Honor Code: How Moral Revolutions Happen* (New York: W. W. Norton, 2012).

11. See http://womeninpublicservice.org/.

12. Francesca B. Purcell, Robin Matross Helms, and Laura Rumbley, *Women's Colleges and Universities in International Perspective: An Overview* (Boston: Center for International Higher Education, Boston College, 2004).

13. For the Balch Nobel laureate lecture, see http://www.nobelprize.org/nobel_prizes/peace/laureates/1946/balch-lecture.html.

14. Patti McGill Smith, ed., *Confronting Challenges to the Liberal Arts Curriculum: Perspectives of Developing and Transitional Countries* (New York: Routledge, 2012).

PART V / Residential Communities and Social Purpose

CHAPTER 14

The Liberal Arts College Unbound

Brian Rosenberg
PRESIDENT, MACALESTER COLLEGE

Demonstrating Value

My opening proposition is relatively straightforward: the continued health and relevance of small, residential liberal arts colleges will be determined by the extent to which such institutions are prepared to focus on quality, distinctiveness, and social purpose. We need to be positioned to demonstrate as concretely as is feasible—and concreteness in these matters can be elusive—that the education we provide has positive outcomes, that it differs in beneficial ways from the education offered in other kinds of institutions (including the virtual), and that it contributes to the collective good.

Together, these factors will determine the value of these high-cost, high-impact colleges to students and to the larger society out of which they have grown. Indeed, I would go so far as to say that the commitment to value not only will answer but *should* answer the question of whether these very resource-intensive enterprises, which in the end can accommodate only a small segment of the American population, deserve to remain a prominent part of the higher education landscape.

I believe firmly that the answer is yes, but I also believe that such an answer should neither be automatically assumed nor based on the expectation that nothing about these colleges will change.

Some would argue that the long history, strong reputation, and distinctively positive educational outcomes of the liberal arts college are evidence that change is unnecessary. I would argue, rather, that these things are all in part results of the fact that liberal arts colleges *have* changed—though rarely quickly and not always obviously to those with a narrow historical perspective—in order to remain effective and relevant. Such change has in the main not undermined but advanced and strengthened central principles and methodologies, and the coming changes I envision would do the same.

I am regularly surprised by the frequency with which not only the general public but also those of us who spend our careers within the world of the liberal arts college are inclined to view that world as fixed and immutable, ignoring Eugene Lang's observation that "pressures for change have been a historic constant" in the lives of these institutions.[1] The successful liberal arts college, like any healthy organization, must in its nature be organic, adapting and evolving in order to fulfill its mission. Fidelity to an important mission does not mean stubborn adherence to particular means to its fulfillment. Technology and globalization are two of many factors that have in recent years altered what it means to be liberally educated, and colleges that fail to alter their work accordingly will not fulfill their responsibility to their students and to the society those students will serve.

Worth noting is the extent to which both those who predict the extinction of the traditional liberal arts college and those who defend its vitality seem to believe that this issue matters. One might argue that such colleges, taken collectively, have already shrunk in relative size to the point where the question of their continued existence is of no great consequence to the future of higher education in America. The percentage of American undergraduates attending liberal arts colleges has declined from about 25 percent in the mid-1950s to about 8 percent in the early 1970s and, by most reckonings, to less than 3 percent today.[2] Using the strictest criteria, one might argue that there are barely more than two hundred "liberal arts colleges," as traditionally understood, still in existence. Even the most sanguine defenders of these institutions are suggesting neither that this number is likely to grow nor that the cost of the educational methods at these institutions will allow them to provide access to many of the new entrants into American higher education, most of these from groups not typically served by high-cost residential colleges. Why spend time either attacking or defending the irrelevant?

The answer, I believe, is that even those who predict the demise of residential liberal arts colleges understand—perhaps on some level just below the conscious— that these institutions have developed an educational model that has been disproportionately successful. According to the National Science Foundation, after normalizing for size, twenty-eight of the top fifty U.S. colleges and universities that produced recipients of Ph.D.'s in science and engineering from 1997 to 2006 were liberal arts colleges, even though such colleges comprise a tiny fraction of all four-year institutions in the country. By contrast, only three of the top fifty were public institutions, one of which, the College of William and Mary, might be described as a public liberal arts college.[3] Richard Arum and Josipa Roska, the authors of the much-cited *Academically Adrift,* which prompted a stream of apocalyptic pronouncements about American higher education, found that students majoring in liberal arts disciplines—identified as areas in the social sciences, humanities, sciences, and mathematics—performed significantly better on a test designed to measure critical thinking, analytical reasoning, problem solving, and writing than did students in other, more vocational and technical fields of study, as did students whose teachers "encourage specific educational practices such as faculty-student contact or engagement in active learning," that is, the practices most common at the small, teaching-oriented college.[4] A recent survey by the consulting firm Hardwick Day found that graduates of selective liberal arts colleges, when compared with graduates of private and public universities, "tended to be more satisfied with their experiences as undergraduates, and more likely to believe that their educations had a significant impact on their personal and professional development."[5]

Clearly, something efficacious is happening at these small institutions that has the potential to inform the practices at institutions very different in kind and scale. Their chief influence is not through size or reach but through example—an example that will remain powerful only if they continue to demonstrate distinctive success.

Changing Boundaries

One might take this subject in a wide range of directions, touching upon topics from the economic model to the curriculum to admissions policies, but here I would like to focus in particular on the boundaries between the liberal arts college and other organizations and communities. These boundaries are in the process of becoming permeable and should become more so. This is a positive development, and as this process continues, it has the potential to enhance the intrinsic value and the utility of the education we provide to our students. I would emphasize three main points regarding the boundaries that delimit the residential liberal arts college.

First, as I note above, the distinctions between what is and is not part of the educational work of the college are becoming less clear. Properly managed, this is a good thing. The education we offer our students will be richer and more relevant if we can establish meaningful educational partnerships among colleges and universities, and between colleges and universities and other entities, including but not limited to businesses, community groups, nongovernmental organizations, and health care providers. We should be able to do more by working together than we can by working alone, offering students not only a larger array of learning opportunities but also programs that are more carefully crafted to prepare them to deal with issues that affect many different sectors of our economy and our communal lives. Without succumbing to the mistaken belief that education is only about vocational training, we should nonetheless be positioned to prepare students more purposefully for local, national, and global workforce needs. And, of course, we should be able to become more efficient in our use of resources. Contrary to what some would argue, there are no easy ways to bend the cost curve in higher education without sacrificing quality,[6] but cooperation and partnerships hold out some hope of productivity gains. We are simply too small individually to do everything comprehensively, economically, and well.

Second, these partnerships and collaborations will only have a deep and lasting impact on our work if they affect the heart of that work, that is, the things that take place in our classrooms, laboratories, and studios. They cannot be add-ons or afterthoughts. They cannot be confined to the realm of the extracurricular, however important that realm is to the development of our students. We do not like to think of ourselves in business terms, even metaphorically, but the fact remains that our core business is made up of interactions between students and faculty and among students in learning environments. We cannot become better at our work if we do not seek relentlessly to improve and advance that core.

Third, we must devote at least as much attention to breaking through and reshaping the boundaries within our institutions as we do to the boundaries between the college and the external world. It is not only the latter that must become more permeable. I am thinking here of internal boundaries of various kinds: those among the departments and disciplines through which we have long organized our curricula; those between faculty and administration; those between what is commonly imagined as academic work and everything else that takes place in a residential community. These internal boundaries can be more stubbornly resistant to alteration than the real or imaginary ones around the borders of the campus. Every campus in America has a large cohort of those who are, in the words of Ann Kirschner, "fierce guardians of the status quo,"[7] and the cohorts may be largest and most determined at those institutions that are the most admired and secure, and therefore the least motivated to do things differently. Some small number of institutions can no doubt survive more or less indefinitely in the absence of meaningful evolution, protected by the power of resources and reputation. But no institution, however many applicants for admission it denies, will through this inertia be serving its students as well as they deserve.

An Example of Change

Altering the boundaries around and within the liberal arts college will not in itself lead to the kind of "disruptive" change that Clayton Christensen and others argue has altered other industries and will inevitably alter higher education.[8] While we wait for disruption to come along and put us all out of business, however, such alteration does seem like an important way of adapting to the current needs of our students and of doing a better job of preparing them for the lives they will lead and the work they will do after they graduate.

One example of such change would be the way we at Macalester have responded to the importance and complexity of the set of issues related to global health, which may be the defining challenge of the next several decades and which touches upon nearly every aspect of our individual and collective well-being. Many of our current and future students will make both their living and their mark on the world by working in this area. We should be preparing them as well as we possibly can to do so.

Here is the way a student interested in global health might have pursued that interest at Macalester only five years ago. She might have majored in biology if she were scientifically inclined, or in economics or political science if she were more interested in matters of public policy. She probably would have found an internship through our Civic Engagement Center with a local organization working on an issue such as reproductive health or the prevention of childhood disease. She almost certainly would have spent a semester studying abroad, probably in one of the less developed parts of the world, and confronted the challenges of global health through both academic and volunteer work. And she might have tied all this together during her senior year in an honors project.

This is a sound and experientially rich educational trajectory that has served students well. What interests me is the question of whether we can do even better by building stronger relationships with organizations outside the college and by rethinking our structures within the college. That is, can we enhance both the quality and the distinctiveness of what a liberal arts college has to offer?

In this case, I believe, the answer is yes. Here is the path the same student might follow today. In addition to pursuing a major, she would add our new academic concentration in Community and Global Health, which brings the disciplines and practices of liberal arts education to bear upon the most important issues related to public health. The concentration crosses traditional disciplinary boundaries, with the core courses alone drawn from biology, anthropology, geography, mathematics, philosophy, psychology, and political science. The curriculum might be described as problem-centered rather than discipline-centered. In addition to its focus on content and theory, the program is designed to develop fundamental skills in areas including critical and quantitative reasoning, writing, and integrative learning. It is (or should be) easier to create such innovative pathways through the curriculum at small colleges than at large universities because our scale allows for more regular social and professional interactions among faculty members and, I would contend, because the grip of the disciplines is (or should be) less powerful.

Four years after its approval by the faculty, the Community and Global Health concentration is the most popular interdisciplinary program in the college, with more than seventy students enrolled and steadily increasing demand. We have been able, through a gift, to endow a new professorship in global health that is not restricted to any particular department. Its initial holder will sit in our geography department and focus on medical and health geography.

Similar problem-centered concentrations have been created in Human Rights and Humanitarianism and in International Development. If I were today creating a liberal arts college from scratch, I would move even more aggressively in this curricular direction.

The student described above might also be able to benefit from partnerships the college has established with various businesses and health care providers in the region, all of whom share an interest in community and global health. Here is one such program:

The Mayo Innovation Scholars Program (MISP) is a collaborative effort between the Mayo Clinic and selected Minnesota private colleges and universities, with financial support from the Medtronic Foundation and Mayo Clinic Office of Intellectual Property, and administrative support from the Minnesota Private College Council.

Teams of four or five undergraduate science and economics majors assist in the assessment of new product submissions by researchers at Mayo Clinic. Each student team is directed by a master's level student and is advised by a licensing manager from the Mayo Clinic Office of Intellectual Property.

The student teams gain valuable insights and experience in the translational process associated with inventions and product development. The experience culminates with a presentation of the team's research findings, in the form of a business plan, to Mayo licensing managers, representatives from the MN Private College Council, the Medtronic Foundation and participating colleges. The presentation is at the Mayo Clinic in Rochester, Minn.[9]

Consider for a moment all of the boundaries being crossed in the creation of this program, which has been a stirring success: boundaries between for-profit and non-profit organizations, between colleges and health care providers, between what might be imagined as purely academic work and product development, and—maybe most challenging of all—those among various private colleges in Minnesota. Making these boundaries more permeable opens up both a world of educational possibilities for students and the opportunity to genuinely reimagine our institutions

Roadblocks

Liberal arts colleges, particularly those with relative financial security and reputational strength, should be the cutting-edge laboratories of U.S. higher education. Many of the conditions most favorable to constant innovation are in place: talented and highly motivated students, gifted faculty members, manageable size, close and regular interactions among members of the community, and—maybe most important—a clearly defined mission focused on the education of undergraduates.

I have tried to demonstrate through the example of Macalester College that the evolution that has marked the history of these institutions is ongoing and that change that is beneficial to students and reflective of the world they will encounter is in fact taking place. But I want to emphasize that such evolution is not happening as quickly, broadly, or consistently as it should. I ponder this matter often, and in doing so I try to move beyond oft-repeated jokes about faculty resistance to change[10] and beyond the dysfunctionality narrative that has distorted so much public discussion of higher education among pundits and policy makers. Whether it is in the area of curriculum or collaboration or technology, why do the liberal arts colleges that should be leaders so often fail to lead?

This is what I do understand: there are virtues to slow, thoughtful, deliberate change and to fidelity to a mission and methodology that have proven effective over time. In many respects, the slow pace of change has served colleges and universities well. Most have survived, even as many of the for-profit companies that take pride in their ability to transform themselves quickly have transformed themselves out of existence. Markets create powerful forces, and by many measures the market for those institutions at the high end of the educational food chain has never been larger or more enthusiastic. Just ask an admissions officer at Harvard. There are very few examples of enterprises opting for significant change while they enjoy such powerful brand strength and an apparently insatiable demand for their services.

And yet, like many others, I cannot escape the sense that economics and technology are combining to create a transformational moment in higher education and that the traditional liberal arts college will be most viable and most valuable if it can use its inherent advantages to make the most of that opportunity for change. I am inclined to set aside the more extreme of the doomsday scenarios for the liberal arts, which, as David W. Breneman and many others have documented, have been around for nearly as long as these colleges themselves.[11] I am even more inclined to dismiss what can only be described as the destructive nonsense coming from those like Peter Thiel and Michael Ellsberg, who argue that a college education itself has become an impediment to financial success.[12] Yet even if liberal arts colleges are not facing a near-term existential threat, they should be actively seeking out those forms of change that will enable them to become better and more productive. The sincere desire to improve may not be as powerful or effective a motivation for change as the fear of extinction—I suspect that most students of the brain would emphasize this point—but it should not be too casually dismissed, and the changes that are born out of aspiration rather than out of fear may in the end be more appropriate and sustainable.

At every gathering of liberal arts college presidents and provosts I attend, at every meeting between administrators and boards of trustees, there is expressed a deep-seated frustration at the inability to move these institutions forward with the agility and creativity the times seem to require. Often these conversations are held *sotto voce,* as if speaking of such frustration, like uttering aloud the name of Voldemort, might bring forth an *Avada Kedavra* curse[13] (which I suppose in the presidential universe is a vote of no confidence). It is that-which-shall-not-be-named.

At the risk of being turned into a toad or an ex-president, let me suggest that the root of the problem lies in our organizational and governance structures. As should by now be evident, I am no fan of the outsized role that the traditional disciplines have come to play in nearly every aspect of the academic life of the liberal arts college. Faculty hiring, faculty evaluation and promotion, the contours of the curriculum, and the allocation of resources are all dominated far too often by disciplinary rather than institutional thinking. It is not at all unusual for a faculty of 150 people to be divided into 20 or 25 semi-autonomous units, some of which are further sub-divided because of disciplinary tensions—think of critics and creative writers in an English department, or physical and cultural anthropologists—or because people simply cannot get along. If it is more difficult to change the direction of a battleship than of a cruiser, it is more difficult still to change the direction of a fleet of small vessels whose captains do not always speak the same language or aspire to reach the same destination.

A version of the same phenomenon has happened within administrations, where we are better at adding divisions and deans than we are at getting them to work collaboratively. This might be expected at mammoth public institutions with multiple schools and an array of different and sometimes incompatible missions. It should not be expected, or at least should be preventable, at a small college.

And then there is shared governance, which can at its best produce broadly embraced, sustainable results but which is all too often not at its best and devolves instead into divided or ineffectual governance. When we speak of shared governance in higher education, we are speaking really of the always complex and often tense interplay between faculties and administrations. Neither group can succeed without the other (although each regularly professes that it would like to give it a try), and no college can reach its full potential if the two are not working effectively together toward at least a general set of mutually embraced goals.

So what goes wrong? In my experience, shared governance works best at the small-group level: put a cohort of faculty and administrators together to address a challenging issue and more often than not you will get a pretty good result. These are by and large smart, well-motivated people who are trained to ask critical questions and solve challenging problems. Shared governance also works best when faculty members embrace the notion of *representative* governance and trust those they have selected to be their representatives.

Shared governance works worst when decision making moves from the level of the small group to the level of the whole, which at a liberal arts college typically means the faculty meeting, and when faith in elected representatives goes missing. Faculty meeting votes on critical institutional questions have become to the governance of liberal arts colleges what ballot initiatives have become to the governance of the state of California. Often those who have spent the least time thinking about a strategic process are given the most power to determine its outcome. As with ballot initiatives, that outcome is more often determined by rhetorical flair and political energy than by extended consideration of the common good.

Accountability also matters. I believe that governance is likely to work best when those responsible for decisions know that there is some reasonable chance that they will be held accountable for the impact of those decisions. While the process of administrative accountability in academia is far from perfect, there are at least formal and informal mechanisms in place for removing presidents, provosts, and deans whose decisions consistently have a deleterious impact on an institution, and the relatively short average tenure of those who hold these positions suggests that these mechanisms are not infrequently employed. There is not and should not be a comparable system in place for faculty, creating a separation between decision making and accountability that is found in few other workplaces and that does not increase the likelihood of good outcomes.

Richard Morrill, president of the Teagle Foundation, has observed that shared governance at colleges and universities is profoundly difficult to revise or even discuss because, for many, it has an ethical as well as an organizational dimension.[14] Challenges to the prevailing governance model are seen as challenges to academic freedom, as administrative power grabs, or as increasing the likelihood that nonacademic influences will unduly shape the curriculum. The best governance models, however, are those that are designed to produce the best results and not those designed chiefly to prevent the worst. While the system in place at most colleges, by passing so much through the blender of relentless campus scrutiny, does a thorough job of smoothing out any impurities, it too often substitutes the broadly palatable for that which is truly original and exciting. One has to balance the ethical imperative that shapes our current governance model against another ethical imperative of perhaps greater weight: the responsibility to serve our students as well as we possibly can.

Because my general preference is for those who are outraged by what I say to be outraged by what I actually say, let me be as clear as I can on this endlessly contentious issue. Good institutional stewardship requires the perspective and understanding that come only through extensive study and thought. Faculty members and administrators who are prepared to devote themselves to this effort should partner in an effective system of shared governance. Administrators who are not so prepared should be replaced; faculty members who are not so prepared should *not* be replaced, but neither should they be the drivers of institutional decision making. It is unrealistic and unproductive to imagine that all or most members of a faculty will be able to do this work, so a system of representative governance, with a subset of the faculty given the time and responsibility to engage with important strategic questions, stands a better chance of achieving good outcomes than does the system of direct democracy in place at so many small colleges.

The bad news is that these problems are real and pervasive. The good news is that because they are rooted in organization and governance rather than in some intractable antipathy between faculty and administration or within faculties, they are fixable. I would begin by centralizing more decisions that have real potential to affect the direction of an institution and by relying more heavily on representative forms of governance, whether through a committee structure or task forces or through a college senate that has genuine rather than nominal decision-making authority. The key distinction, again, is not between faculty and administration, but between those in either group who are prepared to spend time and energy on consequential strategic decisions and those who are not. We should not expect all faculty members, whose central work is teaching and scholarship, to do so; we should also not expect all of them to be well positioned to be stewards of institutional well-being. We might draw some important conclusions from the fact that the one process on most liberal arts college campuses that relies most heavily on representative governance—the reappointment, tenuring, and promotion of faculty—is also perhaps the most consequential and the one that on many campuses works most effectively.

I am keenly aware that much of what I am suggesting is more easily imagined than accomplished. To paraphrase Dickens in *Little Dorrit*, when it comes to structural change on college campuses, we are far more adept at determining How Not [or Why Not] to Do It than we are at Doing It. There are, of course, risks whenever more authority is invested in fewer people, and there are risks—professional and institutional—when one questions a set of governance practices and cultural norms as deeply ingrained as those in academia. But there are risks as well in avoiding change because it is difficult, and these may, for many institutions, ultimately be the greater ones.

In the end, I believe that the future relevance and viability of the liberal arts college may be determined by our ability to create organizations and governance processes that foster more than they inhibit creative change. Fail in this effort, and we do indeed risk obsolescence; succeed, and we have the opportunity to offer to our students an education of unparalleled excellence and compelling social value.

NOTES

1. Eugene M. Lang, "Distinctively American: The Liberal Arts College," in *Distinctively American: The Residential Liberal Arts College,* ed. Steven Koblik and Stephen R. Graubard (New Brunswick, NJ: Transaction, 2000), 138.

2. See Francis Oakley, "The Liberal Arts College: Identity, Variety, Destiny," in *Liberal Arts Colleges in American Higher Education: Challenges and Opportunities,* ACLS Occasional Paper No. 59 (New York: ACLS, 2005), 5. Much of this reduction in percentage, of course, is a result of the proliferation of institutions and the increasing variety of institutional types.

3. "Baccalaureate Origins of S&E Doctorate Recipients," National Science Foundation InfoBrief, July 2008, 6.

4. Richard Arum and Josipa Roksa, *Academically Adrift: Limited Learning on College Campuses* (Chicago: University of Chicago Press, 2011), 109; see also 104–9. The test alluded to is the Collegiate Learning Assessment, or CLA.

5. Kevin Kiley, "Better Than Yours," *Inside Higher Education,* November 16, 2011. An executive summary of the study can be found at http://collegenews.org/news/2011/liberal-arts -college-graduates-feel-better-prepared-for-lifes-challenges-study-finds.html.

6. By far the best discussion of this subject is by Robert B. Archibald and David H. Feldman in *Why Does College Cost So Much?* (New York: Oxford, 2010).

7. Ann Kirschner, "Innovation in Higher Education? HAH!" *The Chronicle Review,* April 13, 2012, B7.

8. See Clayton M. Christensen and Henry J. Eyring, *The Innovative University: Changing the DNA of Higher Education from the Inside Out* (San Francisco: Jossey-Bass, 2011). I am not wholly convinced that Christensen's template for change can be applied as easily to education as to some other enterprises, but he is worth reading.

9. www.macalester.edu/academics/biology/studentopportunities/mayo/.

10. My favorite offering in this genre comes from Jim Collins, who quotes an unnamed university president as describing tenured faculty as "a thousand points of no." *Good to Great and the Social Sectors* (Boulder, CO: Jim Collins, 2005), 10.

11. Breneman writes that "when one reads the literature on private colleges, one discovers a nearly unbroken history of concern for their survival" ("Liberal Arts Colleges: What Price Survival?," in *Higher Learning in America, 1980–2000,* ed. Arthur Levine [Baltimore: Johns Hopkins University Press, 1994], 86).

12. Peter Thiel is the billionaire libertarian founder of PayPal, who, having received BA and JD degrees from Stanford, now argues that students should not attend college. His Thiel Foundation pays a small group of gifted students not to do so. Michael Ellsberg is the author of *The Education of Millionaires: It's Not What You Think and It's Not Too Late* (New York: Portfolio, 2011), in which he argues that a college education is a hindrance to entrepreneurial success. His BA is from Brown.

13. Instant death. Unforgivable.

14. Remarks at meeting of the American Association of Colleges & Universities Presidents' Trust, Washington, DC, April 30, 2012.

CHAPTER 15

"Glowing against the Gray, Sober against the Fire"

Residential Academic Communities in the Twenty-First Century

John M. McCardell Jr.
VICE-CHANCELLOR AND PRESIDENT,
SEWANEE: THE UNIVERSITY OF THE SOUTH

The Wall Street Journal published its "millennial edition" on New Year's Day 2000 with essays about what the future might hold for every sector of American life. One such article had to do with the future of the liberal arts college. "The classroom of the future," it began, "won't have much in common with today's version. For one thing, there probably won't be a classroom." The article went on to discuss the ways in which higher education would be changing—would, necessarily, be forced to change. But toward the end came a telling comment. Todd Nelson, then the president of Apollo Group, which started the University of Phoenix, that avatar of distance learning and unbounded classrooms and high technology, when asked where he planned to send his own children to college, responded that of course they would attend a bricks-and-mortar institution. Why? "There are important social and cultural things [there] that you don't get with us," he explained.[1]

Important social and cultural things indeed: human interaction, for one thing; mentorship, for another; as well as conversation, discussion and debate, lifelong friendships, structure, community—none of them virtual, contrived, or simulated. All of them actual, real—perhaps even transforming. Nelson was, of course, referring to "things" that take place outside the classroom and that add comprehensiveness, coherence and, withal, value to the college experience. Of all the reasons behind the tuitions we charge, this added value makes the most compelling claim and explains why, in spite of our escalating sticker prices, the lines at our admissions offices remain long. Clearly, the public also perceives the value-added proposition that constitutes, and has long constituted, the residential liberal arts college's reason for being. Residential life, in other words, matters and matters every bit as much as the quality of instruction offered in our classrooms.

This summons a well-known quotation, verging on hackneyed, from E. M. Forster's *Howards End:* " '[O]nly connect,' that was the whole of her sermon. 'Only connect' the prose and the passion and both will be exalted. Live in fragments no longer."[2] Could there be a more succinct—or more eloquent—statement about what a liberal arts college seeks to do? It is all about connections, some formulaic, some imaginative, some also serendipitous.

Most of us know that quote, and many of us have probably employed it. But the passage that precedes it is less well known yet just as inspiring. It speaks of building a "rainbow bridge" that connects the prose in us with the passion. "Without it we are meaningless fragments, half monks, half beasts, unconnected arches that have never joined into a man. With it, love is born and alights on the highest curve, glowing against the gray, sober against the fire."[3]

Liberal education, and especially the residential experience, is, or ought to be, that rainbow bridge. Crossing it connects not simply prose and passion but head and heart, hand and eye, adolescence and adulthood. Our campuses are places where young people, not wholly unmade but not yet wholly made, come to continue to learn and to grow.

The residential component of the liberal arts college experience is, arguably, the keystone in that bridge. Liberal education, broadly understood, includes the creation and the nurturing of communities of learning. In these residential communities we go about our work of shaping each individual life to ends that are educational, of course, but more—purposeful, informed, loving, selfless, perhaps even (or what's a heaven for?) noble.

Today's Residential College Experience

But before we begin merely to celebrate, by reiteration, the great benefits to be derived from the residential college experience, we need to take a long, hard look in the mirror. We have aged. Times have changed. Our always rather too self-referential generation, now uncomfortably on the far side of the generation gap, must make the status quo we have created bear at least some burden of proof.

We might begin to take Forster's admonition to heart by considering all the impulses and inclinations to fragmentary living that confront our students daily, routinely. These things are sources of fragmentation and sources also of anxiety. For example, the CIRP freshman surveys have over the years revealed disturbing trends. Between 2007 and 2011 the percentage of freshmen spending three or more hours a week on social networking increased from 45 percent to 57 percent for women and 37 percent to 48 percent for men. And this force that militates so subversively against community is probably understated.[4]

To this might be added, under the general rubric of finance, the discovery that over the last ten years the percentage of students taking on $10,000 or more of debt has risen from 5.6 percent to 13.3 percent. Almost 12 percent have "major" concerns about finance. Another 55.5 percent have "some" such concerns. The average indebtedness for graduates in 2010 was $25,250, a 5 percent increase over the previous year.[5]

In short, the students coming to our campuses are shaped by different influences and preoccupied by different concerns than those that were familiar to us. We have been slow either to recognize this reality or, in recognizing it, to adjust our own behavior. Indeed, it can be argued that higher education has abandoned its students, quite ironically, by giving them greater freedom. On many college campuses there are few adults present between 7 p.m. and 7 a.m. For half the day, in other words, and most weekends, our campuses have virtually no adult presence. Yet we wonder why a disconnect has developed between what goes on in the classroom and what takes place in other sectors of a student's life.

The "adult presence" issue is, of course, sensitive. Students are inclined to believe, even as more of their number visit the counseling office, that to raise it is to question their maturity, their independence, their assumed right to be left alone in the name of learning one's limits or under the equally debatable assumption that they are already adults. Faculty members recoil from the *in loco parentis* role, which begs the question of what moral obligation the faculty ought to have to provide a more supportive environment for students. A wise former colleague once observed that there are in fact some things an eighteen-year-old ought not to be expected instinctively to know.

Some of us are old enough to remember the "new math." Some of us discovered, in the novelty, a penchant for the humanities. But some of it stuck, particularly the Venn diagram, which provides a useful way of understanding what residential life on our campuses ought to be about. The Venn diagram shows separate spheres with greater or lesser points or proportions of intersection. Our students inhabit many different spheres during the course of a single day: the classroom, of course, but also the dining hall, the library, the dormitory, the student center, the playing field, the fraternity or sorority house, the chapel, the music hall, the campus walkways. The purpose of residential life should be to encourage, even insist upon, frequent and multiple points of intersection among these separate spheres. Why ought students to expect, and why oughtn't we to discourage, the notion that one behaves differently depending on where one finds oneself?

Yet mere exhortation won't do. We often teach best by example. We need to make certain that our residential systems in fact address the needs of the current generation of students and that faculty do not abdicate their duty as educators in favor of student life professionals or, far worse, abandon their campuses entirely for large portions of the day and week.

The great nineteenth-century statesman and orator Daniel Webster said it well: "Liberty exists only in proportion to wholesome restraint."[6] There could hardly be a more succinct way of describing how we might approach the general question of student life on our campuses. Liberty without restraint is chaos. Restraint without liberty is oppression. Within those areas where the various elements of campus life intersect, we are most likely to find that balance and, in proportion to wholesome restraint, grant ever more generous portions of liberty.

Features of the Successful Residential College

How might a reformed, revived residential system better meet the needs of students? The successful residential college might be characterized by three distinguishing features. First, the educational experience it offers should be *seamless*. An approach to residential liberal arts education that takes for granted, and therefore creates or maintains structures and policies that reinforce, the continuing existence of separate spheres of activity—with the accompanying separate standards of behavior—is doomed to failure. Such an approach does not prepare students well for the world in which they will live their lives.

Second, the educational experience should be *comprehensive*. It includes an excellent academic program, of course, created and maintained by a faculty of distinction and commitment. But it also includes those other elements of college life that contribute to a superior education and that foster lifelong habits that, for want of a better term, we might call character. Those habits are as apt to be learned on a playing field, in a club, in a choral or theatrical production, or over extended conversations at mealtime—or late at night—as they are in the classroom. The successful residential college acknowledges this reality and provides as best it can for it. For this reason, facilities matter. In response to the assertion that student centers, social and recreational spaces, properly appointed residence halls, athletics facilities, fitness centers, or arts rooms are "frills," we must insist that ours is a mission different from the large public or research institution, and that much of the added value of a residential liberal arts education derives from the kinds of experiences our facilities encourage.

Third, the educational experience offered must be—and here I shudder as I employ a 1960s term—*relevant*. By this I emphatically do not mean trendy or fashionable, bending to the latest set of prejudices masquerading as principles. Rather, I mean relevant in some sense to the lives students have led before they arrive on campus and also to the lives they will lead after they graduate. An old friend and former faculty colleague who has also been a parent of a college student opened my eyes to this point many years ago. The concept of *in loco parentis*, he noted, spoke to a time when there were strong, two-parent families, and opposition to the concept came from students who sought freedom from these constraints. It is far different today. There are ever fewer two-parent households, fewer still where a parent is at home with a child for extended periods. As a result, the concept on which much of the rebellion of the student generation (the generation now populating faculties and administrations) was based is utterly alien to the experience of the current generation of students. And thus we witness, in reaction to stresses we ourselves can hardly comprehend, behavior that suggests that students somehow feel themselves exempt from behavioral rules that give society shape and order, with a license to act as they choose and be protected from the consequences. It is, he concluded, rather like expecting a student to be able to write without knowing the fundamentals of grammar. No one along the way thought grammar was important. So grammar must now, belatedly, be taught, lest writing be juvenile, sloppy, imprecise. This is oversimplified, perhaps, but comes uncomfortably close to describing the attitude that condones excessive drinking, sexual promiscuity, and destruction of property. It is an attitude that is largely formed in other environments and long before students apply to college.

Hallmarks of a Seamless, Comprehensive, Relevant Liberal Arts College

A strong residential system then—seamless, comprehensive, and relevant—ought to offer the best antidote to the centrifugal tendencies that surround the young people we seek to educate. The hallmarks of such a system would include the following:

- It makes clear the objectives of a liberal education. While we assume the importance of study across the curriculum, we also give students more opportunities to consider the long-term consequences of what they have learned in the classroom. A residential community ought to be a place where faculty, staff, alumni, and guests regularly encourage students to look outward from the confines of their own limited experience and to reflect upon how and why education matters. This outward turn is especially important in those institutions, like my own, in isolated or rural settings.

- It establishes an educational environment that is more than simply task-oriented. Students take on challenging academic work every day, and they are graded on their efforts. Indeed, one could argue that academic pressure—being "stressed out"—is a major cause of ethos that demands that one "play hard" in one's free time. A properly designed and functioning residential system should provide a place where students discover the pleasures of learning apart from the process of evaluation, of learning for its own sake.

- It encourages the continuation of conversations between students and faculty, among students, and within the extended college community. There is not enough time in the classroom, in office hours, or anywhere else on many campuses for members of the community to discuss topics—intellectual issues, current events, music, or anything else vital to our culture—not directly relevant to classroom work. Faculty members have interests beyond their own particular disciplines and should welcome opportunities to share these with students. Students, too, have broader interests. Meals, receptions, and other social gatherings, in encompassable settings, provide occasions for such exchange.

- It assumes a broad definition of faculty professional development. To be sure, in order to be granted tenure, faculty must demonstrate both teaching excellence and demonstrated proficiency in research in a chosen field. Of course, those faculty members who prove to be good at producing, and especially eager to produce, research that makes major ongoing contributions to a discipline ought to be encouraged and rewarded. But a liberal arts college ought not to succumb to the research-institution mentality that this is the principal measure of professional or institutional worth. Acknowledging both the changing seasons in a faculty member's life and the many ways in which the faculty can, over the course of a career, contribute to the work of an institution, adroit administrators will find the best fit for each faculty member's particular skills and will especially encourage those interested in the lives students lead outside the classroom to play significant roles in those lives, thereby broadening the understanding of professional accomplishment and rewarding leadership by example.

- It allows students to test ideas and stretch themselves. If college is a place where students experiment and make mistakes in order to grow as individuals, then a residential system ought to enhance this developmental process by supporting activities, from intramural sports to in-house theater, that promote such growth. Moreover, there should be a wide range of opportunities to develop leadership skills and to learn the responsible uses of power and authority through self-government. Whether enabled by adults or fellow students, these activities should encourage intelligent risk taking, which is a significant part of education broadly defined.

- It promotes development by encouraging respect for others. Self-awareness depends on awareness of other people and of how one's own behavior, words, and deeds affect, and are understood by, others. A residential system must build communities that stress the importance of responsibility, accountability, diversity, civility, and integrity. These abstract values will take on concrete importance through routine human interactions, planned and unplanned, that residence in a small community generates naturally.

- It builds a connection to the larger college that extends beyond the undergraduate experience. Continuing residence in a small community gives students a home on campus to which they can return as alumni. Ongoing contact with a dean, a faculty member, a coach, or other staff members or administrators can ensure that no student "slips through the cracks" and that no student graduates without establishing a personal relationship with at least one faculty member. From such relationships a sense of loyalty to the college that made such an experience possible naturally develops.

- Finally, it nurtures students in their individual growth and builds in them the confidence necessary to succeed in the world beyond college. This encouragement comes not only from adults but also from fellow students. As much as the viability of a residential community depends upon strong adult leadership, it must also build upon the active participation of self-educating students.

Examples of Best Practices

I would not presume to contend that the University of the South has satisfactorily attained these lofty goals. But I can assert with conviction that these are goals to which we aspire, and that we are attempting to create an environment aligned with those aspirations.

I offer several examples. The first is in fact simple and fundamental: all students live together and dine together for all four years. That requires residence halls that can comfortably accommodate our entire undergraduate student body, with greater possibilities for more independent living on campus during senior year. Students do not, after freshman or sophomore year, decamp to distant apartments or houses and commute to class. That means a dining hall of sufficient capacity to allow, even encourage, students to linger; they need not be hurried out of concern that other students need to occupy their seats. That means a Greek system that, while shouldering a significant responsibility for social life on our remote mountain campus, does not deploy the "sorting hat" on the day students arrive. Rush is deferred until second semester. Fraternity and sorority houses serve no meals; only one or two responsible students live in them. All parties are open, and as a result one searches in vain for fraternity or sorority decals on the rear windshield of Sewanee student automobiles.

To this might be added the happy reality that, owing to our location, almost all faculty members live proximate to campus. As a result, entertaining students in faculty members' homes is easy and frequent. Some professors still observe the old Sewanee custom of leaving the porch light burning on Sunday evening, which means students are invited to simply drop by.

A second example would be a rootedness in place. We are blessed to have a 13,000-acre "Domain." This precious resource offers virtually unlimited opportunities for research and recreation. To be sure, our curriculum takes maximum advantage of the Domain, and students who enjoy the outdoors are naturally attracted to our university. But encouraging true rootedness does not demand a vast tract of land. It does, however, require attention to the particularity of place and an awareness that history did not begin on the day we were born or the day we arrived. A very wise person once observed that " 'other' takes on meaning only when we know what it is other than." At Sewanee, beginning with new student orientation, we seek to impress upon our students the importance and uniqueness of place, and how place has shaped the university they are attending and will in turn shape them. This endeavor is not outsourced to student life professionals; faculty members play a significant role. From these efforts result better advising, closer bonds, and an understanding of our human interdependence. Our faculty is currently at work on a course to be taken by all new students and, beginning several weeks before other students return, introducing them to the richness of the Domain and incorporating all the features of orientation into an essentially academic enterprise.

Nor has Sewanee distanced itself from the vision of its founders, bishops of ten southern Episcopal dioceses who, in 1857, established on a remote mountaintop what they hoped would become a great national Episcopal university. This is a part of our rootedness, as is the undeniable fact that those founders chose the Confederate side in the Civil War that followed. To this day the university is owned by twenty-eight southern dioceses, representing all points on the theological spectrum. From that springs a genuine commitment to diversity in all its forms, a principle of inclusivity that heeds the scriptural admonition concerning extending hospitality to believers and nonbelievers alike, and an acknowledgment that perhaps especially an institution bearing the name of the University of the South (the University of the twenty-first-century South) has something to say about the humility that comes from knowing what it means to live in a fallen world. This we communicate to our students candidly and unabashedly. It is a part of who we are and, we hope, of what they will become.

A final example, again not unique, is the emphasis placed on honorable conduct. Sewanee, like many institutions, has an honor code, which is not limited to academic misconduct. The code is entirely student administered. Acknowledging that violations are unlikely to be uniform in their seriousness, the code provides a range of penalties. Exams are unproctored. All work is pledged. Investigations do not go on for months. Hearings do not drag into the wee, small hours. Appeals go to the vice-chancellor (at Sewanee, that is the president). None of this is especially noteworthy. But what is striking, and related to the previous two examples, is the emphasis placed upon the honor code from the very moment a student arrives at the university. Nowhere is this more powerful or compelling that at the very end of orientation, when every new student files into All Saints' Chapel, hears a brief talk about honor at Sewanee, and then steps forward, one by one, touches a piece of the original cornerstone (destroyed by soldiers passing over the Domain in 1863), and then signs his or her name to the code. After that, the student is escorted back to a chapel seat by a gowned faculty member who impresses upon the student the gravity of what has just occurred and welcomes that student to the Sewanee community.

These are not radical or dramatic shifts in practice, nor are they in any fundamental way different from what happens on many of our campuses. But students do notice what we choose to emphasize and exemplify, and from these things they take their cues. In such ways is a community formed and sustained, and education, broadly defined, not simply offered but lived.

Shaping the Next Generation of Leaders

Institutions that claim as their mission the education of young men and women in the tradition of the liberal arts must define education broadly and acknowledge that such an education takes place around the clock and in all venues. Faculty and staff need to be encouraged and supported as they fill an adult void in the lives of students, not as policemen but as role models. Facilities must foster the kind of supportive educational environment that will ensure the survival of the residential college. That survival is of little consequence for its own sake. It is of vital importance, however, to a world that desperately needs broadly educated, humane, and purposeful leaders.

As we well know, the current generation of students is quite different from our own. The cultural forces that have shaped it, the aspirations it possesses, its willingness to look beyond or through issues that have preoccupied us, its great promise, offer us more opportunities than ever to deal with them like the adults the law says they are and the adults they seek to be. If our goal is to prepare and produce the next generation of leaders for our country and for our world, leaders prepared to make informed decisions and sound judgments, then we need to consider how best to shape not only their minds but also their souls, and to acknowledge that much of what we seek to accomplish cannot be made to conform with demands that we measure and to quantify what is essentially unquantifiable.

The residential experience can give students liberty while expecting wholesome restraint. It can create an environment where students may learn to balance those two fundamental features of human conduct. It, and it alone, can enable us to build that rainbow bridge connecting the prose and the passion, adolescence and adulthood. And, having crossed that bridge successfully, our graduates in time to come will stand, in a complex and challenging world, in Forster's words, "glowing against the gray, sober against the fire."

NOTES

1. Yochi J. Dreazen, "Student, Teach Thyself," *Wall Street Journal*, January 1, 2000, inter active.wsj.com/millennium/articles/SB944517850742359260.htm.

2. E. M. Forster, *Howards End* (New York: Alfred A. Knopf, 1921), 214.

3. Ibid., 213.

4. Cooperative Institutional Research Program, *The American Freshman: National Norms 2011* (Los Angeles: Higher Education Research Institute, 2011), 13–14.

5. Ibid., 12.

6. Daniel Webster, Speech at the Charleston Bar Dinner, May 10, 1847, in *The Works of Daniel Webster*, ed. Edward Everett (Boston: C. C. Little and J. Brown, 1851), 2:393.

SUGGESTED FURTHER READINGS

Any list of recommended reading is necessarily selective and biased. That said, I have found the following especially useful:

Carter, Stephen L. *Civility.* New York: Harper Perennial, 1999.

Light, Richard. *Making the Most of College: Students Speak Their Minds.* Cambridge, MA: Harvard University Press, 2001.

Ryan, Mark B. *A Collegiate Way of Living: Residential Colleges and a Yale Education.* New Haven, CT: Jonathan Edwards College, 2001.

Willimon, William H., and Thomas H. Naylor. *The Abandoned Generation: Rethinking Higher Education.* Grand Rapids, MI: Eerdmans, 1995.

CHAPTER 16

The Intercultural Connection
Students and the Liberal Arts

Ronald A. Crutcher
PRESIDENT, WHEATON COLLEGE

Private liberal arts colleges have distinguished themselves from larger state universities for many years because of their more intimate size and the high percentage of students who reside on campus. To be sure, this may not be the most cost-effective approach to higher education. As a result, one of the challenges that we as leaders of liberal arts colleges face today is convincing the parents of these students of the value in investing in such an education. This is a new role for many of us. For the last few decades, we have experienced economic growth as well as a growing demand for a liberal arts education in private residential college settings. With the downturn of the economy and the changing demographics of students, we now face an environment in which we must increasingly justify the relevance of the liberal arts in the lives—and careers—of our students.

Fortunately, we have a solid basis for making such a claim. At no time in our history have the benefits of an education within a residential academic community been more important to the development of young people. Today's millennial generation, which covers a range from our incoming students to recent graduates, has grown up in an era of rapid technological changes. They are adept at using the Internet and portable devices for all sorts of resources and, of course, for networking. Surveys reveal that they have progressive social ideas and have developed a strong sense of confidence that they will succeed in the world.

Other studies point to more problematic attributes. According to a study cited in a recent article in the *Chronicle of Higher Education,* millennial students have considerably less empathy than do students from previous generations. Other surveys cited in the article reveal a corresponding increase in narcissism and "a decline in taking responsibility," that is, blaming other forces at work for one's failure.[1] Because this generation is entering the workforce during the aftermath of the Great Recession and at a time when global competition is rewriting the rules of engagement, now more than ever students need to develop a sense of empathy, multicultural understanding, engagement, and responsibility. When they enter our colleges, they are obviously at an extremely vulnerable period in their lives, away from families and meeting people from other backgrounds, many for the first time in their lives. In the right educational environment, this can be a period of great personal transformation and change, giving us an opportunity to prepare them for purposeful consideration of how their actions, values, and beliefs affect the people with whom they interact.

Our job is to make a compelling case that this kind of education—as opposed to a more vocationally centered one—is critical for success in the twenty-first century. We need to remind our students, parents, and alumni that a liberal arts education will not only prepare students to lead successful careers but will enable them to shape lives that embrace meaningful interactions within the intercultural communities with which they will be affiliated throughout their lives.

Demonstrating Successful Outcomes in Liberal Arts Colleges

So is it possible to craft a compelling case for a residential liberal arts education amidst the cacophony of voices advocating for colleges to better educate students for specific jobs—to make higher education much more vocationally oriented? Indeed, this is the very message that we hear from politicians and policymakers on a regular basis. In such an environment, how do we convince parents that a financial commitment that may reach as high as $200,000 (or more!) with no guarantee of a job at the end of four years is worth it? How do we convince students that the ability to be fluent across disciplinary boundaries—in other words, to connect learning from one discipline to another in meaningful ways—may better prepare them for a career in investments, finance, or entrepreneurship than a business degree?

Crafting our case and presenting it in a compelling way is not something that will be accomplished simply by engaging a marketing firm, no matter how good it may be. I believe that leaders of residential liberal arts colleges need first to double down on the core mission and purpose, to gather the evidence and demonstrate the effectiveness of a liberal arts education. The results of the Annapolis Group alumni surveys distributed to the national media last fall are a good start, but more effort is required on our part.

Through the development of honors colleges and other similar programs over the past several years, larger state universities have replicated our approach to undergraduate education, in some cases, quite effectively. Indeed, some of these universities can point to alumni results not too dissimilar from those found in the Annapolis Group Survey. One such case is Miami University in Oxford, Ohio. As provost there, I worked with the faculty to revamp the honors program into a much more rigorous and competitive program. We also developed an ancillary scholars program for those students who did not meet the criteria for the honors programs. Both programs had residential components, and students in both programs were able to develop close relationships with faculty. In other words, both mimicked the kind of education available at small residential liberal arts colleges but at a much cheaper price. Of course, this education was provided for only about 10 percent of a class of 3,500 students, but in the past those 350 students might have been top prospects for a liberal arts college.

We as leaders need to ensure that residential liberal arts colleges are even more intentional in the kind of educational experiences we are offering students. If, in fact, we assert that undergraduate education within a small residential academic community can deeply affect the academic, social, and spiritual development of our students, we need to demonstrate those outcomes to the public.

I propose that we take two of the most vexing challenges facing society in the twenty-first century, diversity and globalism, and become more intentional about the ways in which we assist our students to approach these complex issues. At the dawn of the twentieth century, W. E. B. Du Bois penned these prophetic words: "The problem of the twentieth century is the problem of the color-line—the relation of the darker to the lighter races of men in Asia and Africa, in America and the islands of the sea." Arguably, one could make the case that diversity and globalism are as much of a problem for the twenty-first century as for the twentieth century. Diversity, of course, remains an unresolved vestige from the last century—a challenge for which we in higher education have been unable to find effective approaches beyond, at best, expanding demographic representation. One need only review U.S. military activity over the past decade to understand some of the challenges of globalism.[2]

The goal would be to demonstrate—and show evidence—that small residential colleges are in a better position to help students to develop a repertoire of strategies for living in an intercultural global world: inculcating honesty, integrity, and ethical behavior; learning respect for other cultures and ideas; espousing civic learning and engagement. In short, liberal arts colleges should take a new approach. Throughout the 1970s and 1980s, these colleges demonstrably increased the diversity of student populations but did very little to change the culture beyond the addition of affinity houses or centers and so-called diversity or multicultural courses. Administrators appeared to be more interested in the social justice goal of increasing demographic diversity than in using diversity as an educational asset to change the institution, thus missing an opportunity to add a crucially important component of a holistic education for students.

A recent survey of students suggests there is much room for improvement. Using data of students at six liberal arts colleges and eleven universities collected by the Wabash National Study of Liberal Arts Education beginning in 2006, researchers Jesse Rude and Gregory Wolniak of the University of Chicago, and Ernest Pascarella of the University of Iowa came to the following conclusion: "The longer students are in college, the less likely they are to be interested in promoting understanding across lines of race and ethnicity." They looked at how students answered the same question, "How important to you personally is helping to promote racial understanding?" that was posed three times during their academic tenure: at campus arrival, at the end of their first year, and at the conclusion of their senior year. According to the researchers, this question "attempts to capture respondents' personal commitment to improving racial understanding and may be less prone to social desirability bias." The authors concluded that efforts by racially diverse campuses "to broaden students' racial views should extend beyond multicultural course requirements. Colleges that can take steps that promote environments conducive for cross-race friendship and other forms of positive interaction may have an even greater impact on students' racial attitudes."[3]

Strategies to Deepen Interactions and Relationships on Campus

So what strategies could we use to promote such an environment and to ensure that the benefits of a liberal arts residential experience are made tangible to students, families, politicians, and policy makers? I will share three examples from Wheaton that offer practices with measurable outcomes of success.

Several years ago the President's Action Committee on Inclusive Excellence (PACIE) developed an intergroup dialogue concept based on study circles, which became known as dialogue action teams (DAT). A DAT consists of a small, diverse, and facilitated group of eight to twelve people. DATs could consist of students or faculty-staff. Each DAT, meeting for five two-hour sessions, sets its own ground rules, which helps the group share responsibility for the quality of the discussion. Facilitators also help to manage the flow of the group discussion. The sessions begin with personal stories and examine a particular problem identified by the group, one example being the intersection of race and class. The ultimate goal of the DAT is to take dialogue and turn it into a plan for action and change.[4] Sadly, for Wheaton, the DATs were discontinued during the second year of the economic downturn following staff reductions and have not been resumed. However, to replace the DATs, a series of luncheons was established focusing on issues of difference (the first luncheon was called "Oriental Is a Rug"). This was, in fact, an action step suggested by one of the DATs.

One of the most segregated spaces in the United States remains our residential living areas. Within our residential academic communities, we have an opportunity to influence deeply the quality of the relationships our students will develop in their intercultural world by designing how they live, work, study, play, and eat together. These interactions need to be substantive and enduring, and they must be assessed and monitored on an ongoing basis. One way we are addressing this at Wheaton is with a new theme house, Together We All Prosper (TWAP), which opened in fall 2012. Students at Wheaton may apply to live in houses on campuses, but they must submit a proposal demonstrating how the residents will make a contribution to the broader campus community; they also must identify a faculty advisor. Two of my first-year mentees—one Caucasian and one African American—developed the concept for the house and invited an interracial group of men to reside there with them. TWAP will collaborate with the Black Student Association in developing programs for the house and for the campus. Their primary purpose is "to build strong, educated men for the future" who are prepared to lead in a complex, intercultural society. More specifically, members will develop a relationship with the larger Wheaton community, organizing programs that engage the community in a conversation about the challenges and opportunities inherent when students of diverse racial and economic backgrounds live and learn together.

A third example is based on the NPR series *This I Believe*, in which faculty, staff, and administrators share their core values and beliefs with audiences at Wheaton. Now entering its fourth year, the series has included as featured speakers members of the faculty, a housekeeper, a food service worker, and, most recently, a visiting Jesuit priest from Stonehill College. These sessions provide opportunities for students to hear the beliefs and values of variety of members of the Wheaton community. These individuals serve as models to our student body.

In order to determine whether our students have changed over time, we have used customized questions on surveys (NSSE, SERP, etc.) that are intended to ascertain the extent of change in attitudes and character over a four-year time frame. We are currently in the process of reviewing all of our surveys—student and alumni—for ways to improve them and use them more effectively. At the same time, we are seeking more robust ways to assess the extent of the growth, development, and change of our students.

No One Acts Alone

Addressing the challenges of diversity and globalism should be an essential component of the social purpose of residential liberal arts colleges. I believe that when we address these challenges more intentionally and document our success, we can make a better case for the value of this form of education to current and future generations of students. In an insightful essay, "Qualities of the Liberally Educated Person," William Cronon wrote about the importance of nurturing and engaging people. His words are as true for students as they are for administrators: "One of the most important things that tempers the exercise of power and shapes right action is surely the recognition that no one ever acts alone. A liberally educated person understands that they belong to a community whose prosperity and well-being are crucial to their own and they help that community flourish by giving of themselves to make the success of others possible."[5]

NOTES

1. Jean M. Twenge, "Generation Me on Trial," *Chronicle of Higher Education*, March 18, 2012, http://chronicle.com/article/Generation-Me-on-Trial/131246/.

2. For example, *New York Times* columnist and Pulitzer Prize–winning author Thomas Friedman has written extensively about how globalism is affecting communities and organizations throughout the world.

3. Scott Jaschik, "Backwards on Racial Understanding," *Inside Higher Education*, April 10, 2012, www.insidehighered.com/news/2012/04/10/study-suggests-students-grow-less-interested -promoting-racial-understanding.

4. Find out more about DATs at http://wheatoncollege.edu/president/2009/05/11/what-is -a-dat/.

5. William J. Cronon, "HIV, Health, and Liberal Education," in *Learning for Our Common Health: How an Academic Focus on HIV/AIDS Will Improve Education and Health*, ed. William David Burns (Washington, DC: Association of American Colleges and Universities, 1999).

PART VI / Future Prospects for the Liberal Arts College

CHAPTER 17

More to Hope Than to Fear

The Future of the Liberal Arts College

William G. Bowen

PRESIDENT EMERITUS, THE ANDREW W. MELLON FOUNDATION
AND PRINCETON UNIVERSITY

My aim in this chapter is first to sketch some of the environmental trends affecting liberal arts colleges and then discuss their implications for these colleges. In seeking to discharge this assignment, I am cognizant of the extent to which how one was educated and spent one's formative years affects one's life. I have been extraordinarily fortunate to have lived most of my days on college and university campuses in the company of inspiring teachers and wonderful colleagues and friends. These are thus the thoughts of a happy camper, not those of a disgruntled student, angry faculty member, or disenchanted alumnus. I am also an optimist, as you may infer from the title: "More to Hope than to Fear."[1]

Ten Environmental Trends

Here is my list of ten relevant environmental trends.

First is an indisputable fact: *the ever-increasing importance of brain in today's world.* This is reflected in greater and greater rewards to the well-educated individual—whether measured in lifetime earnings, in the odds of having a satisfying family life, in good health, in lifelong enjoyment of the arts and the pleasures of the mind, or in opportunities for service.[2] The ever-increasing power of trained intelligence, by no means limited to this country, has consequences for entire societies.[3]

Second is a disquieting fact: *since about 1970, educational attainment in the United States has been on a plateau; this stagnation has occurred at the same time that other countries have been making great strides in educating higher percentages of their populations.*[4] There is understandable concern about how this fall-off in our placement in "league tables" will affect this country's competitiveness in years to come.

Third, *worries about international competitiveness are magnified by the globalization of activities of all kinds.* References to a "flat world," shaped by the speed of communication and the ready flow of resources across national boundaries, are by no means all hype.

Fourth, *there is in this country a wide (and apparently widening) gap in educational outcomes related to socioeconomic status (SES).* Put simply, the odds that a young person will graduate from college are dramatically higher if the individual comes from a privileged family. Factoring in both high school and college graduation rates, government panel data show that for the putative high school class of 1992, the odds of earning a BA were more than *seven* times higher for students from high SES backgrounds (i.e., in the top income quartile and having at least one parent who graduated from college) than from low SES backgrounds.[5] It would not be surprising if this same pattern were to be found in other countries, but I don't know if this is the case.

Fifth, *the United States has been experiencing a dramatic increase in inequality of incomes.*[6] The by-now-famous discussion of the "99 percent–1 percent divide" is a vivid illustration of the degree to which this phenomenon has gained traction and caused resentment (witness the "Occupy Wall Street" movement). This does not appear to be only a U.S. phenomenon.[7]

Sixth, *this country is also experiencing major demographic trends; the days of a dominant white majority are rapidly ending.* By 2042, according to projections by the U.S. Census Bureau, the white population will be a minority, with the Hispanic population tripling in growth over the next thirty years.[8]

Seventh, *there is growing political polarization in the United States.* One result is that "middle-of-the-road" thinking is out of favor; there is a poisoning of political discourse that discourages compromises aimed at problem solving.

Eighth, and closer to home, *there are growing economic pressures on much of higher education, especially on the public sector.* This is the result of deep-seated fiscal problems at both federal and state levels marked by an aversion to higher taxes and pressures for more spending on items such as health care and pensions, coupled with calls for austerity.[9]

Ninth, *there is a concurrent growth in concern about the affordability of higher education.*[10] One consequence is that there is great reluctance by universities (especially, but not only, public universities) to use large tuition increases as an "escape valve" when faced with funding cutbacks. A related phenomenon is more emphasis on short-run vocational objectives and sharp increases in professional and pre-professional programs that are expected by students and their parents to yield near-term economic payoffs.

Tenth, *the digital age and rapid technological change are evident everywhere.* There is escalating growth in Internet usage, social networking, and online learning.[11]

Implications for Liberal Arts Colleges

To my mind, the implications of these trends for liberal arts colleges fall into two overlapping categories: implications for their economic viability and for programmatic/budgeting policies, including those affecting tuition and financial aid; and implications for how our colleges teach and what sort of educational outcomes they should seek to achieve.

Impact on Programmatic/Budgeting Policies

My major injunction under the heading of "programmatic/budgeting policies" is *Stay the course; you are playing a winning hand.* The value of a liberal education, as traditionally understood, has never been greater than it is today. Nan Keohane has provided a comprehensive account of the reasons why this is so, and I will not repeat the arguments she makes so eloquently.[12]

I would add only a point of emphasis: as we think about the rapidly changing world our students face, a world in which fewer people follow one career trajectory throughout their lifetime, learning how to do mundane, repetitive tasks is not the way to go. *What counts is both the acquisition of broad-gauged, problem-solving skills and knowing how to function effectively in collaborative settings involving all kinds of people.* Being able to take a new problem, parse it out, and make headway in solving it—all in the company of others—are crucial skills. Such skills can be honed in excellent liberal arts colleges as well as great universities. The president of Yale, Richard Levin, has pointed out the irony that, at the same time that liberal education is under assault by some here at home, it is being extolled and adopted, really for the first time, in other parts of the world such as Asia.[13]

Budgetary choices are always hard, especially when constraints are tight. In choosing how to spend limited resources, it is important not to demean classic offerings that have stood the test of time. Spending money on personalized education and on a high-quality residential experience is wise. An obverse proposition is that colleges should resist spending money on what many will regard as frills—overly elaborate student centers and expensive playing fields, to cite just those two examples. Admittedly, this can be hard to do because of the demand for such "consumer-like" services by prospective students and their affluent parents and because of the intense competition for such candidates.

Here are some thoughts as to where scarce dollars should—and should not—go:

- A high priority should be placed on spending both money and time recruiting exceptional faculty leaders in key disciplines—even if this means bruising the sensibilities of some current faculty by recruiting leaders from outside at senior levels, thereby saying, in effect, "we need stronger leadership." Recruiting opportunities are more promising today than they have been in many years, given the fiscal and other problems facing the country, especially the public sector of higher education.

- Many colleges are wisely investing in approaches designed to help their students gain a good sense of other cultures. This too makes excellent sense in the "globalized" world unfolding before us, especially if real educational values are emphasized and not just the pleasures of brief sojourns abroad.

- Programs that help students understand basic science and its ramifications are more valuable than ever, especially if they involve collaborations with universities as well as other colleges in order to avoid budget-breaking outlays on laboratories and equipment that could be shared. Experimenting with "virtual" laboratories is wise.

- In the digital world of today and tomorrow, students need training in how to use technology and how to learn online—but neither liberal arts colleges nor even most universities should invest in developing expensive interactive online platforms of their own. What is needed is centralized help, the expertise of research universities, and large up-front investments by foundations and/or governmental entities.[14]

- Outlays on financial aid are investments and should be treated that way—not treated merely as discounts used to win bidding wars. The cases for enrolling a diverse student body and for allowing talented students of modest means to get an excellent liberal arts education are, if anything, more powerful than ever before, given the importance of preparing students to function effectively in a multifaceted world in which most people don't look like them. At the same time, tempting as it may be to join the merit-aid wars, I think that this tendency should be resisted, even if that means losing some excellent students.[15] In defining "excellent students," I would emphasize real accomplishments (good grades and high scores on achievement tests), along with leadership potential and coping skills, *not* scores on aptitude tests, which research has shown are poor predictors of almost everything except family wealth! Finally, I remain steadfastly opposed to athletic scholarships, which I think are an embarrassment and an abomination, especially at a time when there are so many needy students.

- I am skeptical that it is wise to go as far as the wealthier institutions such as Harvard and Princeton do in replacing all loans with grants for families above a modest-income threshold—perhaps with exceptions for students who pursue vocations that pay little. Many other students in the higher-middle income range will earn substantial returns on their educational investments, and there is no reason they should not repay some of the funds that were, in effect, "advanced" to them. Reasonable amounts of educational debt are not bad things, and sustained efforts should be made to spread the costs of higher education across a wide population of direct beneficiaries.

- Finally, in the face of much furor over allegedly high tuition charges and "affordability," I would not overreact. I believe that strong colleges and universities that emphasize the right kinds of learning and the right values will continue to attract sufficient numbers of outstanding students, regardless of modest variations in the level of tuition.[16] Many of these students will come from families that can pay, and that *should* pay—even if that means, horror of horrors, sacrificing an occasional winter vacation in order to make a lifetime investment on behalf of their children. A quarter of a century ago I wrote a pair of essays on tuition that stressed the risks of charging too little as well as too much.[17] I stand by those essays today. It is by no means *infra dig* to remind families that higher education is much more than a consumer good and that, thanks to the generosity of those who attended in earlier years, many of the best colleges provide an implicit subsidy, often a large one, to every current student. I recognize, however, that all of higher education faces serious political risks from escalating tuition, even when higher tuition levels are justified and accompanied by generous financial aid. It is imperative, I think, for all colleges and universities to intensify efforts to transform teaching methods in order to reduce instructional costs—and then to pass on at least some of the savings to students and their families.

Impact on Teaching Methods and Desired Educational Outcomes

Based on the preceding discussion, there are clear implications for what students attending good liberal arts colleges should learn. Woodie Flowers, a highly regarded teacher at MIT (not a liberal arts college, to be sure, but a very good teaching institution), has encouraged us to distinguish "education" from "training." There is much in what he says (even as I think he fails to see how blurry the lines are between his categories). Flowers suggests that "codified knowledge" is susceptible to "training," whereas "education is much more subtle and complex. . . . Learning a CAD program is training, while learning to design requires education; learning spelling and grammar is training, while learning to communicate requires education. In many cases, learning the parts is training, while understanding and being creative about the whole requires education."[18]

Henry Adams has taught us that in thinking about education, all of us are autobiographical. In that spirit, I hope I may be allowed to share an example of what should be learned that is taken from my own educational history (albeit at the graduate level). I took a beginning course in economic theory from William Baumol, a distinguished economist and one of my closest friends to this day. We used a text by J. R. Hicks (*Value and Capital*) that is one of the most densely packed and worst-written books I have ever encountered. (I always suspected that Professor Baumol chose it in part for that reason.) We covered, if my memory serves me, about thirty-five pages in an entire semester. When we were studying a particularly inscrutable passage, Professor Baumol would say to the class: "Your assignment for next week is to take this passage and write me a three-page paper explaining, in clear English, what it means." I would go back to my room and struggle and struggle—until I realized (if I were fortunate, and often in the middle of the night) "I've got it!" I vividly remember leaping out of bed and writing down the key insight before I lost it. The course also included excruciating sessions at the blackboard in which students attempted to explain concepts to their classmates under the relentless prodding of Professor Baumol, who insisted that we speak, as well as write, in clear sentences. (He would ask: "What is a demand curve? Please answer in a simple sentence that begins 'A demand curve is. . . .'"). Not everyone survived this regimen.

Fortunately, I did survive, and that at-times searing educational experience taught me lessons that I have never forgotten. One is that clear thinking has to precede clear writing but that the former does not guarantee the latter. A second lesson was that it might take me quite a while to understand something—longer than it took some of my classmates—but that if I persevered, I could figure most things out. Thanks to Professor Baumol's friendly but demanding tutelage, I gained a quiet confidence that was (is) a gift of incredible value. An impersonal educational setting, or studying with a much less gifted teacher, would not have permitted that kind of learning.

I am certainly not saying, however, that all teaching, even at liberal arts colleges, requires this one-on-one character (though much of it should). There is also a place for sophisticated online learning that is largely machine-guided, especially when used in courses in which there is more or less one answer to basic questions and when they are part of a hybrid mode of instruction that includes some opportunities for face-to-face interactions between teacher and student. To be sure, systems that provide "interactive learning online" have less to offer to liberal arts colleges than to financially hard-pressed public universities that must teach introductory courses in subjects such as statistics and pre-college math to large numbers of students. Still, students attending all kinds of institutions will benefit from learning how to learn in online environments.[19]

My plea is for the adoption of a "portfolio" approach to curricular development that provides a carefully calibrated mix of learning styles. This mix will vary by institutional type, and liberal arts colleges can and should put much more weight on seminars, discussion groups, and directed study than large institutions can hope to do. Nonetheless, even the wealthiest, most elite colleges and universities that can afford to stay pretty much as they are should ask if failing to participate at least to some degree in the evolution of online learning models is to their advantage in the long run. Their students, along with others of their generation, will expect to use digital resources—and to be trained in their use.

More generally, there is everything to be said for heeding Derek Bok's admonition that a determined effort should be made to help faculty teach better, in part by being sure that they are aware of, and take account of, the insights of recent research in fields such as cognitive science.[20] Liberal arts colleges, in particular, should put a real premium on doing all that can be done to ensure that excellent teaching actually occurs, and is not reflected solely in the language of promotional materials, abstract pronouncements, and inspirational talks.

Next, I want to say a few words about styles of teaching in the personalized settings that are, and should continue to be, the hallmarks of liberal arts colleges. Another great teacher of mine, Jacob Viner, echoed Jeremy Bentham in decrying "nonsense on stilts," which Professor Viner described as "a type of sophisticated nonsense, of ignorant learning, which only the [well] educated are capable of perpetuating." Viner loved to tell this story: "A woman in a shop asked for a drinking bowl for her dog. When the clerk replied that he had no drinking bowls especially for dogs, the woman said that any drinking bowl would do. The clerk, having found one for her, suggested that he have the word 'dog' painted on it. 'No thanks,' said the woman. 'It is not necessary. My husband doesn't drink water [from a bowl] and my dog can't read.'" Viner's conclusion: "Learning should be kept in its place."[21]

There is, of course, a critically important role for learning, assuming that it is "kept in its place." In the best selective, residential institutions, the right kind of learning occurs more or less constantly just as often, or more often, outside of the classroom as in it. This cliché, repeated by all presidents of strong residential colleges and universities, conveys real truth. Late night peer-to-peer exchanges offer students a hard-to-replicate access to the perspectives of other smart people. As Professor Viner never tired of warning his students, "There is no limit to the amount of nonsense you can think, if you think too long alone."

Grasping complexity—embracing it—is a critical capacity to be learned earlier rather than later in life. Liberal arts colleges should do all in their power to encourage students to avoid the polarized thinking that is, sad to say, becoming the standard of our day. Einstein was right in asserting: "Everything should be made as simple as possible ... *but not more so!*"[22] Dilemmas are real and should be acknowledged, not dismissed by sloganeering. Isaiah Berlin's famous book *Russian Thinkers* is full of examples of the dilemmas faced by nineteenth-century Russian writers as many of them sought to balance a yearning for absolutes with the complex visions that they simply could not push from their minds—and to do so in a terribly troubled time. Berlin writes with special empathy about Alexander Herzen and others, "who see, and cannot help seeing, many sides of a case.... The middle ground," he wrote, "is a notoriously exposed, dangerous, and ungrateful position."[23] So it is. Nonetheless, students need to be both thoughtful enough and courageous enough to occupy it when that is where hard thought takes them.

Mining this same vein of quotable quotes with enduring lessons, I will next tell you tales of two horses (sorry about the "tales"), one from Maine and the other from Arabia. Each has a moral. When I referred earlier to the need to inculcate in students an appreciation for the way scientists think, I had in mind the need to develop a healthy skepticism that includes a deep-seated respect for evidence—an incorrigible need to "find the facts." There is a wonderful little book called *The*

Fastest Hound Dog in the State of Maine that illustrates this mindset. It is "thoroughly Maine," the author suggests, "to want the full facts before negotiating an opinion." He provides this exchange between two people riding on a train:

> "Is that a white horse?"
> "Seems to be from this side."[24]

There is also great value in recognizing what one does not know and realizing when it is time "to punt." A great friend of mine, Ezra Zilkha, grew up in Baghdad and is fond of telling stories from the Arabian Nights. This is the story of the Black Horse. A prisoner who was about to be executed was having his last audience with the Sultan. He implored the Sultan: "If you will spare me for one year, I will teach your favorite black horse to talk." The Sultan agreed immediately with this request, and the prisoner was returned to his quarters. When his fellow prisoners heard what had happened, they mocked him: "How can you possibly teach a horse to talk? Absurd." He replied: "Wait a minute. Think. A year is a long time. In a year, I could die naturally, the Sultan could die, the horse could die, or, who knows, I might teach the black horse to talk." When telling this story, Mr. Zilkha always described himself as an "adaptive pessimist." The lesson of the story, he said, is this: "If you don't have an immediate answer, buy time. Time, if we use it, might make us adapt and maybe, who knows, find solutions." If speaking to a college or university audience (and he himself is a graduate of Wesleyan), Mr. Zilkha would add: "It is the job of the college to learn to teach the black horse to talk."

I end now with another admonition, easier to state than to follow. Do not be reluctant to accept the obligation of the college to teach students to think about values as well as about how to achieve more mundane ends. This is most definitely not a plea for indoctrination; nor is it a plea for pontification. I remember well the comment of Robert Hutchins when he was urged to teach his students at Chicago to do this, that, or the other thing: "All attempts to teach character directly will fail. They degenerate into vague exhortations to be good, which leave the bored listener with a desire to commit outrages which would otherwise have never occurred to him."[25]

Assuming, however, that we are wise enough to avoid such excesses, my admonition about the desirability of putting an emphasis on values suggests another dimension along which the best liberal arts colleges can differentiate themselves from other institutions that may be afraid even to allude to something as ineffable and sometimes controversial. Again, I have a text. This time it is from a Baccalaureate address given in 2010 by Jeff Bezos, the hugely successful CEO of Amazon, who is apparently cut from a different cloth than other alleged "exemplars" of corporate leadership about whom we have been reading of late (though I cannot judge the accuracy of these often harsh portrayals). The title Bezos gave to his talk is: "We Are What We Choose."[26] He began by relating a poignant story of a trip he took with his grandparents when he was ten years old. While riding in their Airstream trailer, this precocious child laboriously calculated the damage to her health that his grandmother was doing by smoking. His conclusion was that, at two minutes per puff, she was taking nine years off her life. When he proudly told her of his finding, she burst into tears. His grandfather stopped the car and gently said to Jeff: "One day you'll understand that it's harder to be kind than clever."

Bezos went on to talk about the difference between gifts and choices. "Cleverness," he said, "is a gift; kindness is a choice. Gifts are easy—they're given after all. Choices can be hard." He then challenged the graduating students to think carefully about their future range of choices. He asked: "Will you be clever at the expense of others, or will you be kind?"

There is, of course, an all-too-real limit to what colleges can do to shape the thinking of their students. But it is well to recognize that colleges, at their best, can and should encourage their students to learn to choose wisely—and to learn to be kind. Colleges should do this at the same time that they seek to inculcate in their students an insatiable appetite to learn new things, in new ways, while always respecting evidence; and to inculcate in them, too, a capacity to occupy, when their best thinking takes them there, "the notoriously exposed, dangerous, and ungrateful middle ground." These avowedly subjective goals will always elude the quantifiers among us (and within us). Still, if they can be embraced, the future of liberal arts colleges will offer, without question, more to hope than to fear.

NOTES

1. This is an inversion of the famous comment made by John Maynard Keynes. He said that when interest rates are as low as 2 percent (and of course they are lower than that today), there is "more to fear than to hope" (*The General Theory of Employment, Interest and Money* [Delhi: Atlantic Publishers and Distributors, 2006]). But Keynes was talking about prospects for bond holders—which are indeed grim these days—whereas I am talking about prospects for a certain kind of college.

2. See Richard C. Levin, "Why Colleges and Universities Matter," American Council on Education meeting, March 6, 2011. Some argue that these returns are in part fictitious in that they reflect the advantages of institutional prestige and credentialing. But this is an odd line of

argument. Graduating from a strong, well-respected college or university definitely gives a graduate a "leg up" in recruitment competitions of all kinds. However, this is entirely proper in that giving weight to where someone went reduces the cost of search for a prospective graduate school or employer. The head of a major law firm explained that his firm routinely concentrates on graduates of a half-dozen leading law schools. "Might we find a top person at a lesser-known school?" he asks. "Of course. But the odds of that are low enough, and the costs of search high enough, to make that an unattractive approach." Similarly, in searching for research assistants, my practice (and the practice of many others) is to turn first to the most accomplished teachers of prospective candidates—without, of course, excluding anyone from applying. I have wanted to reduce the costs of search, which can be daunting, as everyone knows. These costs are real, and in no sense "fictitious."

3. In speaking at his installation as chancellor of the fledgling University of Guyana in January 1967, the Nobel Prize–winning economist Sir W. Arthur Lewis described the evolution of thinking about the processes of economic growth in these words: "Poverty is not primarily due to people not working hard enough, or to inadequate land, or even to inadequate capital. It is primarily due to inadequate knowledge and primitive techniques which keep output per head low." He then noted the "tribute that men pay to brain." "Let me put this into historical perspective," he said. "Not very long ago men lived in caves, or under the shadow of trees. Their lives were dominated by fear—fear of the elements, of drought and flood and fire; fear of other animals; and fear of other men, who wandered around in families or tribes ready to exterminate each other. The human race has pulled itself up from this by handing down from generation to generation knowledge of two sets of principles, those relating to controlling nature, which we call science, and principles relating to controlling human behaviour, which we call ethics. Human life as we know it today is based on accumulated science, and accumulated ethical principles enshrined in laws and in the conventions of decent behaviour" (quoted in William G. Bowen, "Remarks at the Memorial Service for Sir W. Arthur Lewis," November 10, 1991, Princeton University Archives).

4. See William G. Bowen, Matthew M. Chingos, and Michael S. McPherson, *Crossing the Finish Line: Completing College at America's Public Universities* (Princeton, NJ: Princeton University Press, 2009).

5. See *Crossing the Finish Line*, p. 21, fig. 2.2. There is no reason to believe that this disparity has narrowed since then. For a reference to broader and more recent studies, see Sabrina Tavernise, "Education Gap Grows between Rich and Poor, Studies Say," *New York Times*, February 9, 2012. See also Martha J. Bailey and Susan M. Dynarski, "Gains and Gaps: Changing Inequality in U.S. College Entry and Completion," National Bureau of Economic Research Working Paper No. 17633, December 2011, www.nber.org/papers/w17633.

6. See Carmen DeNavas-Walt, Bernadette D. Proctor, and Jessica C. Smith, "Income, Poverty, and Health Insurance Coverage in the United States: 2010," United States Census Bureau, www.census.gov/prod/2011pubs/p60-239.pdf (accessed March 15, 2012), and Laura D'Andrea Tyson, "Tackling Income Inequality," *New York Times*, November 18, 2011, http://economix.blogs.nytimes.com/2011/11/18/tackling-income inequality/?scp=4&sq=income%20inequality&st=cse.

7. See Liz Alderman, "Ranks of Working Poor Grow in Europe," *New York Times*, April 1, 2012, www.nytimes.com/2012/04/02/world/europe/in-rich-europe-growing-ranks-of-working-poor.html?_r=1&hpw.

8. CB08-123, "An Older and Diverse Nation by Midcentury," Bureau of the Census, August 14, 2008, www.census.gov/newsroom/releases/archives/population/cb08-123.html

9. A recent report by the State Higher Education Executive Officers indicates that per-student state and local expenditures for higher education have reached their lowest point in 25 years. See "State Higher Education Finance Report FY 2011," 19.

10. Barack Obama, "Remarks by the President on College Affordability, Ann Arbor, Michigan," January 27, 2012, www.whitehouse.gov/the-press-office/2012/01/27/remarks-president-college-affordability-ann-arbor-michigan.

11. According to the 2011 Sloan Consortium-Babson Survey Research Group report, "Going the Distance: Online Education in the United States, 2011," online enrollments at degree-granting postsecondary institutions increased from about 1.6 million in fall 2002 (about 9.6 percent of total enrollments) to 6.1 million in fall 2010 (31.3 percent of total enrollments) (p. 11). Even traditionally taught courses routinely utilize the tools of online learning. For example, institutions are capturing lectures through video, archiving them on the web, and making them available to students (and in some cases the public) in an asynchronous format. Homework is routinely being submitted and evaluated online. Video conferencing is also becoming common.

12. See Nannerl O. Keohane, "The Liberal Arts as Guideposts in the 21st Century," in *Chronicle of Higher Education*, January 29, 2012. See also Andrew Delbanco, *College: What It Was, Is, and Should Be* (Princeton, NJ: Princeton University Press, 2012).

13. Richard C. Levin, "The Rise of Asia's Universities," The Royal Society, London, England, February 1, 2010, http://opac.yale.edu/president/message.aspx?id=91.

14. See the paper by Lawrence Bacow et al., reporting the results of a study by Ithaka S+R, "Barriers to Adoption of Online Learning Systems in U.S. Higher Education," April 2012.

15. I recognize that some colleges may need to provide certain kinds of merit awards to "seed" the campus population with exceptional students who can set a tone and a standard.

16. Leaders of private colleges and universities should examine carefully projections that allegedly show very small numbers of prospective candidates with a combination of high test scores, ability to pay, and interest in liberal arts institutions. Such projections are often overly mechanistic and do not allow for dynamic factors such as the effects of woes in the public sector on the appeal of private colleges and universities. See Beckie Supiano, "In California, Private Colleges Benefit from Public System's Shrinking Capacity," *Chronicle of Higher Education*, March 28, 2012. Nor do such projections always take into account another dynamic: the growing appeal of strong U.S. colleges and universities to foreign students. More generally, there has been much discussion of the growing stratification of higher education over the last three or four decades. As Caroline Hoxby has emphasized, the clustering of top students at small numbers of highly selective colleges and universities is a natural consequence of deep-seated factors such as faster and cheaper communications and readier access to information about both schools and students—both of which have led to a "nationalization" (and now "internationalization") of markets for the top students. See Professor Hoxby's seminal paper, "The Changing Selectivity of American Colleges," in *Journal of Economic Perspectives*, Fall 2009.

17. See William G. Bowen, "Thinking about Tuition" and "The Student Aid/Tuition Nexus," in *Ever the Teacher* (Princeton, NJ: Princeton University Press, 1987), 528–43.

18. Woodie Flowers, "A Contrarian View of MIT: What Are We Doing?" *MIT Faculty Newsletter,* January/February, 2012.

19. More and more of the most selective colleges and universities grasp this important point. See the description of initiatives at Princeton in Rebecca Zhang, "U. Explores Interactive Learning," *Daily Princetonian*, March 28, 1012, www.dailyprincetonian.com/2012/03/28/30389/.

20. See Harvard President Derek Bok's book on higher education (forthcoming from Princeton University Press), which is full of excellent advice for all of us concerned about how to teach, as well as what to teach.

21. Jacob Viner, "A Modest Plea for Some Stress on Scholarship in Graduate Training," *The Long View and the Short: Studies in Economic Theory and Policy* (New York: Free Press, 1958).

22. Quoted in Albert W. Alschuler, *Law without Values* (Chicago: University of Chicago Press: 2000), 191, italics mine.

23. Isaiah Berlin, *Russian Thinkers* (New York: Viking, 1978), 279.

24. John Gould, *The Fastest Hound Dog in the State of Maine* (Thorndike Press, 1953), 92.

25. Robert Maynard Hutchins, *No Friendly Voice* (Chicago: University of Chicago Press, 1968), 93. Hutchins added: "Hard intellectual work is doubtless the best foundation of character, for without the intellectual virtues, the moral sense rests on habit and precept alone."

26. Jeff Bezos, "We Are What We Choose," Remarks as delivered to the Class of 2010 at Princeton University, May 30, 2010, Princeton University Archives.

Contributors

William G. Bowen, president of The Andrew W. Mellon Foundation from 1988 to 2006, was president of Princeton University from 1972 to 1988, where he also served as professor of economics and public affairs. A graduate of Denison University (AB 1955) and Princeton University (PhD 1958), he joined the Princeton faculty in 1958, specializing in labor economics, and served as provost there from 1967 to 1972.

Rebecca Chopp is the chancellor of the University of Denver, where she is leading a comprehensive effort to transform the student experience, expand the design of knowledge, and engage with the liberal arts in new ways. Previously, she served as the president of Swarthmore College and Colgate University, Titus Street Professor of Theology at Yale Divinity School, and provost and executive vice president for Academic Affairs at Emory University.

Carol T. Christ is the director of the Center for Studies in Higher Education at the University of California at Berkeley. She served as the president of Smith College from 2002 to 2013. She went to Smith from Berkeley, where she was a professor in the English Department and held a number of administrative positions, among them dean of humanities, dean of the College of Letters and Science, and executive vice chancellor and provost.

Joanne V. Creighton served as interim president of Haverford College (2011–2013), president of Mount Holyoke College (1996–2010), and provost and interim president of Wesleyan University (1990–1995). Currently, she is professor of English at Mount Holyoke and is completing a three-year appointment as a Five College Fortieth Anniversary Professor, teaching successively at University of Massachusetts Amherst, Amherst College, and Hampshire College.

Ronald A. Crutcher became the tenth president of the University of Richmond on July 1, 2015. He is also a professor of music and president emeritus of Wheaton College in Norton, Massachusetts, where he served from 2004 to 2014. Crutcher also served as provost and executive vice president for academic affairs and professor of music at Miami University in Oxford, Ohio.

Adam F. Falk became the seventeenth president of Williams College in April 2010. A fellow of the American Physical Society whose research focuses on elementary particle physics and quantum field theory, he joined Williams from Johns Hopkins University, where he served at the Zanvyl Krieger School of Arts and Sciences as the James B. Knapp Dean and earlier as dean of the faculty.

Susan Frost is a consultant and researcher who works with college and university leaders to form and execute strategic plans, engage faculty in shaping the institution's future, and develop academic programs as major fundraising targets. She has traveled extensively to China, India, and the Middle East, forging closer connections between top universities in those countries and those in the United States. For thirteen years, Frost served in the administration at Emory University, most recently as the vice president for strategic development.

Kevin M. Guthrie is an executive and entrepreneur with expertise in high technology and not-for-profit management. He was the founding president of JSTOR in 1995 and ITHAKA, which helps the academic community use digital technologies to preserve the scholarly record and to advance research and teaching in sustainable ways. Previously, Guthrie cofounded a software development company and served as a research associate at the Mellon Foundation, where he authored *The New-York Historical Society: Lessons from One Nonprofit's Long Struggle for Survival*.

Catharine Bond Hill became the tenth president of Vassar College in 2006. She is a noted economist who studies higher education affordability and access. During her presidency, Vassar has become a national leader in providing access and support for students from all socioeconomic backgrounds. In recognition of that work, in 2015 the Jack Kent Cooke Foundation awarded Vassar its inaugural million-dollar prize for Equity in Educational Excellence. In 2012, Hill established a first-of-its-kind veterans admission program with the Posse Foundation. Now twenty-nine veterans attend Vassar through the program, with Wesleyan University and Dartmouth also participating.

Wendy L. Hill became the Head of School at The Agnes Irwin School, an all-girls' independent day school serving prekindergarten through twelfth grade in Rosemont, Pennsylvania, in 2014. Previously, Hill was a member of the faculty at Lafayette College since 1989 and was appointed the William C. '67 and Pamela H. Rappolt Professor of Neuroscience. She served as the provost and dean of the faculty at Lafayette College from 2007 to 2014.

Jane Dammen McAuliffe is director of National and International Outreach at the Library of Congress. She is the immediate past president of Bryn Mawr College and former dean of the College of Arts and Sciences at Georgetown University.

John M. McCardell Jr. is vice-chancellor and president of The University of the South, Sewanee, Tennessee. He came to Sewanee in 2010 after thirty-four years at Middlebury College, including thirteen years (1991–2004) as its president. At Middlebury, he championed the creation of a residential Commons System, which included continuous membership, proximate dining, and a faculty presence. At Sewanee, he has taken steps to address the sustainability of the "high tuition/high discount" economic model.

David W. Oxtoby became the ninth president of Pomona College in July 2003. An internationally known physical chemist, he previously served as dean of the Division of Physical Sciences at the University of Chicago, where he was William Rainey Harper Distinguished Service Professor. At Pomona, he is also professor of chemistry and annually teaches a course in environmental chemistry. He has served as a member of the Board of Overseers at Harvard University, the Science Education Advisory Board of the Hughes Medical Institute, and the boards of the Toyota Technological Institute and the Claremont University Consortium.

Daniel R. Porterfield became Franklin & Marshall College's fifteenth president in 2011. Since joining F&M, he has strengthened support for faculty scholarship, launched new initiatives to broaden access to low-income and first-generation college students, and enhanced the holistic student experience. Prior to this appointment, he served as senior vice president for strategic development at his alma mater, Georgetown University.

Brian Rosenberg is the sixteenth president of Macalester College. Under his leadership, Macalester completed a historic five-year campaign to raise $150 million, launched the Institute for Global Citizenship, diversified its student body, and upgraded its facilities in areas that include the arts and wellness. Prior to coming to Macalester in 2003, Rosenberg was the dean of the faculty and an English professor at Lawrence University.

Shelly Weiss Storbeck is a managing partner at Storbeck/Pimentel and Associates, LLC. She was previously the managing director of the education practice of A.T. Kearney, Inc., an international search and consulting firm. She has conducted more than four hundred searches for public and private universities, colleges and schools, and not-for-profit associations and organizations. Before joining A.T. Kearney, Storbeck was a senior associate and administrative officer for the education practice at Korn/Ferry International. Prior to working in search, she was an administrator at Haverford College.

Jill Tiefenthaler became Colorado College's thirteenth president on July 1, 2011. She was previously provost and professor of economics at Wake Forest University. Before joining Wake Forest, she taught economics at Colgate University, where she chaired the Economics Department and served as associate dean of the faculty. Tiefenthaler is a noted economist, specializing in labor economics, economics of the family, and the economics of higher education.

Eugene M. Tobin is senior program officer in Higher Education and Scholarship in Humanities at The Andrew W. Mellon Foundation and a former president of Hamilton College. He is the co-author with William G. Bowen of *Locus of Authority: The Evolution of Faculty Roles in the Governance of Higher Education* (2015).

Daniel H. Weiss is the president of the Metropolitan Museum of Art. For over a decade, he led liberal arts institutions, serving as the president of Haverford College and Lafayette College. He was also the James B. Knapp Dean of the Krieger School of Arts and Sciences at Johns Hopkins for three years. A graduate of George Washington University (BA), Yale University (MBA), and Johns Hopkins (PhD), he served on the faculty at Johns Hopkins from 1992 to 2005.

Suzanne P. Welsh was vice president for finance and treasurer of Swarthmore College from 2002 until her retirement in 2014. She joined the college in 1983 and was named treasurer in 1989. Before coming to Swarthmore, she spent six years in corporate finance and accounting with a Fortune 500 company.

Index